The Entrepreneur's Guide To...

CAPITAL

Over 150 Proven Ways to Finance New & Growing Businesses

Revised Edition

Jennifer Lindsey

PROBUS PUBLISHING COMPANY
Chicago, Illinois

This publication is designed to provide accurate and authoritative information in regard to the subject matter covered. It is sold with the understanding that the publisher is not engaged in rendering legal, accounting or other professional service.

Library of Congress Cataloging-in-Publication Data Available

ISBN 1-55738-075-9

Printed in the United States of America

BOMC offers recordings and compact discs, cassettes and records. For information and catalog write to BOMR, Camp Hill, PA 17012

Dedication

To J. Michael Jeffers

Contents

Acknowledgements

A work of this magnitude is rarely compiled by the author alone, and this book is no exception. Literally hundreds of financial, legal, investment and accounting professionals have added vital information to the emerging body of knowledge available to entrepreneurs who need to recapitalize their businesses. Most of the information in this book was gleaned from personal interviews, and the number of specialists interviewed was legion.

More than a few deserve grateful acknowledgement by name for the effort and enthusiasm they contributed in unique and thoughtful ways. J. Brian Stockmar lent his considerable legal talent and knowledge of emerging entrepreneurial practices to the arduous task of editing the contents of the book. His commentary, incisive and always on the mark, refined the book in immeasurable ways.

Dr. Douglas J. Collier provided an invaluable overview of long-range financing strategy as it is practiced by some of the most successful companies of the 1980s.

David P. Sutton gave unconscionable amounts of time to suggest, digress, point out, rephrase, add, delete and polish. No draft of this book was spared his diligent professionalism.

Others who shared their expertise generously and always graciously include Stanley Pratt and his top-notch research staff, Tomi Simic, Stephen M. Stoffel, William E. Lewis, Edward Pfohl, Alan S. Danson, Alan Wetzell, John Jordan, Graham E. Hollis, Gary Powell and John F. Childs.

Also appreciated are executives, too numerous to mention by name, from Deloitte Haskins + Sells; Merrill Lynch; Peat, Marwick, Main; Boettcher & Co.; First Interstate Bank of Denver; Hein + Associates and Dean Witter Reynolds.

Special thanks are due Robert Flaherty and Robert Sheue for being writers who exemplify integrity by any standards, and editors who know how to demand the best.

And finally, special thanks to Tory Brown for sharing his wealth of experience.

Jennifer Lindsey

Introduction

The small business impetus that has characterized American business history in the 1980s will be fueled in the next decade by creative ways to raise money. The availability of old and new forms of financing will determine The health of small business and the direction in which it leads the nation's economy.

The comparative net costs of raising the capital needed to support the entrepreneurial trend, therefore, are of utmost importance to business owners at every stage of corporate development. Even more important is a financing strategy from day one that emphasizes planned, balanced and possibly global growth. The key to a long-range financial blueprint is at least a basic knowledge of the comparative advantages—and disadvantages—of the ways to raise capital anywhere in the world.

This book is meant to be used as a reference by business owners who need a basic knowledge of financing techniques. It provides a big-picture perspective of techniques that are currently used to capitalize small business. The book can help readers become a part of the financial planning process, rather than victims of no planning.

The information is geared to the managers of companies with under $25 million in annual revenue, to managers with little formal financial or investment training, and to business owners who want to direct the company's growth by doing their own homework before consulting the professionals. The cost ranges,

1

comparative advantages and disadvantages, and overall perspective have been distilled from interviews with small business specialists who adapted the data for companies that fit the under–$25 million category. Many of the rules of thumb, costs and planning strategies differ significantly for large companies.

Although many owners are driven by their need for capital in the short term, diligent thought should be given to the long-term ramifications of how to raise money. At what price can owners cash out? How will passive investors "exit" the investment? Does going public preclude using other financing sources in the future? The assumptions underlying these questions are beyond the scope of this book, but the what-if scenarios for each technique can be examined by management in accordance with updated investment, legal and accounting practice.

The ever-expanding U.S. economy continues to be supported by a still-growing number of small businesses, of which more than 13 million are sole proprietorships and about 2 million are partnerships. And significant private- and public-sector studies indicate that, over the next decade, self-employment—as distinguished from asset-building small businesses—also will increase due to the aging of the baby boom generation as it peaks into the self-employment era.

With any luck, this growth trend in the small business sector will attract new sources of funding in the 1990s to help finance-seeking owners keep their doors open in the coming global economy. After the October 1987 stock crash, lots of equity capital fled the stock market and landed in the private market. So there was more of it, but it became harder to get—the rules got stricter—and more expensive. The net/net was zero growth in equity capital for entrepreneurs.

But during the same era there was a silver lining: while offshore competitors have put American innovators and marketers on the run since the mid-1980s, their native lands also serve as lucrative new markets for American products, technology and know-how. In fact, foreign investors already have put more than $65 billion into direct U.S. investments, which is a 61 percent increase over the past year. This is unabashed good news for

American entrepreneurs because this hefty increase clinked right into America's corporate coffers, not its stock exchanges.

And while the stock crashes of 1987 and 1989 may have slowed the initial public offering market to a near-standstill—for all but the most fundamentally profitable companies—other market indicators suggest that small companies still have what it takes to lure investors. The National Association of Securities Dealers now trades up to 300 over-the-counter stocks at 4 A.M. Eastern time in direct competition with the London and other stock exchanges.

These and other market developments like the new Globex trading system from Reuters and the Chicago Mercantile Exchange are another determined push toward 24-hour global securities trading, a definite boon for small companies that make the market grade.

For those that don't, there are innovative ways to access the same old sources. Many banks around the courntry, plagued by lingering recession-like effects, offer loans to small companies once again in order to comply with stringent community-reinvestment guidelines passed by their municipal governments.

Although new sources like these are coming available with impeccable timing as the new decade unfolds, it would be wise for entrepreneurs to see that their dilemma remains constant through rapid economic changes, mixed recession/inflation signals and the globalization of world markets: how to access the new, and sometimes the old, financing sources; and how to look, feel and act credible to increasingly asset-hungry equity investors and cash-conscious lenders.

If there is one clear signal for entrepreneurs in the 1990s it is this sequence: know who the appropriate financing sources are, know how to chase capital correctly (by their rules) and don't be afraid to swim around in international waters.

Capital is nearly always available to well-run companies, but the competition is more fierce than ever. About 19 million Americans have opted for self-employment, up 50 percent since 1979. To meet their need for financing, venture capital funds have increased in number to 450, with only $2.81 billion by dollar amount raised to $4.2 billion in 1987; franchisors have increased the number of franchises to 462,000, with $457 billion in sales (one-third of all retail sales) in 1984, compared to 442,000 franchises with $334 billion in sales in 1980; investors traded 15.9 billion shares in 3,900 NASDAQ-listed companies in 1983, compared to 6.7 billion shares in 2,894 companies in 1980.

Measures of Business Formation, 1981–1988, Second Quarter

	Incorporations	Percent Change
1988 (January-September)	522,247	
1987 (January-September)	523,820	–0.3
1987	683,686	–2.7
1986	702,101	5.0
1985	668,904	5.3
1984	634,991	5.8
1983	600,400	5.9
1982	566,942	–2.5
1091	582,661	—
	Business Starts*	Percent Change
1988 (January-June)	102,586	
1987 (January-June)	118,583	–13.5
1987	232,948	–7.6
1986	252,111	3.1
1985	244,387	—
1984	102,329	1.4
1983	100,868	11.1
1982	90,757	–1.5
1981	92,161	1.5

*Dun and Bradstreet revised the business starts series in 1985. Data through 1984 are based on D&B industry coverage prior to 1980. Data since 1985 are based on current D&B industry coverage, which is presently about twice the previous coverage.

Source: Adapted from Dun and Bradstreet Corporation press releases by the U.S. Small Business Administration, Office of Advocacy.

Composition of Net Acquisition Announcements
Payment Breakdown

	1984	1985	1986	1987	1988
Divestitures					
Cash	152 (57%)	354 (71%)	186 (59%)	88 (60%)	99 (59%)
Stock	15 (5%)	26 (5%)	31 (10%)	12 (8%)	7 (4%)
Combination	96 (36%)	114 (23%)	95 (30%)	45 (31%)	58 (35%)
Debt	5 (2%)	3 (1%)	2 (1%)	2 (1%)	4 (2%)
Total	268	497	314	147	168
Acquisitions of Publicly Traded Companies					
Cash	134 (65%)	182 (57%)	171 (56%)	127 (57%)	250 (76%)
Stock	34 (16%)	78 (25%)	78 (25%)	60 (27%)	52 (16%)
Combination	35 (17%)	56 (18%)	57 (19%)	35 (16%)	29 (8%)
Debt	4 (2%)	1 (–)	0 (–)	0 (–)	0 (–)
Total	207	317	306	222	331
Acquisitions of Privately Held Companies					
Cash	167 (29%)	170 (28%)	180 (27%)	78 (23%)	85 (31%)
Stock	226 (39%)	234 (39%)	295 (45%)	173 (51%)	107 (39%)
Combination	180 (31%)	195 (33%)	188 (28%)	89 (26%)	80 (30%)
Debt	4 (1%)	1 (–)	0 (–)	0 (–)	0 (–)
Total	577	600	663	340	272
Acquisitions of Foreign Sellers					
Cash	12 (45%)	36 (67%)	8 (40%)	5 (33%)	3 (50%)
Stock	6 (22%)	6 (11%)	7 (35%)	3 (20%)	0 (–)
Combination	9 (33%)	12 (22%)	5 (25%)	7 (47%)	3 (50%)
Debt	0 (–)	0 (–)	0 (–)	0 (–)	0 (–)
Total	27	54	20	15	6
All Transactions					
Cash	465 (43%	742 (51%)	545 (42%)	298 (41%)	437 (56%)
Stock	281 (26%)	344 (23%)	411 (32%)	248 (34%)	166 (21%)
Combination	320 (30%)	377 (26%)	345 (26%)	176 (24%)	170 (22%)
Debt	13 (1%)	5 (–)	2 (–)	2 (1%)	4 (1%)
Total	1,079	1,468	1,303	724	777

All totals are based on those transactions providing information on form of payment.

Source: *Mergerstat Review.*

Perhaps more significant is the trend toward self-financing: in 1984, business owners raised $775 billion to finance their own companies, an increase of about 55 percent from 1980. Corporate conglomerates are slimming down by divestiture; leveraged buyouts are on the rise, spurred by entrepreneurialism; and intrapreneurs are changing the structure of America's largest corporations.

By these, or any, measures, the end of the twentieth century promises to be the most entrepreneurial era in our history. To the financial strategists belong the spoils.

Section 1
Partnership Techniques

Section 1
Introduction

Five partnership techniques described in Section 1 are viable strategies for a small business in the under–$25 million category. In addition, there are many variations on the joint venture theme, which can be structured in any number of ways to provide not only capital, but also combinations of technological expertise, management advice, facilities and/or distribution assistance.

Limited partnerships, in particular, can be hybridized to provide income (an income partnership) for investors or to allow time for a research and development program to gestate (a research and development partnership).

Research and development partnerships are highlighted in this section because of their usefulness to the many low- to high-tech companies that were formed in the '80s. Venture capital is included in this section because the nature of the partnership between management and venture capitalists is an important component of the financing package.

Partnerships are an extremely flexible strategy for a company of any size, from the startup concern that needs venture capital to the mature company that joint ventures with a Fortune 500 firm. Franchising is another partnership form that provides not only immediate capital, but also instant growth through a network of franchisees.

The gain in popularity by all forms of partnership is due to flexibility (there are as many different terms as there are companies) and to inherent advantages such as management assistance from investors (excluding limited partners), access to research from corporate partners, immediate expansion into new markets through franchising and tax advantages in addition to returns.

Glossary

Benchmark Goal: a development stage the company must meet, signifying the completion of a task specified in the partnership agreement as a financing stage, i.e., financing is approved as benchmark goals are met.

Distributor: a wholesaler of products that are sold to dealers who, in turn, sell directly to the public.

Equity Kicker: a convertible feature or stock warrant that accompanies a debt or equity offering to provide partial ownership in the company as an inducement to buy the offering.

Equity Stake: a percentage ownership in the company paid to venture capitalists, lenders or investors in compensation for financing, management advice or other services.

Feasibility Study: an analysis conducted to determine how successful the potential product, technology or corporate relationship will be in terms of design, financing opportunities, R&D, pricing, market, demand, competition, company strength, break-even costs, revenue and profit projections.

Income (Limited) Partnership: a structure designed for high, taxable income in the real estate, oil and gas or equipment-leasing industries. Usually used for tax-sheltered accounts like IRAs, Keoghs or pension plans.

Licensing Agreement: a document signed by the owner of a technology or product in which the right to make, use or sell the product is granted to another party for a specific time and under specific terms in exchange for compensation in the form of fees, royalty payments or a percentage of income.

Master Limited Partnership (MLPs or publicly traded limited partnerships): oil and gas drilling partnerships or income partnerships that are rolled into one instrument and spun-off by a large company to current stockholders or sold via a public offering to raise cash. It establishes a market value for the company's oil and gas operations.

Patent: protection of a proprietary claim to make, use or sell a product, technology or idea.

Royalty Payment: compensation paid to the owner of a product or technology for the right to make, use or sell it. Royalties are established in advance as a percentage of income earned when the product is sold (commercialization).

Royalty Trust: an account created when an oil and gas company transfers royalty interests to a new trust. The company still manages the properties, but the trust unit-holders receive tax deductions for depletion and abandonment losses. The investors usually receive larger distributions than they would have as corporate shareholders because the trust doesn't have to pay income taxes.

Technology Transfer Agreement: outlines what part of an incomplete technology remains under company control and what part is transferred to any party. It establishes the compensation for that part of the technology sold to limited partners.

Trademark: a device, word or sign that signifies ownership of a product or name to which it is applied or legally reserved, for the exclusive use of the owner as maker or seller.

CHAPTER 1

Venture Capital

DESCRIPTION

Venture capital is early stage risk financing offered by private individuals or funds, publicly held funds, or subsidiaries of banks or corporations (Small Business Investment Companies or SBICs) to private startup companies with above-average aftertax profit potential in exchange for a combination of stock, profits and/or royalties. Most venture capital funds finance a specific growth stage, i.e., startup or mezzanine level, or a specific industry. It should be considered only one financing strategy among many that may be required simultaneously with additional debt or equity financing. Venture capitalists expect a return on investment in three to seven years, either from profits or royalties, by taking the company public or by selling it off.

PROFILE OF A SUCCESSFUL VENTURE CAPITAL CANDIDATE

The best candidate for venture capital is a company that has a low current valuation, but above-average opportunity for future aftertax profits at the 30 percent level. The company is seeking at least $1 million in financing. For long-term potential, the company has room to grow in a rapidly accelerating industry that has few competitors. The company has a unique technology, unusual sales/dis-

13

tribution opportunity or some other factor that distinguishes it from the competition.

When used as startup or seed financing, venture capital can be a viable option even if the company is still in the concept stage. If the company is a startup, management has strong credentials in the industry.

When the equity market is not appreciating enough to attract investors, later-stage companies that represent less risk are more successful with venture capital. The more mature company must be able to offer value to investors, including management credentials in the industry, a stable operating history showing quarterly and annual growth for at least two years, and a solid revenue/earnings track record.

New Commitments, Disbursements, and Total Capital Pool of the Venture Capital Industry, 1980–1987 (Billions of Dollars)

Year	New Commitments to Venture Capital Firms	Disbursements to Funded Companies	Total Investment Capital Pool At End of Year*
1987	4.9	3.9	29.0
1986	NA	2.9	24.1
1985	NA	2.6	19.6
1984	4.2	3.0	16.3
1983	4.5	2.8	12.1
1982	1.7	1.8	6.7
1981	1.3	1.4	—
1980	0.9	1.1	—

NA = Not available.
*The capital pool at year end should equal the total pool at the end of the previous year plus new commitments, minus the amount of net withdrawal (or liquidation) from the funds. For 1983, an additional $600 million was identified which had not been included in the prior estimate.
Source: Capital Publishing Corporation, *Venture Capital Journal*, various issues.

The company should show current income appropriate to its current stage if financing is sought from an SBIC. It supports a range of 25 to 30 percent return compounded annually for investor compensation. Return on investment ranges from 5 to 10 times investment in five to seven years for a startup company to five times investment in five years for a more mature company.

Examples of successful venture capital financing include:

Custom Silicon, Inc.
Petrophysical Services, Inc.
Signal Processing Circuits, Inc.
Apollo Computer, Inc.
LaserData, Inc.

RESULTS OF VENTURE CAPITAL FINANCING

Depending on the experience level of management and the company's size and operating history, management will give up a significant percentage of equity (up to 70 percent) as a result of venture capital financing. That equity percentage is directly proportionate to the perceived risks involved. Often, startup management will lose effective control of the company. If venture capitalists decide to retain a minority position, they will usually prefer that the majority interest be divided among key managers.

Most venture capital funds abstain from day-to-day management of the operation, although they may seek representation on the board of directors. Some funds, however, will require hands-on management opportunity if the company flounders or if projected returns diminish.

If convertible notes are included in the financing deal, venture capitalists can become creditors to the company. In addition, notes reduce future debt capacity, even if they are subordinated to other debt. This can be detrimental to the company's future financing needs. If the contract includes preferred stock in the compensation package, the relationship between company and fund is less complicated.

One way to estimate the cost of venture capital is to estimate the venture capitalist's return: project ten times the initial investment in five years for a startup, or five times the initial investment in five years for a mature company.

One risk is that if the money raised in any given round of financing is not sufficient to achieve present goals, or the company has not negotiated staged financing before maturity or going public, additional future financing may be required, which can further erode share price and management's equity stake/control.

WHEN TO SEEK VENTURE CAPITAL

The best time to look for venture capital is when (1) the company has a unique technology, product or characteristic distinguishable from the competition, if any, (2) it needs financing as well as management direction early on to achieve rapid growth for high returns, (3) the company's industry can support long-term growth potential to at least $25 million in revenues, (4) the company has few competitors for a new product or technology, (5) it needs short-term financial and management assistance before going public or being acquired or (6) after-tax profit potential is above-average at about 30 percent.

THE HOW-TO TIMETABLE

One Year before Financing (Startup Companies)

1. *Market Research.* Determine that there is a need for the product or technology at a price that earns a significant profit for the new company and its future investors.

2. *Product Protection.* Patents, trademarks, copyrights and trade secret protection should be sought by third-party professionals before the new company is structured.

3. *Third-Party Professionals.* A professional team of attorneys, accountants, advisors, strategists and financial planners should be assembled to assist in business formation, first-round and later-stage financing, estate planning and legal consulting.

Venture Capital Investments*

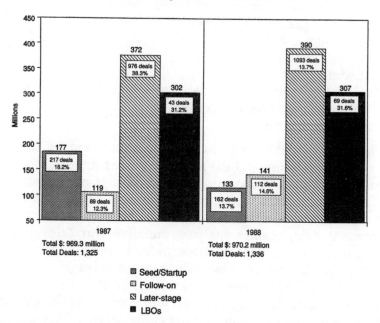

4. Business Formation. Incorporation should be planned by a professional who has expertise in the most beneficial ways to structure a new business.

Six Months before Financing (Startup and Mature Companies)

1. Business Plan. Outline the product, company, industry and market highlights on which venture capitalists will evaluate the potential of the company, including:

Executive summary with a description of the product, its market and the management team, projected financial data including annual revenue and net income for five years, and financing needs and use of proceeds

Background data on the founders and key management
Market statistics, domestic and overseas
Analysis of potential customer base
Competitive analysis
Labor and material cost data
R&D data
Product/technology protection program including patents, trademarks and/or copyrights
Regulatory information

The length of the business plan is determined by the complexity of the company and the amount of financing desired. If the company is a high-tech manufacturing firm that needs more than $1 million in first-round financing, the business plan will require more in-depth information including detailed research and development data, market analysis, and five-year sales and cost projections. If management requires under $1 million for a simpler operation, the plan can be about fifteen pages in length.

2. *Financial Projections.* If the company is in the concept or startup stage, financial projections should start with sales estimates based on extremely accurate assumptions, from which all other analysis flows. Data on manufacturing, administrative and sales costs, and cash flow projections should be included. More mature companies should also include profit and loss statements, balance sheet projections and a five-year cash flow. Most projections can be based on:

Capital expenditures
Gross margin by product line/total
Sales increases by product line/unit or total dollar volume
Interest rates on debt and interest income on temporary investment of excess funds
Income tax rate
Accounts receivable collection
Accounts payable payment
Inventory turnover
Depreciation schedules and usefulness of assets

3. *Financial Request.* State how much financing is requested, why it is needed, and use of proceeds, which should be consistent

with financial projections. Startup companies need to explain capitalization, enumerate shareholders and their position within the company, how much stock they own and their share cost. Management of mature companies needs to outline the capital structure and how venture capital funding will affect it. Also, simultaneous and future financing sources should be described, including immediate financing and/or staged financing, as various corporate development goals are met. Finally, an analysis of the debt/equity capital mix should be included, which outlines the company's ability to repay (debt) and/or grow (equity).

Three Months before Financing

1. Fund Selection. A third-party professional can give referrals for the funds that most closely match the company's development stage, size and industry, the amount of financing required and future development needs. It is critical to match the goals of the company with the capabilities and preferences of the venture capital investors. Successful venture capital candidates most often are referred to an appropriate fund by an outside professional. There are many kinds of venture capital funds to choose from:

SBICs: Small Business Investment Corporations are bank- or corporate-owned, invest up to $50,000 in a company, and will not be the largest investor in the deal.

Private Funds: Investors include individuals and/or institutions like pension funds or insurance companies. Private funds typically invest more heavily in later-stage companies that are less risky, putting at least $1 million into the deal with or without other investment partners. Larger private funds tend not to participate in the company's affairs to the extent that a public fund would to help manage a startup.

Publicly Held Funds: Venture capital funds whose stocks are traded publicly invest more often in startups, require a more substantial equity position in the company and become far more involved in management. Most public funds invest from $500,000 to $2 million in any one company.

BDCs: Business Development Companies are either public or private, and by law must put 70 percent of their capital in venture equity investments and provide significant managerial assistance to portfolio companies.

Public Partnerships: Offered by large brokerage houses to small investors, these partnerships generally will invest up to $2 million in a startup or mature company.

FILING REQUIREMENTS

Venture capital is early-round financing for a private, startup company or small, later-stage company. There are no federal or state disclosure/reporting requirements when venture capital is invested in a private company. State incorporation papers must be filed when a new business is created.

COSTS

1. *Management Fee.* Most venture capitalists charge from 2 to 4 percent of the total capital committed for management services.

2. *Equity Stake.* Startup management may lose up to 70 percent of its equity in the company. Later-stage management retains up to 60 percent of its equity. Equity loss varies widely, depending on the amount of risk involved. Venture capitalists typically take one of three forms of equity: convertible debt or debt with a warrant to buy common stock, convertible preferred stock or common stock.

3. *Capital Gains.* When the company is sold or goes public, venture capitalists may get up to 30 percent of the capital gains as a result of the transaction.

4. *Return on Investment.* Although public funds look for returns of up to 30 percent and private funds often seek 50 percent returns, a more realistic estimate is about 20 percent.

5. *Out-of-Pocket.* These expenses include preparation and production of the business plan, finder's fees and upfront costs, which total up to 5 percent of the amount invested.

Capital Commitments to Independent Private Firms

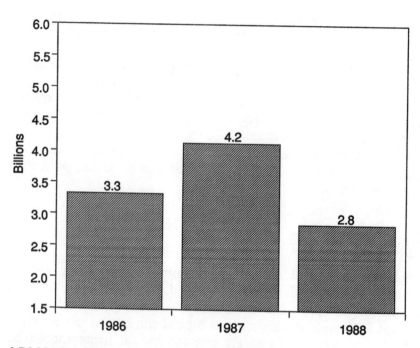

ADVANTAGES AND DISADVANTAGES

Advantages

1. Management assistance is available to startup firms, including access to bankers, suppliers, potential customers and management recruitment services.

2. Staged financing can be negotiated for startup, execution and expansion-phase funding, which reduces the risk of stalled growth and reduces the amount of return on investment required to initiate separate financing.

3. Venture capital is one of the few financing sources available to startup or concept-stage ventures.

4. Venture capital financing is more immediate and less costly in the short term than most other forms of startup financing.

Disadvantages

1. In the long term, venture capital can be very costly in return on investment, which averages between 20 percent and 50 percent.

2. Management of a concept-stage operation often loses effective control in exchange for seed capital to get started.

3. Future valuation of the company based on faulty projections can cost owners more equity and/or lawsuits if the company does not perform to expectations.

4. Excessive debt/equity servicing as a cost of acquiring venture capital can reduce company valuation as an initial public offering or acquisition.

TESTING THE WATERS

There is no specific guideline that determines when venture capital will be most successful. Common sense dictates that when interest rates are high or traditional startup sources like banks have tightened loan restrictions, venture capital can be the most beneficial financing source. However, venture capital firms should be reviewed and selected carefully on the basis of their track record in the industry.

ALTERNATIVES TO VENTURE CAPITAL

1. *Friends and Family.* For a startup company that needs less than $100,000, the least costly financing source in the short and long term is usually a personal loan from supporters who are familiar with the company and its management.

2. *Mezzanine Financing.* This capital falls between ground floor financing from equity investors and the roof, topped by senior bondholders. Mezzanine financing provided by institutions like pension funds often supports highly leveraged buyouts, and is generally less costly than venture capital. See Section 5.

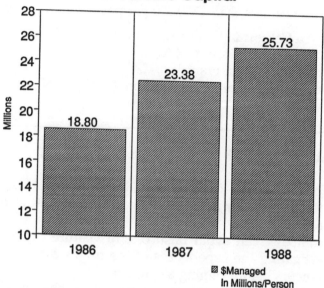

Per Person Investments in Venture Capital

Source: From a survey of the venture capital industry conducted by Boston Capital Ventures Inc.

3. Research and Development Limited Partnership. Rather than give up partial ownership of the company, an R&D partnership can provide some of the necessary funds at a lower cost. Gamma Partners created a partnership in which the founder was the general partner and a venture capital fund was the limited partner. It raised $670,000 in staged financing in exchange for a graduated profit allocation between 25 percent and 45 percent. See Chapter 4.

4. Incubator. In addition to offering lower overhead and administrative costs, some university and corporate incubators make limited financing available to promising startups. Lamb's Information Systems, Inc., began manufacturing antistatic computer devices in 1985 at the Business and Technology Center in Pueblo, Colorado, at a rental cost of $8.50 per square foot. This protected the company's cash flow from standard marketplace costs. See Chapter 8.

SOURCES

Funds that invest less than $750,000 per portfolio company:

Southern California Ventures, Los Angeles, CA.
Zero Stage Fund, Boston, MA.
Coast Ventures, San Francisco, CA.
Yegen Venture Capital Corporation, Paramus, NJ.

PITFALLS TO AVOID

Management should know the liquidity of the venture capital fund, and whether or not the fund can support future rounds of financing.

The company can avoid unsuccessful venture capital firms by investigating the experiences of the fund's other portfolio entrepreneurs before signing a contract.

Public funds may be under pressure from shareholders to achieve capital gains before the company is ready to be sold, merged or taken public.

CHAPTER 2

Joint Ventures

DESCRIPTION

A joint venture is a partnership between two or more parties to research, develop, produce, market or distribute a product for profit by forming a separate project that is owned, operated and controlled by a small group of investors. A joint venture can be organized as a corporation, partnership or undivided interest. Typically, a small company that has incorporated will contract with a larger company to merge only one complementary technology or product. Joint venture compensation to the large company takes the form of an equity stake in the small company.

In contrast, a partnership shares in all combined products or technologies, and pays compensation in the form of a royalty interest from sales, a percent of profits or a combination.

A joint venture can include, but is not limited to, a licensing agreement or an effective research and development partnership with the joint venture party. A joint venture also is known as a research and development contract, a joint venture marketing, manufacturing or distribution agreement or a collaborative agreement.

PROFILE OF A SUCCESSFUL JOINT VENTURE CANDIDATE

The most viable joint ventures are formed (1) by an entrepreneur with a proprietary technology that is at least fully conceptualized, if not fully developed, (2) after the small, developing company has been incorporated, (3) by an owner who has come from a larger corporate culture and who knows how to attract the attention of funding executives, (4) when the undeveloped technology or product is complementary to a technology or product proprietary to the large corporate entity, (5) between a small firm and a larger corporate entity that is not an industry giant (e.g., Apple Computer is more accessible than (IBM), (6) when there is the potential for a long-lasting relationship in which future product ideas can be merged and (7) if commercialization of the undeveloped technology or product is enhanced by the know-how of the large company's market-driven strategies.

Successful joint ventures include:

International Athletic Clubs of America
AgriCapital Corporation
Energy Reserve, Inc.
MPSI Systems

RESULTS OF A JOINT VENTURE

In a joint venture with a larger corporate entity, most entrepreneurs (1) give up a 20 percent or less equity stake in their new company, (2) can develop a technology or product and get it to market more quickly as a result of support by the joint venture partner, (3) benefit from advanced management, marketing and production strategies proven by the larger company, (4) have at least the potential for developing second-, third- and fourth-generation products more easily in a proven relationship, (5) can concentrate on developing the product rather than on raising future financing, (6) retain the control necessary to continue the joint venture relationship, go it alone, go public or create another relationship that may be more supportive of the owner's goals and (7) can expand into foreign markets easily with an overseas joint venture partner.

The Innovation Process—
The Product Life Cycle

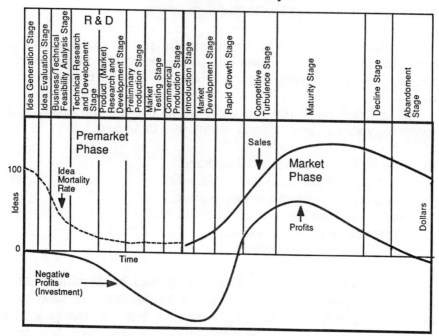

Source: The Innovation Assessment Center.

WHEN TO CREATE A JOINT VENTURE

An entrepreneur should structure a joint venture when (1) additional financing and/or assistance is needed quickly to develop the product expeditiously for competitive or financial reasons, (2) startup or development capital is expensive or scarce, (3) the undeveloped product is complementary to a product offered by a large company in the same or a related industry, (4) recessionary economic effects warrant a joint venture as the least expensive way for a large company to develop a product, (5) the entrepreneur has good contacts within larger corporations that are joint venture candidates or (6) a foreign entity needs the company's product and will be competitive to obtain it.

THE HOW-TO TIMETABLE

Nine Months before Contract Signature

1. Incorporation. The entrepreneur should incorporate in order to simplify the joint venture agreement and to more easily assign the joint venture responsibilities to specific corporate entities.

2. Market Analysis. The potential market for the product or technology should be analyzed extensively including:

Size and value of potential demand
Existing and potential target markets
Market-share analysis of competitors
Technical evaluation of competitors
Potential for future products
Condition of the industry

3. Business Plan. This document should be developed as a strategic outline for potential joint venture partners who will evaluate not only the emerging company, but also the potential products, the market and the complementary aspects of their own product or technology. The plan should include:

Extensive analysis of the proposed project, what is to be developed, any base technology already available, how the new product can be merged with existing corporate products, and the equipment, facilities, financing and personnel necessary to complete the project.

Feasibility analysis of the technology or product based on a technical evaluation by an outside professional.

Market analysis developed by the company including potential demand, existing and potential markets, estimated revenues, estimated production costs and the competition.

Project budget with line-item costs and the development stages to be covered. Manufacturing plan that explains how the new project will be produced, set-up costs and financing sources.

4. Complementary Products. Management should begin the search for potential joint venture partners with complementary products and/or technologies among larger companies in the same or a related industry.

Six Months before Contract Signature

When a list of prospective partners is compiled, management can begin to interview and screen companies that may be compatible. Negotiation points should cover the following questions:

> How large an ownership stake will each candidate want in the company in exchange for financing and production assistance?
>
> Is the large company's product or technology compatible with the product to be developed?
>
> Is there a potential for an ongoing relationship that includes future products? How much control will the joint venture partner want of day-to-day development and operations in the emerging company?
>
> Is the large company willing to define specific responsibilities for and rights to development, manufacturing, marketing and distribution?
>
> Who gets the tax credits for research and development?
>
> What happens to the joint venture partnership on liquidation?

Three Months before Contract Signature

1. Third-Party Professionals. When the joint venture partner has been identified and final-stage negotiations are imminent, the entrepreneur should obtain the professional assistance of an attorney and an accountant who are knowledgeable in the company's industry and familiar with joint venture structures. Their job is to project the tax implications of the joint venture, develop the necessary contracts and file the required disclosure/reporting documentation. Although the larger company will have in-house and outside counsel, the emerging company also should retain outside professionals to represent its interests.

2. *Intermediary.* Most small companies find that using an intermediary for final negotiations is helpful and time-saving. The intermediary can be the attorney or accountant retained to assist management, or it can be a deal broker or underwriter interested in the future development of the company.

3. *Filing.* In many cases, management will structure a joint venture with a larger public company that must file reporting/disclosure documents with the SEC and state regulatory bodies. This will be done by the public company's legal counsel, but the documents should be reviewed by the entrepreneur.

After the Joint Venture Is in Effect

Many large joint venture partners require the entrepreneur to achieve benchmark development goals at specified intervals and to keep the project within budgetary and time constraints. If applicable, management will be expected to keep the partner(s) informed of progress, cost overrides and glitches that may surface while the product is in development.

FILING REQUIREMENTS

An emerging private company is not subject to SEC and/or state filing requirements in a joint venture; a public joint venture partner is. Private companies are governed by the Uniform Partnership Act. If the company is a public entity, it is subject to the reporting/disclosure requirements of the SEC; management must inform shareholders of the funding commitment via a footnote in financial statements contained in annual and quarterly reports to the shareholders.

COSTS

1. *Sweat Equity.* The largest cost of a joint venture to the entrepreneur is the sweat equity time invested in the product or technology before and after the joint venture is created.

2. Compensation. Most large joint venture partners require up to a 20 percent equity stake in the emerging company as compensation for financing and production/management assistance. The equity stake generally doesn't exceed 20 percent because of the reporting requirements that ensue for the large company when that percentage is exceeded.

3. Legal. The cost of legal assistance is highly variable depending on the complexity of the product or technology and the nature of the joint venture agreement. Most entrepreneurs pay about 5 percent of the amount financed through the joint venture.

4. Accounting. Usually a flat fee of between $2,000 and $10,000 is charged for a tax analysis of the joint venture.

5. Marketing. The entrepreneur can spend a variable amount on marketing and travel expenses to interview potential joint venture partners.

ADVANTAGES AND DISADVANTAGES

Advantages

1. A joint venture can be one of the least costly ways for an entrepreneur, or large company, to develop a product or technology. Management usually gives up less than 20 percent ownership in the emerging company as compensation.

2. Product development can proceed rapidly, with supplementary assistance and financing from the larger partner.

3. Foreign joint ventures permit rapid expansion in foreign markets, with resulting rapid company growth.

4. A joint venture can be structured virtually at will, with terms that are tailored to the needs of both the entrepreneur and the larger company.

5. There are no filing requirements associated with a joint venture for the emerging company.

6. Long-term potential in future products, financing, revenue, profit and growth are practically assured if the joint venture partners are compatible.

Disadvantages

1.   It can be difficult and time-consuming to find an appropriate joint venture partner within a large organization unless the entrepreneur has good contacts within that organization.

2.   The entrepreneur may not be open to the market-driven theories of the larger partner, thus endangering the efficacy of the joint venture or its future prospects.

3.   Foreign joint ventures can be costly to the entrepreneur who has not researched and been advised of all the ramifications of doing business with a foreign concern (see Chapter 11).

4. Regulatory agencies are increasingly concerned about antitrust issues, which can negatively impact the goals of the joint venture.

TESTING THE WATERS

A common interest in a technology or product on the part of both the entrepreneur and a large company in the industry is the surest guideline for evaluating the success potential of a joint venture. The prospect of an entire line of products that can be developed from a technology or new product is even more conducive to a successful joint venture.

ALTERNATIVES TO A JOINT VENTURE

1.   *Research and Development Partnership.* If management wants assistance only to develop a product, an R&D partnership may be a better option. Holographics, Inc. raised $432,000 in two R&D partnerships over two years to build test models of its medical imaging device (see Chapter 4).

2.   *Licensing Agreement.* Management can limit the participation of a business partner by spinning off a technology or product to another company for sale or distribution. Integrity Solutions, Inc. had strong overseas sales of its proprietary software program to protect the loss of computer data. To increase domestic sales

without incurring extensive marketing costs, the company signed a licensing agreement that allowed Sterling Software, Inc. to sell the product in exchange for $1 million (see Section I).

3. *Private Placement.* By giving up equity in the company, management can sell shares to a limited number of private investors or to an institution in order to meet specific marketing goals. Ribi ImmunoChem Research, Inc. sold a $1.8 million offering to Executive Life Insurance Co. to commercialize several new immunotherapeutic products and market existing biomedical agents (see Chapter 23).

PITFALLS TO AVOID

Antitrust issues can become important if the joint venture creates a seemingly monopolistic operation.

The interests of a small venture partner can be lost if the large corporate partner gains control of the product or technology, directs the momentum of the project to suit its needs, or does not provide enough financing or other assistance.

Joint venture terms can be extremely flexible. Tax advantages and profits should be negotiated carefully to avoid inequities.

CHAPTER 3
Limited Partnerships

DESCRIPTION

A limited partnership is a for-profit business entity composed of a small number of general partners and a larger number of limited partners. The general partner(s) manage the day-to-day activities of marketing the product or service and the limited partners finance the project. The chief characteristics of a limited partnership, and the most important reasons for structuring it, are the resulting structural flexibility and tax benefits. Limited partnerships allow a more flexible allocation of profits and losses, in contrast to the corporate structure. Without these benefits, it does not make sense for a startup or early-stage company to form a limited partnership.

The general partner typically collects a management fee and a percentage of capital gains and/or income in exchange for providing management services and assuming liability for debt repayment, if any. The limited partners are at risk only for the amount of their capital contribution, and receive capital gains, income and tax benefits as compensation for that investment.

Partners share all earnings before taxes, whereas the owners of public corporations—shareholders—receive only a percent of after-tax earnings as dividends.

Public limited partnerships are accessible by any number of investors, who generally make an investment of about $5,000 each. Private limited partnerships are sold to a maximum thirty-five nonaccredited investors and an unlimited number of accredited investors, who each contribute $50,000 or more.

There are many specialized limited partnership structures, developed primarily for service organizations, that are subject to additional regulatory and tax requirements, including oil and gas partnerships, master limited partnerships, income partnerships, and research and development partnerships (see Chapter 4).

Although federal tax law changes in 1987 caused sales of master limited partnerships to plunge 73 percent to $771 million in 1988 from $2.87 billion in 1987, MLPs still are legal. Under the tax revisions, new MLPs are taxed as corporations unless they are engaged in energy, natural resources or real estate.

PROFILE OF A SUCCESSFUL LIMITED PARTNERSHIP

A successful limited partnership is a private, early-stage company with tangible assets that can be developed for future profit, and for current depreciation or tax deductions. Industries that derive optimal limited partnership benefits include real estate, high-tech, biomedical and cable television, among others.

Although an early-stage concern is the best candidate because potential appreciation is greatest early on, the company should have strong profit potential from product sales in addition to tax deduction opportunities. Therefore, the company's debt-to-capitalization ratio should fall below 50 percent in order not to burden future profit with debt repayment.

The product or asset to be developed by the limited partnership should be marketable and, ideally, have unique qualities or a strong, if potential, market niche among competitors. The most successful limited partnerships develop an asset that is easily appraised or has an existing market with which to compare value.

In addition, the company should allow tax deductions only for the amount of capital contribution or initial investment, excluding the value of letters of credit issued by the limited partners. Multiples, or partnerships that offer deductions equal to the capital contribution plus the value of the letter of credit, often are disqualified for tax deductions by the Internal Revenue Service. Successful limited partnerships include:

Standard Microsystems
Bega Biotechnologies
Chyron Corporation

RESULTS OF A LIMITED PARTNERSHIP

By structuring a limited partnership, management can (1) raise between $250,000 and $20 million plus in development capital, (2) attract investors more easily with pass-through tax benefits for depreciation during the early years of the project and with a strategy for converting ordinary income to capital gains, which are taxed at a lower rate, (3) negotiate more favorable terms for development capital than those usually associated with venture capital or bank borrowing, (4) retain ownership of the company and future assets or technology while receiving assistance for a current project and (5) share in the gain when the asset is developed and sold.

WHEN TO STRUCTURE A LIMITED PARTNERSHIP

The best time to do a limited partnership is when (1) the company's industry is young and growing, but mature enough to establish fair market valuation of the asset, (2) the asset will meet a future demand, (3) there is little competition for market share in the industry, (4) market research indicates that potential for profitability exists, (5) other sources of startup capital are resistant to financing new ventures or (6) borrowing rates are high.

THE HOW-TO TIMETABLE

Nine Months before Effective Date

1. Feasibility Study. Before outside professionals are brought in, management should complete a feasibility study to determine the marketability of the asset or product. Some of the questions that need to be answered early on are:

Is there a market, or a demand, for the asset?

What kind of profit potential exists for the asset at the time of sale?

To what extent will the asset have to be developed before profit is achievable?

How long will development take?

Can the limited partners provide enough financing to see the project through the development stage?

Will outside or supplementary financing be necessary to complete development?

How many competitors divide market share?

2. *Business Plan.* The results of the feasibility study should be compiled into a business plan to help potential investors analyze the merits of the proposed project. This strategic outline should include 10 to 30 pages of:

Extensive information about the product to be developed, and the facilities, equipment and personnel necessary to complete development;

Market analysis including potential demand, existing and potential markets, estimated profit, development costs, a description of the competition and a sales plan;

Manufacturing plan explaining how the product will be made, set-up costs and specific responsibilities, if applicable;

Budget items including line-item costs of the work to be covered;

Development plan that outlines what has to be done, by whom and in what time frame;

Investment analysis of how profits and losses will be allocated, cash-flow projections and investor tax consequences.

Six Months before Effective Date

1. *Appraisal.* A professional appraiser should be contacted for an evaluation of the asset or product that will be sold. The appraiser should be a specialist in the company's industry and be able to provide industry standards for appraisal. References should be required and contacted.

2. *Syndication.* Although most limited partnerships are structured and sold by a lead underwriter who forms a syndicate of secondary underwriters to help sell the investment, a limited partnership can be self-underwritten via a contractual sales arrangement with a registered broker/dealer who is retained by management. Many states require that a limited partnership be sold only by a registered broker/dealer.

If management delegates the sales job to a broker/dealer, several should be interviewed before selection in order to determine:

Fees: Most underwriters charge a percentage of the amount raised by the limited partners, and some charge upfront retainers or nonrefundable, nonaccountable expenses of up to 2 percent of the amount raised.

Qualifications: The lead underwriter should be a specialist in limited partnerships and have knowledge of the company's industry.

Style: Management should try to match the level of aggressiveness among the brokers with corporate style, i.e., will the deal be syndicated among colleagues and acquaintances or will brokers cold-call the public to sell the deal?

3. *Accounting.* An accounting firm should be selected to help structure the limited partnership, giving particular attention to tax implications for the investors. The accounting firm should be chosen with the same qualifications that applied to the underwriter. When the accounting firm has been selected, management should arrange a meeting between accounting and underwriter professionals to structure the deal.

4. *Legal.* The last stage is contracting for outside legal assistance to complete filing and other requirements. Legal representation should be queried about fees, capability in limited partnerships in the company's industry, and style.

Three Months before Effective Date

1. *Contracts.* Specific limited partnership agreements should be drawn up so that both the company, or general partner, and the limited partners are adequately protected and intended tax benefits actually result. These include:

Limited Partnership Agreement: Terms and conditions must be specified, including terms for forming and dissolving the partnership, rights and obligations of the limited partners, and the company's rights, obligations, responsibility and authority. Limited partnership documents are among the most complex of all financing agreements.

License Agreement (if applicable): To meet the holding period requirement for long-term capital gains to investors on the proceeds received from selling the product, asset or technology, the partnership must hold for one year before selling. To enable the company to use the product during that period, the partnership signs a developed technology or product license agreement including terms and conditions.

Stock Acquisition Option: If the partnership is given warrants to buy stock in the company as part of the contract, called an "equity play" terms and conditions must be outlined in a separate agreement.

2. *Optional documents* may be required, including:

Feasibility study
Tax opinion
Legal review
Securities opinion for public offerings
Budget

3. *Offering Circular or Sales Document.* If the limited partnership is sold as a public offering through an underwriter (seldom done except in the oil and gas industry), a prospectus (see Chapter 1 for prospectus requirements) and appropriate documentation must be prepared to meet SEC requirements. If the limited partnership is sold as a private placement limited to 35 nonaccredited investors and an unlimited number of accredited investors, an offering circular or placement memorandum must be produced, including:

Description of the asset or project
Use of proceeds

Risk factors
Company background
Market analysis
Analysis of competition
Summary of the contract and all related agreements
Partnership agreement summary including profit and loss allocation
Tax opinion including deductibility of costs and the tax treatment of proceeds to the partnership

One Month before Effective Date

The offering circular will be filed with the SEC, and state regulatory bodies, if applicable. Before the SEC issues an effective date, at which time the underwriter can begin selling the limited partnership, revisions will have to be completed.

After the Limited Partnership Is Sold Out

Ongoing management of the partnership is the responsibility of the general partner(s), who monitors the project, distributes royalties or income if any, and provides progress reports and tax updates to the limited partners. In some cases, an affiliate of the sponsoring company acts as general partner.

FILING REQUIREMENTS

The Uniform Partnership Act and the Uniform Limited Partnership Act govern the creation and operation of partnerships in most states. All public partnerships are subject to the federal reporting/disclosure requirements of the SEC. Reporting documents include a quarterly financial report (Form 10-Q), annual financial report (Form 10-K), annual report to shareholders, proxy statements, reports about current material events in the company (Form 8-K) and other reports for audited financial statements, the sale of control shares and tender offers.

Public partnerships also must meet any reporting/ disclosure requirements of the states in which the company is located and the limited partnership is sold.

If the limited partnership is sold as a private offering to no more than 35 nonaccredited investors, or any number of accredited investors, the company is subject to S-1 or S-18 SEC requirements and state requirements as applicable. If the limited partnership is sold to more than 35 nonaccredited investors, additional and on-going SEC filing requirements apply, and the offering will become a public entity.

COSTS

The key to the cost of a limited partnership is this: the smaller the number of investors and the more accredited investors sold, the lower the underwriter cost (the biggest portion of the total cost). Nearly all limited partnerships cost from 10 percent to 15 percent of the total amount raised. Multimillion dollar partnerships cost closer to 20 percent of the amount raised.

1. Appraisal. Depending on the complexity of the asset or product to be sold and the availability of industry comparisons, appraisers usually charge 2 to 4 percent of the value of the asset.

2. Underwriter. The largest portion of the total cost, syndication commissions total about 6 percent of the amount raised. In addition, some underwriters may charge up to 2 percent of the amount raised for upfront, nonaccountable expenses, and/or underwriter legal and filing expenses.

3. Accounting. The second largest portion of the total cost, accounting assistance costs about 4 percent of the amount raised.

4. Legal. Outside legal representation costs about 3 percent of the amount raised.

5. Printing. Between $50,000 and $100,000 is charged to produce a prospectus for a public partnership. If an offering circular is produced for a private limited partnership, the cost will range between $10,000 and $50,000.

6. Filing Fees. For a public offering, SEC filing costs .02 percent of the amount raised. NASD filing costs $100 plus .01 percent, with a $5,100 maximum. State fees vary up to $15,000, and registrar and transfer agent fees cost between $5,000 and $10,000.

7. *Capital Gains.* Capital gains are based on the assets the partnership is entitled to profit from, which are highly variable and distributed on an annualized after-tax basis. Limited partnerships generally are more costly to owners than debt financing, but less costly than equity techniques.

8. *Ongoing Costs.* Between one-third and one-half of the initial cost of the partnership must be paid annually for legal, reporting, tax compliance, accounting, filing and hidden costs.

ADVANTAGES AND DISADVANTAGES

Advantages

1. Investors are attracted by the pass-through tax advantages of early-stage depreciation deductions and the lower capital gains tax rate when the asset or product is sold.

2. Investors risk only the amount of capital contribution, excluding multiples that offer deductions equal to the amount of capital contribution plus the letter of credit issued by the investor.

3. If investors qualify, the limited partnership is not subject to extensive SEC filing requirements.

4. A limited partnership can be an inexpensive way to raise startup capital well before the product or asset goes to market.

5. If losses occur in the development stage, they are passed through to investors who can deduct them from ordinary income.

Disadvantages

1. The company must be able to show potential profit, in addition to tax deductions, in order to sell a limited partnership successfully and/or extensively

2. Most limited partnerships extend from three to eight years before the partnership makes a profit.

3. Regulatory bodies like the Internal Revenue Service often can greatly affect the terms and the desirability of the partnership. Federal tax law changes in 1987 helped cause a 23 percent drop in the sale of public partnerships in 1988 to $10.5 billion from $13.5 billion in 1987.

TESTING THE WATERS

The best indicator for forming a limited partnership is possession of an asset or technology that is certain to appreciate in value as a result of further development. With the prospect of capital gains, together with profit or loss tax advantages that result in deductions and conversion of ordinary income, limited partners who need deductions are usually attracted to the investment.

ALTERNATIVES TO A LIMITED PARTNERSHIP

1. Venture Capital. Many of the newer venture capital firms specialize in startup companies. American International Communications, Inc. raised more than $1 million in two rounds of financing during 1983 and 1984 from Columbine Venture Management, Inc. for early-stage product development (see Chapter 1).

2. Convertible Debt. No longer a strategy used primarily by mature companies, convertible debt is becoming a popular tool for raising capital among emerging companies. In 1982, Gish Biomedical, Inc. sold more than $1 million in convertible subordinated debentures, including common stock and a warrant for common shares (see Chapter 19).

3. Networking. American Information Systems raised $2 million in early-stage capital by selling shares of the company through a network of accounting firms. See Chapter 7.

SOURCES

McCown DeLeeuw, New York, NY and Menlo Park, CA.
Business and Industry Association of New Hampshire, Concord, NH.

PITFALLS TO AVOID

Limited partners are passive investors. The company will receive no management or other assistance except financing.

Internal Revenue Service guidelines should be adhered to so that the partnership is not endangered. Deals that propose sheltering more than twice the amount invested by each limited partner are most likely to be audited.

The potential for success should be high. If losses occur, the general partner must cede resulting tax deductions to the limited partners, who are at-risk only for the amount of their capital contributions.

CHAPTER 4

Research and Development Partnerships

DESCRIPTION

A research and development (R&D) limited partnership, the most common R&D contract form, is an agreement between a sponsoring company with a technology or research that needs to be funded, and a group of limited partners who function like stockholders in a corporation. The company (general partner) agrees to complete research and development for the partnership on a best-efforts basis (results are not guaranteed) for fixed-fee or cost-plus compensation. An R&D partnership can be structured as a public offering or as a private placement. Alpha, Inc. raised $750,000 from investors for its R&D partnership, Alpha Partners.

The primary characteristic of an R&D partnership is the tax benefit package that limited partners can take advantage of because they own the technology. If the general partner, or inventor of the technology, wants to buy the technology back after developing it, the limited partners receive cash or equity in the company as remuneration for it.

A blind pool R&D partnership is an investment in a group of companies rather than in a specific venture. A blind pool, which is managed by a brokerage house, R&D group or venture capitalist, functions like a venture capital fund. Near Space Communications, Inc. raised $3.4 million from PruTech Research & Development Partnership, a blind pool fund.

A tax-advantaged startup partnership is an agreement between a startup company, whose founder serves as the general partner, and venture capitalists, who purchase limited partnership units. The partnership develops a product to the brink of profitability, when the partners can choose to incorporate and convert the partnership units, tax-free, into shares of the new corporation.

A hybrid R&D partnership is an agreement in which the company issues warrants that entitle the partnership to purchase stock. The partnership receives both royalties and a right to acquire equity in the sponsoring company.

Small Business Innovation Research Program, FY 1983–FY 1987

	Phase I			Phase II		
Fiscal Year	Number of Proposals	Number of Awards	Thousands of Dollars	Number of Proposals	Number of Awards	Thousands of dollars
Total	53,027	7,216	359,873	4,953	2,151	640,512
1987	14,723	2,189	109,585	2,390	768	240,883
1986	12,449	1,945	98,494	1,112	564	199,394
1985	9,086	1,397	69,126	765	407	130,003
1984	7,955	999	48,020	559	338	60,422
1983	8,814	686	34,648	127	74	9,810

Source: U.S. Small Business Administration, Office of Innovation, Research and Technology, Results Under the Small Business Innovation Development Act (Washington, D.C.: U.S. Government Printing Office, annual reports for FY 1983–FY 1987).

In 1983, Cetus issued warrants to purchase stock at $23 per share, exercisable for four years, at a time when its common stock was trading at $20 per share.

A corporate R&D partnership is an agreement between two or more companies to pool their resources and share research results. Microelectronics and Computer Technology Corporation, the largest combined R&D group in the country, was formed by 12 mega-company sponsors like Honeywell, Digital Equipment and Motorola, among others.

PROFILE OF A SUCCESSFUL R&D PARTNERSHIP CANDIDATE

Virtually any company, regardless of size or maturity stage, can utilize an R&D partnership beneficially. A promising candidate is an emerging growth company with existing products in the

Royalty Partnership

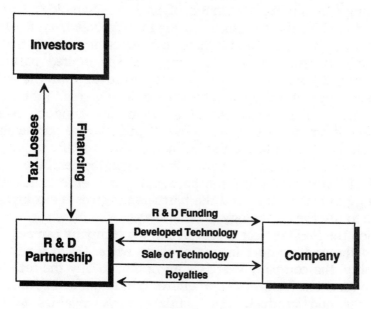

marketplace, or a company that can support at least a 45 percent aftertax rate of return on the investors' net investment. A successful R&D partnership operates in an industry that is growing and promises longevity, such as electronics or high-tech. It can attract other financing sources that will support expenses additional to research and development while the company is engaged in research. The ability to attract debt financing for working capital, for example, or equity financing to acquire fixed assets, presupposes the existence of value in the company.

Other R&D partnerships include:

MEC Industries, Inc.
Genentech Clinical Partners Ltd.
Trilogy Computer
Development Partners

RESULTS OF AN R&D PARTNERSHIP

In exchange for giving ownership of its base technology to the R&D partnership, the sponsoring company receives from $50,000 to $50 million (a maximum, for large companies) in funding that is earmarked for research and development. The limited partners receive current tax benefits, as well as future royalties in the 45 to 55 percent range. If management wants to keep access to the technology, for use in products other than the product being developed, it can do one of two things. It can give the partnership a nonexclusive license to use the technology in a specific project in exchange for a license fee. In a cross-licensing agreement, the other method, the company gives the partnership a license to use the technology in the venture and the partnership gives the company a license to use the technology in other ways.

When the R&D project is completed, the company can acquire rights to the end product in one of three ways. (1) In a royalty partnership, the company exercises an option to buy the technology with an exclusive license that allows it to manufacture and/or market the end product. The company pays royalties to the partnership based on product sales. (2) In a joint venture, the company and the R&D partnership form a joint venture to manufacture and market the end product. (3) In an equity partnership, the partnership and the company form a new company after the technology is developed, with a future conversion right in which partnership interests are converted to equity in the new company in a tax-free transaction. Equity partnerships are used primarily to start up new companies.

Equity Partnership

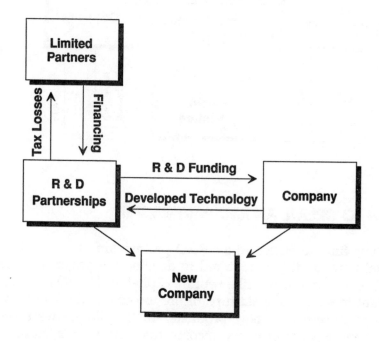

Joint Venture

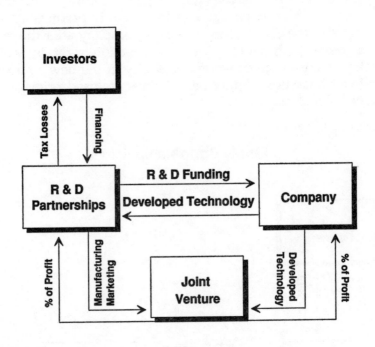

WHEN TO CREATE AN R&D PARTNERSHIP

The best time to structure an R&D partnership is when (1) substantial new funding is required to develop the project and traditional financing sources, like venture capital or the IPO market, are resistant to supporting startups or are too costly, (2) the company has a track record in new products, (3) the IRS allows investor deductions against ordinary income that represent a substantial portion of their investment (85 to 95 percent), (4) the aftertax return to investors can be in the 45 to 55 percent range, with income at long-term capital gains rates, (5) there is little dilution of stock, (6) there is a high probability of getting a product successfully to market or (7) interest rates are high.

THE HOW-TO TIMETABLE

Eight Months before Contract Date

1. *Business Plan.* This strategic outline not only serves as the cornerstone of limited partnership documentation, but it must also help potential investors assess the proposed R&D venture. It should include:

Extensive analysis of the proposed project, covering what is to be developed, base technology available, and equipment, facilities and personnel necessary to complete the project.

Feasibility study of the technology based on a technical evaluation by an outside firm like SRI International.

Market analysis, covering potential demand, existing and potential markets, estimated revenues, estimated production costs and the competition.

Budget for the project, covering costs and work to be completed.

Manufacturing plan with target sales, costs, strategies to reach target markets and sales projections.

Investment analysis with profit and loss allocation, cash-flow projections, assumptions and investor tax consequences.

2. *Third-Party Assistance.* Several experts should be retained to give specialized assistance in finding investors, marketing the partnership, developing the documentation and satisfying filing requirements. They should be interviewed about their expertise in R&D partnerships. These experts can include:

Underwriter: Depending on how much capital the company needs, any one of several professionals can develop the partnership, including accountants and attorneys (who typically raise up to $500,000), professional general partners that function like venture capital funds (who raise $500,000 to about $5 million), regional brokerage firms (for $1 million to $15 million) and national brokerage firms (for $15 million to $100 million).

Attorneys: Experienced professionals should be selected for familiarity with R&D agreements, related documentation and the offering documents. Accountants: A working knowledge of the tax consequences that result from all forms of R&D partnerships is essential.

Financial Printer: Look for a specialized ability to produce SEC-related documents.

Three Months before Contract Date

1. Contracts. R&D agreements should be structured by the underwriter so that both the company and the investors are adequately protected, and so that intended tax benefits actually result. R&D partnership documents are highly complex as compared to most other financing documentation, and include:

Limited Partnership Agreement: Terms and conditions must be specified, including terms for forming and dissolving the partnership, rights and obligations of the limited partners, and the company's rights, obligations, authority and responsibility.

Technology Transfer Agreement: Cover what portion of the incomplete technology remains under company control as well as the compensation for that portion sold to the partnership.

R&D Contracts: Define terms under which the company agrees to do specified research on a best-efforts fixed-costs or cost-plus basis.

License Agreement: To meet the holding period requirement for long-term capital gains allocated to investors on the proceeds from the sale, the partnership must hold the technology for one year before selling it to the company. To enable the company to use the technology during that period, the partnership signs a developed-technology license agreement that describes terms and conditions.

Purchase Options: This agreement allows the company one of three ways by which to buy the technology back from the partnership when development is complete.

Stock Acquisition Option: If the partnership is given warrants to buy stock in the company as part of the contract, called an "equity play," terms and conditions must be outlined in a separate agreement.

2. Optional documents may be required, including a feasibility study of the project, tax opinion, securities opinion for public partnerships and a project budget.

3. *Sales Document.* If the R&D partnership is sold as a public offering, a prospectus must be prepared (see Chapter 1 for prospectus requirements) and appropriate documentation must be filed to meet SEC and state requirements.

If the partnership is a private placement (limited to 35 nonaccredited investors and an unlimited number of accredited investors), an offering circular or placement memorandum must be prepared. In either case, the sales document should include:

Description of the project
Use of proceeds
Risk factors
Analysis of competition
Market analysis
Company background
Summary of the R&D contract and all related agreements
Partnership agreement summary with profit and loss allocations
Tax opinion with deductibility of costs and the tax treatment of proceeds to the partnership

After Contract Date

Ongoing management of the partnership is the responsibility of the general partner, who monitors the R&D project, distributes royalties if any, and provides progress reports and tax updates to the limited partners. In some cases, an affiliate of the sponsoring company acts as general partner.

FILING REQUIREMENTS

An R&D partnership is governed by the Uniform Partnership Act and the Uniform Limited Partnership Act. All public partnerships are subject to SEC reporting/disclosure requirements. Reporting documents include proxy statements, annual report to the shareholders, quarterly financial report (Form 10-Q), annual financial report (Form 10-K), reports about current material events in the company (Form 8-K) and other reports for audited financial statements, the sale of control shares and tender offers.

In addition, public partnerships must meet any reporting/disclosure requirements of the states in which they are sold. State requirements differ widely. If the R&D partnership is a private offering, the company must meet simplified filing requirements of the SEC and state regulatory bodies, if applicable.

COSTS

The total annualized costs of an R&D partnership average between 25 and 50 percent of funds raised.

1. *Underwriter.* The commission varies between 7 and 15 percent of the funds raised, depending on the size, track record and growth potential of the company, the growth potential of the industry both here and overseas and general market conditions. As a rule, small companies with a short operating history pay commissions on the high end of the 7–15 percent scale.

2. *Expenses.* Upfront, nonaccountable underwriter expenses are usually between 1 and 3 percent of the funds raised. They may be billed to the company in addition to as much as $50,000 in underwriter legal and filing expenses, and the commission.

3. *Out-of-Pocket.* These expenses range up to 20 percent of the funds raised for the company's legal and accounting fees.

4. *Printing.* Up to $100,000 may be spent to produce a prospectus for a public partnership, and up to $50,000 for a private placement offering circular.

5. *Video Production.* Some high-tech companies use a video prospectus to illustrate sophisticated concepts. The cost ranges from $1,000 to $5,000 per minute.

6. *Filing.* For a public offering, SEC filing costs .02 percent of the funds raised. NASD filing costs $100 plus .01 percent, with a $5,100 maximum. State fees vary up to $15,000, and registrar and transfer agent fees cost between $5,000 and $10,000.

7. *Royalties.* Between 25 and 45 percent will be paid out on an annualized, aftertax basis. Because R&D partnerships are perceived to be riskier than most other investments, their returns must be higher. R&D partnerships are more costly than debt financing, but less costly than many equity techniques.

8. *Ongoing.* Public partnerships pay between one-third and one-half of the initial partnership costs annually for legal, accounting, tax, compliance, printing and hidden costs.

Effect of $1 Million R&D Contract on Earnings:

	R&D Partnership	Equity	Debt
Contract Revenue	$1,100,000		
R&D Expense	(1,000,000)	$(1,000,000)	$(1,000,000)
Interest Expense			(150,000)
Pretax Effect	100,000	(1,000,000)	(1,150,000
Income Taxes at 50%	(50,000)	500,000	575,000
R&D Tax Credit*			100,000
Aftertax Effect on Earnings	$50,000	$(400,000)	$(475,000)

(*Assumes that 80% of expenditures qualify)

Source: Anthony P. Spohr and Leslie Wat, Forming R&D Partnerships—*An Entrepreneur's Guidebook* (New York: DH&S, 1983). Used by permission of Deloitte Haskins & Sells.

ADVANTAGES & DISADVANTAGES

Advantages

1. The risk inherent in an R&D venture is borne by the limited partners. The company (general partner) pays no cost if the technology fails; it pays market costs for the technology if it succeeds.

2. There is less dilution of company stock with an R&D partnership as compared to equity or other joint venture arrangements that convert partnership interests into equity interests. Although dilution may occur eventually, it will not be as significant as an equity play.

3. The company retains greater control over the technology when there is less dilution and the general partner can afford to buy back the technology.

4. The company's financial statements will be influenced favorably by the results of a successful R&D venture, but they will not be penalized if the venture fails. Debt-service requirements are nonexistent, freeing up cash flow to pay royalties after the product is commercialized.

5. R&D partnerships are tax-driven; most R&D expenses can be passed through to investors for attractive write-offs.

Disadvantages

1. Unless the company can set its gross margin at about 50 percent to attract investors who want 25 to 45 percent returns, an R&D partnership may be too expensive to the general partner. Typically, the longer the project takes to develop, the higher the percentage of royalties paid.

2. An R&D partnership may be as time-consuming and expensive as an initial public offering, including adherence to SEC requirements for a public offering, the development of a prospectus and the underwriter's commission.

3. Future royalty obligations may prevent the company from going public eventually if earnings are penalized severely in order to fulfill royalty commitments.

4. This partnership provides capital only for earmarked expenses as outlined in the contract. Mandatory collateral expenses may have to be financed through additional sources.

5. On going expenses for a public partnership are the responsibility of the general partner if they cannot be paid from the partnership.

TESTING THE WATERS

For a small, development-stage company that needs R&D financing at low risk, the best test is the relative cost of capital from other sources as measured against prevailing interest rates for a startup. In general, the higher interest rates are, the more beneficial a short-term R&D partnership is—providing it can pass-through tax advantages to investors.

ALTERNATIVES TO AN R&D PARTNERSHIP

1. Debt. Debt financing costs about half as much as R&D funding if the venture takes three to six years to develop. If the venture takes six years, debt financing costs about 25 percent as much as an R&D partnership See Section 5.

2. Borrowing. When interest rates are high, even a guaranteed bank line of credit or lump-sum loan can be less costly than royalty payments. Mentor Technologies, Inc. borrowed $300,000 in 1984 in exchange for giving up a 28 percent stake in the company. See Chapter 17.

3. Venture Capital. By itself, or in combination with an R&D partnership, venture capital can decrease the negative effects of future royalty payments, although the company usually gives up some ownership. Circadian, Inc. arranged $120,000 in initial financing from venture capitalists in 1979, supplemented with three later rounds to boost capitalization to $7 million (see Chapter 1).

SOURCES

Venture capital hybrid funds that offer R&D financing:
 Daleco Technologies, Inc., Newport Beach, CA.
 Technology Funding, Inc., San Francisco, CA.
 Crosspoint Venture Partners, Palo Alto, CA.
 United Investment Groups, Inc., Fairfield, IA.

PITFALLS TO AVOID

Limited partners are passive investors who receive most of the pass-through tax benefits.

The R&D partnership owns the technology. If management wants to buy the technology back after development, it will have to negotiate affordable terms to reacquire rights to the developed product.

R&D terms and documentation are among the most complex of any financing structure. Management has to negotiate carefully to retain the right to use, adapt or spin off the technology while the partnership still owns it.

CHAPTER 5

Franchising

DESCRIPTION

Franchising is the right of a dealer (franchisee) to sell the product or service of a manufacturer or service organization (franchisor) in a specific geographic area with or without exclusivity. The franchisee usually pays a down payment and a percentage of profits or sales to the franchisor in exchange for the franchisor's expertise and assistance, including financing, marketing, supplies, operations instructions or management consultation among other things. The franchisor may sell any number of such rights to market its products under one of two primary franchise systems: (1) a single franchise is sold to a franchisee, or (2) a specific geographic area is sold to the franchisee, which can be a group of investors, who in turn finds individual franchisees to open a given number of outlets within that area (master franchising).

When franchisors are faced with higher marketing or development costs, they usually decide it is better to sell in quantity to fewer customers than to sell less volume to a larger market. This can be done with master franchisees and area-development programs, through which franchisors lure better-capitalized, seasoned business owners who develop regional, statewide and sometimes international territories for the franchisor: the trend is now toward deep-pocketed multi-unit operators who have staying power.

In area-development agreements, franchisees buy bigger territories and then open a specific number of units within an agreed-upon time period. This differs from master franchises, in which franchisees assume some of the sales and service responsibilities of the franchisor. Area developers are franchisees only, so they do not sell or service products—nor do they split royalties or franchise fees.

The franchisor helps area developers by providing a systematic approach to running an operational business, giving them time to plan and execute expansion strategies. Master franchisees can grow exponentially, too, by establishing mini-franchise companies of their own.

Other innovative franchisors have developed a third way to expand the franchise network: joint-venture franchise programs. Joint-venture programs suit real estate developers primarily. The franchisor kicks in about 50 percent of the initial capital and provides the management expertise to open and operate a center. In exchange, the developer-franchisee must locate and develop the site, as well as commit to open a certain number of locations within a specified area that cost about half of the initial investment. Both parties then split the profits.

PROFILE OF A SUCCESSFUL FRANCHISOR

Companies that can most easily franchise are those with (1) at least a three-year track record of general operating success, (2) enough profitability by specific industry standards to be attractive to would-be franchisees, (3) an operating system that can be "boiler-plated" and easily taught to others, (4) a unique product or service, (5) market share growth potential in diverse geographic areas and (6) an operating system appropriate for middle-management level, nonentrepreneurial franchisees.

Successful franchisors include:

K-Bob's Steakhouse
Jitney Jungle

Sir Speedy Printing Centers
Video Biz, Inc.
PNS, Inc.
International Tours Inc.

RESULTS OF FRANCHISING

A franchisor can expect (1) cost-free capital with which to expand or revitalize without losing equity or incurring debt, (2) lower general and administrative expenses per unit sale, (3) generally a higher-than-average return on investment and profits compared to similar nonfranchised products/services in the industry, (4) an automatic system of product distribution, (5) increased and automatic sales of supplies if they are cost-competitive, (6) increased name recognition via franchisee mass marketing, (7) limited but cost-free research and development opportunities from franchisees and (8) to position itself favorably to be bought out by a large firm or go public if the franchise is successful.

WHEN TO FRANCHISE

The time most conducive to franchising is when (1) local and/or national unemployment is on the rise, (2) the company is ready to expand but does not want to pay the cost of raising capital, (3) the company wants to expand and management is willing to trade its expertise/patent/system for growth, (4) the company is profitable and has a product or service that can be boiler-plated for sale by others, (5) the cost of raising capital is high (interest rate, Fed funds or private funds have become scarce), (6) the industry is poised for growth with little target market penetration by competitors or (7) the company has few competitors for a product or service that is in great demand.

THE HOW-TO TIMETABLE

Nine Months before Franchising

1. Selection. There are three ways to franchise. One method should be selected and carefully scrutinized before making a commitment to franchise:

Do-It-Yourself: This method is extremely time-consuming and requires extensive effort in legal and accounting reviews. It is not recommended.

Development: This is a piecemeal method in which the company hires each franchise service separately and administers the "professional team," which consists of attorneys, accountants, franchisee sales/marketing reps, operations analysts and management consultants. This method takes longer and is usually about 50 percent more costly than hiring a franchise consultant to complete the franchise process.

Full-Service: Franchise consulting firms will package the process and coordinate the entire professional team under one roof. Many firms also offer ongoing services like advertising, institutional marketing production and follow-ups.

2. Interviews. After selecting the franchise method, management should identify and interview several candidates before selecting a professional team or consulting firm to initiate the franchise process. Candidates should have specialized expertise in franchising and offer a client list to call for referrals.

Six Months before Franchising

1. Financial Review. Accountants will have to analyze all company financial statements to construct an operating history model on which to base the feasibility of spinning off franchise operations.

2. Marketability. If the company is deemed to be financially sound, its product or service will be researched for sales and profit potentials under various circumstances and in numerous geographic locations.

3. *Feasibility Study.* Based on the financial analysis, projections will be made with regard to break-even, specific costs, staff needs, sales, seasonality and other aspects of franchise operations.

Three Months before Franchising

1. *Development.* If company and product prospects are sound, the management team (hired individually or as a group from the consulting firm) will begin putting an operations prototype together that includes accounting techniques, operations model, management infrastructure and legal documentation.

2. *Legal.* Disclosure documents must be filed in accordance with Federal Trade Commission and various state requirements. Most reputable franchising consultants recommend that the company meet full registration disclosure requirements, whether needed or not, in the state of registration. Disclosure documents include:

Complete product/service description
General description of the franchisor company
Description of company management
Trademark or copyright certification
Franchise costs including startup fee, ongoing fee, inventory
    provided to franchisee, working capital requirements
Available locations, territorial rights and/or site selection as-
    sistance
Training and/or startup assistance
Operating practices and controls
Marketing procedures and controls
Required equipment
Rights to sell
Terms of agreement, renewals and termination
 Lawsuits against the business and previous bankruptcies

Ten Days before Signing a Franchisee

At least 10 days before a franchisee contract is signed, franchisees must be presented with the disclosure documentation described above.

FILING REQUIREMENTS

Most franchisor companies are organized as corporations, so management must file appropriate documentation with the state in which the company is located and/or does business.

To sell a franchise in a nonregistration state, the company must meet minimal Federal Trade Commission disclosure requirements. Registration states require the company to file a complete Uniform Franchise Offering Circular, as outlined in Step 3 above.

Publicly held franchisors are subject to the registration and reporting/ disclosure requirements of the SEC, Reporting documents include a quarterly financial report (Form 10-Q), annual financial report (Form 10-K), reports about current material events in the company (Form 8-K), annual report to the shareholders, proxy statements and other reports for audited financial statements, the sale of control shares and tender offers.

In addition, public companies must meet any reporting/disclosure requirements of the states in which franchises will be sold. State requirements differ widely.

COSTS

1. *Third-Party Professionals.* Hired independently, outside legal and accounting assistance averages between $50,000 and $100,000 over four to six months. Most consulting firms that package franchise services charge between $25,000 and $40,000, depending on the nature and complexity of the services rendered.

2. *Marketing and Disclosure Documents.* The cost of producing a marketing brochure on which to sell franchises, plus the agreement, disclosure documents and operations manual, can range between $5,000 and $20,000, depending on the number printed and the quality of the materials.

Total New Incorporations (in Thousands)

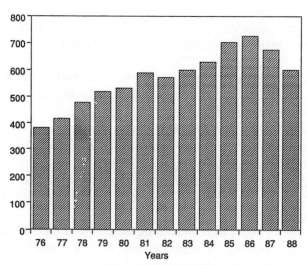

Source: Dun & Bradstreet.

ADVANTAGES AND DISADVANTAGES

Advantages

1. Additional capital for expansion or revitalization can be obtained cost free from franchisees who pay a down payment and some percentage of sales and/or profits for the right to market the company's product.

2. Expansion and market share growth can be achieved relatively quickly with limited risk via a franchisee network. Franchisees not only put capital into the operation, but also pay all their own operations expenses.

3. Name recognition, and presumably sales, increase with each new franchisee added to the system.

4. Economies of scale in operating expenses are attained as franchisees are added.

5. With the help of competent franchise consultants, the company can effectively run itself leaving management free to pursue other interests or growth.

Disadvantages

1. Some franchisors lend funds to borrower/franchisees. Lending criteria must be professionally established to avoid credit problems.

2. Company performance is no longer controlled by management; franchisees determine sales and profits within their own operations to a great extent.

3. The company loses proprietary control over patents, trademarks and/ or copyrights by having to disclose related information to franchisees.

4. Management must share quality control of the product, store conditions and marketing efforts with franchisees, despite franchise agreement restrictions.

5. Because of particular state regulations, it can be difficult for a franchisor to sever its relationship with a franchisee if the franchisee fulfills its contractual responsibilities.

TESTING THE WATERS

A good rule of thumb for projecting franchise success and for attracting franchisees to the network is to expect return on investment (ROI) to measure at least 45 percent, the median ROI for the top Venture 100 franchisors. To achieve at least the median ROI, service companies with low startup fees and high initial work investments are favored over fast-food and restaurant franchises, which require higher initial cash investments and inventory.

ALTERNATIVES TO FRANCHISING

1. *Distributorship.* Companies that wholesale products for others who sell to the public can realize many similar franchise benefits. Technitron GMBH in Munich paid $2 million to become the West German distributor for Miniscribe Corporation's computer storage system.

2. *Licensing Agreement.* Teledyne, Inc. signed a licensing agreement in 1985 that allowed Technology Development Corporation to distribute its LASAR program, an automatic digital test program generator which Technology Development uses to develop test program sets. See Section I.

3. *Going Public.* Edac Technologies, Inc. went public in 1985 to join Cade Industries, Inc. in acquiring Gros-Ite for cash and notes (see Chapter 20).

SOURCES

Francorp, Chicago, IL and Los Angeles, CA.
International Franchise Association, Washington D.C.
United States Department of Commerce Franchise Division, Washington, D.C.

PITFALLS TO AVOID

Franchising only works well when both the franchisor and the franchisee operate in good faith. If the franchisor expands too fast and decreases infrastructure services, many franchisees litigate to retrieve lost sales revenues.

The success of the franchise operation depends primarily on the abilities of the franchisee. The franchisor should be prepared to provide whatever is necessary in marketing, accounting, management and other assistance to help the franchisee succeed.

If the franchisor charges too high a franchisee fee and requires the franchisee to buy high-priced supplies from the parent organization, lower returns on investment may inhibit the sale of new franchises.

Section 2
Organizational Techniques

Section 2
Introduction

Three forms of organizational assistance described in Section 2 are helpful and supportive resources for a small business in the under–$25 million category. Although most offer equity or debt financing packages, their collateral benefits can be even more useful: gestation time outside the competitive demands of the marketplace, access to appropriate contacts for financing or advice, long-term resources, reduced overhead expenses for increased cash flow and contacts for future growth.

Although the management of a small company may perceive the need for additional capital as paramount, resource organizations can supplant the perceived need for capital with what the company really needs: facilities, time, expertise or equipment. In this way, management often can acquire necessities without giving up equity or committing to debt repayment. Resource organizations, therefore, can play a key role in the development of an early-stage company.

One advantage of organizational assistance is a broader base of resources that combines tax dollars from the public sector with individual or corporate investments from the private sector. The reason is that both sectors increasingly acknowledge the important role they play in the success of local small business.

Networking is an effective technique for service companies that are difficult to value in the early stages of development. This

strategy creates a buffer between the marketplace and a seed company that needs extra time to acquire or develop resources to increase the company's market value in the future.

Section 2
Glossary

Champion: an incubator manager who administers the organization, and provides general direction and guidance to all tenant and nontenant members of the incubator.

Development Corporation: a private-public sector partnership in which a government agency like a city council will use federal, state or local funds to encourage economic development in specific geographic areas by investing in or loaning seed financing to private-sector startup companies. These entities also may include large banks, the SBA and/or venture capitalists or any combination.

Product Life Cycle: multistaged development of a product or technology that includes the research and development phase, premarket phase and market (sales) phase.

Prototype: an original model on which a later version is patterned, with all the essential features of the later version. Often required for certain kinds of financing including R&D partnerships, joint ventures or technology transfer.

Technology Transfer: a mass movement of technology from advanced to underdeveloped countries via the licensing, joint venture or sale of U.S. technology or products to a foreign country or company.

Tenant: a company that leases space in an incubator facility like a warehouse or office park and receives such packaged administrative services as typing, computer time and bookkeeping.

CHAPTER 6
Small Business Administration

DESCRIPTION

The Small Business Administration (SBA) is a federal government agency created in 1953 to provide direct loans and loan guarantees to small businesses that lack creditworthiness and/or access to larger capital markets. The SBA also provides venture capital to startup companies through licensed and funded small business investment companies (SBICs), senior and graduate school assistance at universities through small business institutes (SBIs) and combined government, private sector and university managerial or technical help through small business development centers (SBDCs).

In addition to funding from direct grants approved by Congress, the SBA offers management assistance, as well as specialized counseling and training, and small business advocacy to small businesses owned by the disabled, minorities, veterans and the economically disadvantaged. Small Business Innovation Research Programs, added in 1983, emphasize technological innovation and research and development in joint efforts between the government and the private sector.

Procurement Preference Programs

A description of small business administration financing programs
by minority follows:

For Qualified Small Businesses—"Small Business Set-Asides": This
program requires federal agencies to limit competition on certain
contracts to small businesses qualified by the SBA. Because the law
requires awards to be made at competitive prices, set-asides are
applied only when enough small business are expected to bid to
ensure adequate competition.

*For the Socially and Economically Disadvantaged—"Business
Programs"*: The SBA contracts the performance of work to socially
and economically disadvantaged small business owners who have
been certified by the SBA as eligible to receive these contracts. The
agency also provides management, technical and financial support
to participating firms. The advantage of this program is that it permits socially and economically disadvantaged firms to receive
government contracts on a noncompetitive basis.

For Firms that Work Off-Site—"Labor Surplus Area Set-Asides":
Under this program, competition is restricted to firms that agree to
perform most of the contract work in labor surplus areas (areas of
higher-than-average unemployment) even if their headquarters is
not located in these areas. Contracts are set aside when enough
qualified firms are expected to bid to ensure that awards will be
made at fair and reasonable prices. Consult the publication "Area
Trends in Employment and Unemployment," which is available
from the U.S. Department of Labor, Employment and Training
Administration, Room 9304, 601 D St., NW, Washington, D.C.,
20013.

*For Small and Disadvantaged Firms—Subcontracts for Small and
Disadvantaged Businesses"*: Federal agencies are required to ensure
that their prime contractors establish goals for awarding subcontracts to qualified small and disadvantaged firms. Each prime
contract with a total value of $500,000 ($1 million for construction)
must include percentage goals for subcontracts with such firms
and a description of how the goals will be achieved.

For Women—"Women-Owned Businesses": Federal agencies
must take affirmative action in support of businesses owned by

women. To carry out this order, agencies are making special efforts to advise women of business opportunities and eligible women-owned firms are strongly encouraged to participate in the programs.

For Vietnam Veterans—Government contracts and all programs listed above: Although there are no statutory requirements for awarding contracts to businesses owned by Vietnam veterans, federal agencies actively encourage them to seek government contracts and to participate, where eligible, in the above programs. The SBA alone, or with the help of veterans' organizations, offers special business training workshops and assistance from a veterans' affairs specialist for loans, training and/or procurement.

For Low-Income Owners—Special Loans: (see page 81).

For Handicapped Owners—Handicapped Assistance Loans: These are awarded to physically handicapped small business owners and private nonprofit organizations which employ handicapped persons and operate in their interest.

For Local Development Companies—Special Loans: These loans are awarded for the purpose of helping small businesses in rural or urban communities.

For Exporters—Export Credit Insurance Programs, special loans and lines of credit, Overseas Private Investment Corporation, ERLIC, Agent/Distributor Service, Trade Opportunities Program, Commodity Credit Corporation's Export Credit Guarantee Program, and various Eximbank programs including the Commercial Bank Guarantee Program, Small Business Credit Program, Working Capital Guarantee Program, Eximbank/SBA Working Capital Company Guarantee Program, and the Engineering Multiplier Program. The federal government has established a number of programs to help make it easier for small companies to enter or expand into international markets: although each $1 billion in U.S. exports provides about 31,000 jobs, very few of the nation's 300,000 manufacturing firms export offshore. It is estimated that at least several thousand other firms offer goods and services which could compete successfully in foreign markets.

For ESOP Owners—Guaranteed Loans for Owners of High-Growth-Potential Firms: Small Business Investment Companies and Small Business Investment Research programs. Federal agencies are directed to divert a certain percentage of their annual SBIR research and development contracts to small high-tech firms. Also, funding for venture or risk investments must be made available through SBIC's to small, qualified, profit-making firms in the form of equity capital, unsecured loans and loans not fully collateralized. Many SBICs also provide managment assistance to the companies they finance.

For General Contractors: Small General Contractor Loans and Surety Bonds: These programs assist small construction firms with short-term financing. Loan proceeds can be used to finance residential or commercial construction or rehabilitation of property for sale. Proceeds cannot be used for owning and operating real estate for investment purposes. The SBA also guarantees to a qualified surety up to 90 percent of losses incurred under bid, payment, or performance bonds issued to contractors on contracts valued up to $1 million. These contracts may be used for construction, supplies, or services provided by either a prime or subcontractor for government or nongovernment work.

For All Small Business Owners: Pollution Control financing, seasonal line of credit guarantees, energy loans, disaster assistance, Physical Damage Natural Recovery Loans and Economic Injury Natural Disaster Loans. These specific programs are available to any qualified small business owner.

How It Works

Eligibility: Most small, independent businesses are eligible for SBA assistance. Under the Disaster Loan Recovery Program, owners of both small and large businesses are eligible. Also eligible are homeowners, renters, nonprofit organizations, veterans, minorities, the disabled and economically disadvantaged.

Availability: There are two primary ways to get SBA backing:

1. Direct funding is provided by Congress-approved grants to the agency. To qualify for direct funding, management must be unable to get private financing or an SBA-guaranteed or participation loan. The maximum amount loaned directly is $150,000 per applicant.

2. The SBA also has a participation program called the "7(a) Loan Guarantee Program." There are approximately 15,000 lending institutions in the country that guarantee 90 percent of long-term loans up to $500,000 to qualified small business owners. These authorized lenders can charge borrowers 2.25 points above the prime rate as long as the loan is for seven years or less. Lenders usually sell the guaranteed portion of the loans to an active secondary market. About 4,000 of the 15,000 authorized lenders carry no SBA loans in their portfolios. Only about 1,000 carry more than five or ten loans a year.

In addition, the SBA offers other specified programs:

Local Development Company loans to groups
Small General Contractor loans
Seasonal Line of Credit guarantees
Energy loans
Handicapped Assistance loans
Disaster Assistance
Physical Damage Natural Disaster Recovery loans
Economic Injury Natural Disaster loans
Pollution Control financing
Surety Bonds

Qualification: Requirements vary according to the individual guidelines of the 15,000 authorized lenders who guarantee, and actually lend, to SBA applicants. Most guarantors are banks that look for:

Good character
Ability to operate a business successfully
Enough capital in the company to operate successfully with the infusion of SBA funding
Ability to repay the loan and other fixed debt from profits, as determined by past earnings and projections
Enough personal resources to have a reasonable stake against possible losses, particularly during startup

Process: Many states now act as a secondary market for the SBA Loan Guarantee Program, and offer lower interest rates than the SBA itself offers. The Quality Investment Capital Program in

Colorado buys 90 percent of the small business loans that the SBA guarantees. A state agency, Colorado Housing Finance Authority, administers the program in Colorado by collecting the loans from banks and then selling them to the state treasurer's office. Customers qualify for these special programs at local authorized banks by indicating interest in a specific program.

PROFILE OF A SUCCESSFUL SBA CANDIDATE (SBA LOAN TERMS)

A business owner must meet specific requirements for either a direct loan or the loan guarantee program. He or she:

Meets the credit requirements listed above

Has been turned down for credit at two financial institutions and cannot get funds from private sources

Owns a business that is independent, operated for profit (except sheltered workshops) and is not dominant in its industry

Does not permit discriminatory employment practices

Does not own a speculative business, newspaper or gambling operation

Other SBA requirements the company must meet by industry:

Manufacturing: Employees must number between 500 and 1,500, depending on the industry in which the applicant is primarily engaged.

Wholesale: The maximum number of employees must not exceed 500.

Service: Annual receipts cannot exceed $3.5 million to $14.5 million, depending on the industry.

Retail: Annual sales cannot exceed $3.5 million to $13.5 million, depending on the industry.

Construction: General construction average annual revenues cannot exceed $17 million for each of the last three completed fiscal years.

Trade Construction: Average annual revenues cannot exceed $7 million for each of the last three completed fiscal years, depending on the industry.

Agriculture: Annual revenues cannot exceed $100,000 to $3.5 million, depending on the agricultural sector.

The successful SBA candidate also must be able to provide collateral in one of the following categories:

A mortgage on land, a building and/or equipment, chattels

Assignment of warehouse receipts for marketable goods

A guarantee, personal endorsement or assignment of current receivables

Examples of successful SBA borrowers:

Video Company
Evergreen Lawns Corporation
Regency Cards and Gifts

SBA Loan Terms

The SBA may offer an entrepreneur beneficial loan amounts unavailable from other capital sources, depending on the applicant's history, the creditworthiness of the company and general market conditions. Most SBA loans fall within these ranges:

1. A direct loan maximum is $150,000; the loan guarantee maximum on funding advanced by a bank is $500,000. The handicapped assistance maximum is $150,000; a Local Development Company loan maximum is $500,000.

2. Working capital loan payout is generally 7 years. Regular business loans have a maximum maturity of 25 years.

3. The SBA regularly sets a maximum allowable interest rate that banks can charge on guaranteed loans. Interest rates on direct loans and the SBA's share of an immediate participation loan are tied to the cost of money to the federal government and are adjusted periodically. The interest rate is 3 percent for SBA's share of a handicapped assistance loan.

RESULTS OF AN SBA LOAN

When management elects to get financing from the SBA, it will have a limited amount of long-term funding at a cost slightly over the current U.S. Treasury rate or prime rate, and, in many cases, lower than bank rates. SBA financing is often the only source available to disadvantaged groups who have been denied private credit. The funding can be used to start up or expand and, contrary to other forms of financing, can be used as working capital. Along with capital, an SBA loan guarantees a certain amount of management assistance, in the form of training, budgeting, marketing or corporate counseling. Most SBA applicants are closely scrutinized to ensure compliance with agency regulations and completion of quarterly paperwork.

WHEN TO GET AN SBA LOAN

Company management should apply for an SBA loan when it (1) needs startup or long-term, early-stage financing, (2) cannot get bank credit, (3) is not in a hurry for financing, (4) qualifies for a special small business program, such as the Small Business Innovation Research Program, (5) elects to provide a product or service to the U.S. government, thus qualifying for special SBA assistance or (6) has not defaulted on other state or federal loans.

THE HOW-TO TIMETABLE

Three Months before SBA Funding

1. *Business Plan.* To meet SBA requirements for a concept-stage business, this outline should include:

Description of the business
Description of management experience and capabilities

Estimation of owner's investment in the business and financial need

Preparation of a current financial statement listing all owner assets and liabilities

Preparation of a detailed projection of earnings for first year operation

Listing of collateral to be offered as security for the loan, indicating present market value for each

2. *Balance Sheet.* A current financial statement should be prepared, listing all business assets and liabilities.

3. *Earnings Statement.* A profit and loss statement should be prepared for the current period to the date of the balance sheet, covering a minimum of three years for an existing or acquired business.

4. *Owner Financial Statement.* A current personal financial statement should be compiled for each owner, partner or stockholder who owns 20 percent or more of the corporate stock in the business.

5. *Revised Collateral.* List all collateral to be offered as security for the loan, estimating the present market value of each item.

6. *Use of Proceeds.* State the amount of the loan requested and the exact purposes for which it will be used.

One Month before SBA Funding

1. Take the paperwork listed above to a banker and ask for a direct bank loan. If a direct loan is declined, ask the bank to make the loan under SBA's Loan Guarantee Plan or Immediate Participation Plan. If the bank is interested, ask the banker to contact the SBA for discussion of the application.

2. If the banker is interested in lending to management, he or she will require that a set of SBA forms be completed and returned to the bank. The banker will send the forms to SBA.

3. Additional information or financial data may be required while the bank and the SBA consider the loan. Some paperwork may have to be revised.

SBA Funding

If the SBA approves the loan, the bank will advance the owner money, which is repaid to the bank just like a standard bank loan.

FILING REQUIREMENTS

SBA funding does not require that a business owner meet federal or state disclosure/reporting regulations. An incorporated business must file incorporation documents in accordance with individual state requirements.

Small Business by Industry

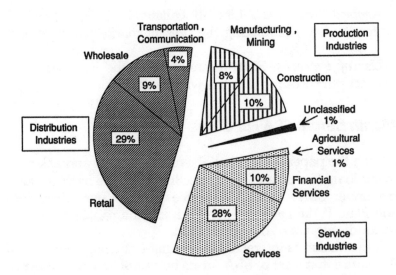

Source: National Federation of Independent Business.

COSTS

SBA financing usually costs from 1 to 3 percent over the current U.S. Treasury rate or prime rate.

ADVANTAGES AND DISADVANTAGES

Advantages

1. Research-oriented companies, and minority, economically disadvantaged and disabled entrepreneurs (among others) are given special assistance by the SBA.
2. Funding, training and counseling are offered to management that meets research or other criteria, or is unable to get credit elsewhere or has defaulted on a private loan.
3. Special programs that promise less paperwork and shorter processing times are available to qualified companies.
4. Some SBA loan guarantors have a reputation for speedy and specialized service. One is Money Store Investment Corporation, the nation's second largest SBA lender, which created a 300-loan, $140 million portfolio in 1984 under the 7(2) loan guarantee program.

Disadvantages

1. A company must have 500 or fewer employees to qualify.
2. Most SBA loan rates are based on prime or U.S. Treasury note rates and many are set several points above these volatile benchmark rates.
3. Management assistance, training and disadvantaged counseling in many cases is offered by academically trained professionals, not hands-on entrepreneurial specialists.
4. Loan processing can be a lengthy process, often taking six months to a year, and company management is required to complete an extensive amount of paperwork during and after application.

5. The SBA becomes a silent business partner, in effect. Less day-to-day scrutiny characterizes other financing strategies like a limited partnership or convertible debt offering.

TESTING THE WATERS

There are several SBA programs that offer special financing to companies that can meet specific qualification requirements. SBA guidelines for these special programs are available on request.

ALTERNATIVES TO AN SBA LOAN

1. State Bond. Many states have special bond programs that offer lower interest rates and take less time to process. One is Industrial Expansion Capital (or Index II from the Colorado Housing Finance Authority), with a Triple-A rated industrial development bond that lends at the seven-year U.S. Treasury note rate on a seven-year payout schedule. Benchmark Woodworks and RNL, Inc. applied to the program and got loans of up to $220,000 (the maximum is $1.2 million total). See Section 5.

2. Borrowing. Banks often provide lower interest rates to creditworthy small businesses that have been long-term customers. Central Fence, Inc. and Ready-Mixed Concrete Company both have been financed in part since inception by bank borrowing (see Chapter 17).

3. Private Placement. For short-term, early-stage capital that doesn't take long to raise, a private placement can be beneficial. Three-year-old Mainstay Software Corporation raised $1 million in 1984 for expansion capital (see Chapter 23).

4. Networking. High-tech companies in any industry can apply for grant contracts offered at many research-based institutes and universities. Stolar, Inc. got a $400,000 contract from the New Mexico Energy Research and Development Institute in order to further develop its proprietary mining technology (see Chapter 7).

PITFALLS TO AVOID

It is a safe assumption to double, or even triple, the amount of time projected to complete the loan process.

To avoid duplicating the application process, management should identify specific SBA programs the company can qualify for.

Not all banks are efficient or willing loan guarantors for the SBA program. Apply at financial institutions that are known to do a large volume of SBA business.

CHAPTER 7

Networking

DESCRIPTION

Many entrepreneurial programs that finance seed companies are funded by a state legislature and offered through a local university as a public/private partnership. A network combines the talents of university faculty, outside venture capitalists in some cases, industry-renowned experts and management professionals to help an inventor develop and market his product. A network relationship may result in outside financing by another capital source. Examples of successful networks include:

Wharton Innovation Center, University of Pennsylvania

Center for Management Studies, Fairleigh Dickinson University, Rutherford, N.J.

Institute of Entrepreneurship Development, Point Pleasant, N.J.

New Mexico Energy Research and Development Institute, Santa Fe, N.M.

Another kind of network provides only initial evaluative services for the inventor/entrepreneur, which helps with more thorough preparation for seeking other sources of capital. Evaluative networks include:

MIT Enterprise Forum, Cambridge, Mass.

The Tarrytown Group, Tarrytown, N.Y.

Innovation Assessment Center, University of Washington, Seattle, Wash.

PROFILE OF A SUCCESSFUL NETWORK CANDIDATE

The most successful network candidate is a company currently developing a product (1) in popular industries like high-tech or biomedical, (2) that has strong current marketing potential, (3) has sales and profit growth potential, (4) can be easily modified or updated and (5) reviews favorably on the following criteria:

Legality
Environmental impact
Product life cycle
Product visibility
Durability
Functional feasibility
Development status
Product line potential
Promotion
Price potential
Payback period
Consumer/user compatibility
Safety
Societal impact
Usage learning
Serviceability
New competition
Production feasibility
Investment costs
Perceived function
Appearance
Protection
Profitability
Product interdependence
Distribution

Examples of companies successfully backed by either an evaluation or development network include:

Bar UI Ranch Co.
Energy Optics, Inc.

Solac Builders, Ltd.
Immunomedics, Inc.
Monitor Systems Group, Inc.

RESULTS OF NETWORKING

Most companies that work with a network benefit from services that range from initial product evaluation to assistance with business plan development, marketing strategies, product development, patent protection, sales and/or financing. In exchange, a network will ask for up to 50 percent of owner profits, an equity stake in the new company of up to 25 percent or royalties of up to 50 percent, depending on the development stage of the product, the profit potential of the company and the corporate structure.

When management works with a prestigious network, associated with a renowned university business school for example, not only is product development made easier, but future financing can be easier to obtain. Also, suppliers and customers are more willing to do business with a vigorously scrutinized startup.

When requested by management, the product or company can be listed in a computerized disclosure file in which other companies seek new products or ideas.

WHEN TO APPROACH A NETWORK

Company management can use network services effectively from the time its product is still an idea on paper through most stages of product development. Later-stage development must be adaptable to modifications that may be required by the network's evaluation team. Management of concept-stage companies, or entrepreneurs who have not yet incorporated, should have their plans and projections on paper, but a business plan or even a patent is usually not required during application.

THE HOW-TO TIMETABLE

Three to Six Months before Networking

1. *Commercial Viability.* Seek general outside opinions on the commercial prospects of the product or idea from a government small business agency, corporation in the industry, business firm, brokerage house or commercial idea broker.

2. *Innovation Problems.* Get an evaluation of the potential problems that are likely to be encountered during the innovation process from a technical specialist who is well known in the industry.

3. *Prototype.* Find out from outside professionals whether or not a prototype will be helpful when presenting the product idea to specific networks.

4. *Investors.* Conduct advance market research that will substantiate the interest of outside investors in the product. Good sources are friends, suppliers, related companies or brokerage firms.

One Month before Networking

1. *Inventor Background.* Prepare an inventor/owner biography that outlines credentials, education, work history and related expertise. Most networks will want to know how suited the inventor or product developer is to carrying the idea through to completion.

2. *Selection.* Research the available networks and select those most appro priate to the product. Most networks specialize in specific kinds of products like biomedical, high-tech or retail.

FILING REQUIREMENTS

Product development through a network requires no disclosure or reporting to federal or state regulatory bodies. When the product is ready to be marketed and the inventor/owner decides to incorporate or patent the product, most networks will assist with incorporation, export trade or Federal Trade Commission requirements.

COSTS

Most nonprofit networks charge a minimal fee within the $100 to $200 range for an initial product evaluation. There are extra charges for special materials or services requested by the inventor/owner. Although these networks merely evaluate a product, their value is in the computer listing of new products that other companies seek and in the interest of investors who inquire about the most promising candidates.

For-profit networks that assist technical product development usually charge a retainer, plus one of the following:

1. Up to 50 percent of the owner's profit, depending on the development stage and viability of the product, and the condition of the company.

2. Up to 50 percent of royalties, depending on the corporate structure of the company that sells the new product.

3. An euity stake in the new company of up to 25 percent, sometimes more.

ADVANTAGES AND DISADVANTAGES

Advantages

1. Networks do not charge large, upfront fees, in contrast to patent or idea brokers who charge up to $10,000 for product development assistance.

2. Most networks utilize top experts in specific industries as research consultants, ensuring the highest level of evaluation for the new product.

3. Networks usually combine the best commercial marketing strategies with impeccable product research to ensure a successful product that also can be profitable.

4. There are very few capital sources available to seed companies, or to product ideas that are still conceptual. Networks offer not only evaluation and funding opportunities, but also management advice, product development assistance, equipment and/or facilities.

Disadvantages

1. Networks that merely evaluate potential products may be unduly pessimistic about their marketability or suitability. However, most are willing to work with an entrepreneur who is willing and able to modify the product.

2. For-profit networks may require a large percentage of ownership in the new company in exchange for product development assistance and financing.

3. Inventors or entrepreneurs may disagree with any of several aspects of the evaluation, even a positive evaluation, advanced by the network. It is important to find a network compatible in product research and development as well as in corporate principles and style.

4. Although large networks are capable of assisting an entrepreneur from idea to marketplace, they may not get the product to market as speedily as competition or other factors require.

TESTING THE WATERS

The best way to determine whether or not a new product will be successful is to research the existing marketplace: Does the product already exist? Can it be modified or improved for profit? Is there foreign competition? Can it be produced profitably, with a beneficial performance-to-cost ratio? Does management intend to work closely with the sales force and initial customers during the critical first year? Can the product be marketed effectively? Will it be marketed continuously? If these questions are answered favorably, chances are good that the product will be a success.

ALTERNATIVES TO NETWORKING

1. Venture Capital. Some venture capital firms specialize in financing startups, but they usually require a large ownership stake in the company in order to protect their investment. Immunomedics, Inc. raised $1.5 million from Johnson and Johnson Development Corporation in exchange for 9.9 percent of the company, which develops cancer-imaging technology (see Chapter 1).

2. Private Funding. Many private investors will finance a startup idea. Cultural Services, Inc. raised $700,000 in 1984 to create a database on arts and entertainment (see Chapter 23).

3. Bank Loan. Geographic Systems, Inc. raised $500,000 in bank loans and tripled sales from 1984 to 1985 on its computer-generated maps for strategic planning and marketing. The bank loans resulted from a company evaluation performed by MIT Enterprise Forum (see Chapter 17).

4. SBA. SBA funding can provide limited help to a startup entrepreneur, and technological expertise for specialized product development through the Small Business Innovation Research programs. Ophir Company has received 17 SBIR grants for high-tech research in the atmospheric sciences (see Chapter 6).

SOURCES

National Federation of Independent Business, Washington, D.C.

Innovation and Entrepreneurship Institute, University of Miami, FL.

Small Business United, Waltham, MA.

Venture Network, Inc., Denver, CO.

PITFALLS TO AVOID

Some venture capital networks function like incubators at first, but also require large amounts of equity in the company in exchange for financing. The equity stake should not exceed 49 percent unless management has been unable to find a more favorable source of financing.

Networking can delay commercialization of the product or technology if a large number of experts must approve unrealistic benchmark stages of development.

The technological and commercial portions of the feasibility study required by many networks should be analyzed separately, even by different professionals. Many studies are turned down because one or the other portion is judged to be unworkable.

CHAPTER 8
Incubators

DESCRIPTION

An incubator is an organization, physical facility or other special environment that supports, and in some cases finances, small business startups and expanding operations by providing inexpensive office and manufacturing space, office services, management and marketing assistance, a business library and/or funding. It enables a company to move from the garage to a business park in less than two years.

A smokestack incubator such as Fulton-Carroll in Chicago is a physical facility for light industrial companies that tenant in a converted factory or manufacturing plant. It provides lower-than-market rentals, and emphasizes renovation and the creation of new jobs, particularly for unemployed factory workers who have been displaced by the nation's economic shift to service industries.

A university-based incubator such as The Wharton Innovation Center at the University of Pennsylvania is a gestation facility that helps evaluate potential startups and early-stage companies that need business plans, marketing strategies and access to management and technology resources. Other university-based incubators help franchise products and services, raise capital, and provide high-tech and/or academic assistance.

An adaptive business incubator is created by a private corporation or city government to achieve specific geographic goals. They assist service-oriented businesses, and sometimes include a physical facility for light industrial companies. Richmond Square Technology Park Associates in Providence, R.I. caters to high-tech startups.

A recent incubator development is the formation of venture capital funds around client companies. The Seed Company in Philadelphia and IncuTech Venture Fund in Providence, R.I. invest up to $100,000 in an incubator company for an equity stake of between 10 and 50 percent.

PROFILE OF A SUCCESSFUL INCUBATOR CANDIDATE

Virtually any startup company or expanding small business can be a good incubator candidate. The key is that the company have enough potential to generate income and be able to survive in the open market after one to three years. Most incubators expect tenants or clients to incubate for about two years and then move into the marketplace.

An exception is the R&D incubator, usually university-based, that nurtures long-term research for up to seven years. A venture-capital backed incubator generally funds a company that has the potential to generate 10 times its initial investment over 5 years.

Successful incubator companies include:

Amphora Systems, Inc.
IKAN Systems, Inc.
Advanced Energy

Successful incubators include:

Prospect Park East
Center for Management Studies
Institute of Entrepreneurship Development

RESULTS OF INCUBATOR TENANCY

If a light manufacturing company tenants in a smokestack incubator, monthly charges are greatly reduced for the no-frills rental ($1.50 to about $5 per square foot). For warehouse space and some office services, rents range up to about $12 per square foot. Employees typically are recruited from within a few miles of the incubator for greater efficiency. Pooled services for tenants include typing, telephone answering, mailing, meeting facilities and copying.

A service-oriented company in an adaptive business incubator may tenant in a special building for rents that are 50 to 75 percent of the local market rate. Pooled administrative services are low-cost and include bookkeeping, typing, telephone answering, computer time, copying and meeting facilities.

Growth of Small-Business Incubators in the U.S.

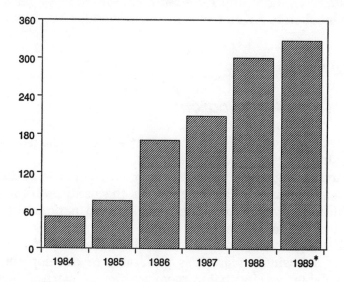

*As of January.

States with the most incubators: Pennsylvania, 42; Illinois, 26; New York, 24; Michigan, 18; Wisconsin, 16; Ohio, 15; N. Carolina, 12; Indiana, 11; Minnesota, 10; Washington, 10.

Source: National Business Incubation Association.

Most business incubators, particularly if they do not provide inexpensive office space, offer specific management assistance: marketing, financial planning, strategy consulting and capital formation.

University-based incubators that specialize in R&D assistance usually offer lab space, technological and equipment support, access to faculty and product development over a longer period of time.

WHEN TO APPLY TO AN INCUBATOR

The best time to use an incubator is when the company is in the concept, startup or low capital-intensive stage. Unless the company needs a large amount of capital, it can develop more quickly without outside financing because of low-cost rent, office services, facilities, equipment and/or technical assistance. New companies that normally would apply for a bank line of credit to get started may find incubators a better way to afford initial costs.

THE HOW-TO TIMETABLE

One Year before Application

1. Develop a viable company concept that can support a sound business for the medium-term.

2. Structure growth objectives that will provide substantial revenue and increasing employment for the medium-term, especially a business with a large local market or a national business with strong local employment.

3. Although some companies need incubator support while developing a business plan, it is preferable to develop the plan before applying for incubator membership. A startup business plan should include:

Executive summary
Business description

Market analysis
Product/service description
Marketing/sales strategy
Manufacturing/service operation and distribution plan
Financial data
Assistance desired/growth timetable

Six Months before Application

1. Recruit a management team with strong credentials in the company's industry and a good employment track record.
2. Begin capital formation from within the community. Most incubators prefer a company that is locally owned and financed in part by the founding entrepreneur. A personal financial and resource commitment from the founder is considered by the incubator to be assurance of tenacity and stability in the management of the new company.

Three Months before Application

1. Review available incubators in order to match their goals with company goals. Interview several and select one that supports the company's business, goals, growth pattern and style.
2. Apply to the board of directors or manager of the incubator by requesting application information and an initial interview.
3. Submit the company's business plan with a cover letter summarizing the operation. Be ready to work with an incubator specialist who will review the business plan and, at times, suggest revisions that will enhance the success of corporate membership.

FILING REQUIREMENTS

There are no federal or state reporting/disclosure requirements for incubator membership. If the company is to be incorporated, ap-

propriate application must be made with state government. The
incubator manager generally will assist an entrepreneur with the
appropriate documentation.

COSTS

There is no cost associated with incubator membership. In fact,
costs are reduced by about 50 percent for space and services in
most incubators. The exception is a venture capital–backed incubator that provides small amounts of capital in addition to
reduced costs for facilities and services. These venture incubators
invest up to about $100,000 in seed companies, in exchange for an
equity stake in the 10 to 50 percent range. Most venture firms
hope to get returns of 10 times initial investment over a 5-year
period.

ADVANTAGES AND DISADVANTAGES

Advantages

1. For a company that does not require a lot of capital investment, an incubator provides a receptive environment for the concept or startup stage, as well as for more mature companies that
need time to grow carefully.
2. In most cases, rent for office, warehouse or manufacturing
space is reduced by up to 90 percent, depending on the category
of incubator. Office services like typing and copying are included
in the rent.
3. Other incubator tenants or members often provide a ready
market for the company's goods or services.
4. Adaptive business incubators provide free or low-cost
management assistance in marketing, sales, distribution, estate
planning and future growth.
5. Networking opportunities among the board of directors,
manager and other incubator companies provide a springboard for
entering the marketplace.

Disadvantages

There aren't any. If a company has made good use of the protective incubator environment to develop sound business practices, a move to the open marketplace will demonstrate that the company has become stable and positioned for growth at virtually no cost to management.

For-profit venture capital incubators may require an equity stake of up to 50 percent in exchange for space and services.

TESTING THE WATERS

A good test of readiness for a seed company is the approval of the company's business plan by outside consultants and lenders. Before applying to an incubator, submit the plan to a few banks, venture capitalists and brokerage houses. If one or two like the plan, even with alterations, chances are good the incubator will approve membership.

ALTERNATIVES TO AN INCUBATOR

1. Friends and Family. During the startup stage, it is imperative to have enough capital and support to ensure getting to the production or later-round financing stage. Capital commitment from friends and family is a good, and inexpensive, place to start. Three-year-old Integrity Solutions, Inc. was initially financed by a second mortgage on the founder's house.

2. Venture Capital. Many funds, both private and public, specialize in seed companies. A specialist in sophisticated high-tech and biomedical operations, Johnston Associates in Princeton, N.J., helped develop Genex Corporation in 1977 from the ground up, beginning with a business plan (see Chapter 1).

3. Borrowing. If interest rates are reasonable, a bank line of credit or startup loan can be the simplest way to raise a small amount of initial capital, as well as to get ongoing management assistance. United Bankers, Inc., a 10-bank holding company in

Waco, Tex. has a $10 million lending limit per customer without participations. Most of it is lent at 1.5 points over prime to small businesses (see Chapter 17).

SOURCES

Utah Innovation Foundation, Salt Lake City, UT.
The National Association of State Development Agencies (lists state incubator organizations).
Many municipal governments help finance incubators.

PITFALLS TO AVOID

Some incubators offer such inexpensive services that management is not realistically prepared for the intense competition of the open marketplace.

Venture capital incubators require an equity stake in the company. Management should avoid giving up more than about 30 percent of the company for temporary incubator services.

There is a temptation to market only to other incubator tenants while the company is still growing. The company should have as many or more customers outside the incubator.

Section 3
Foreign Market Techniques

Section 3
Introduction

The 10 foreign partnership techniques described in Section 3 can be profitable financing strategies for a small public or private business in the under–$25 million category. The significant trend toward proliferation of foreign partnership strategies has been created by U.S. business owners, hampered since the beginning of the decade by high domestic interest rates, dwindling markets and increased competition from abroad.

Similar to domestic partnerships, an arrangement with a foreign partner can yield not only current financing, but also flexible terms tailored to the company's specific needs. Beneficial extras are also possible like instant growth, in-place distribution, and built-in demand for future products and technology.

In most cases, a foreign investor is more willing than a U.S. investor to accept technology transfer or expertise in lieu of equity in the company or a percentage of future profits. This means that a foreign partnership can be potentially more profitable to the business owner, despite the increased risks and higher expenses sometimes associated with doing business abroad.

Although foreign investors and potential partners are becoming more sophisticated and discriminating about investing in U.S. companies, a small business in the United States that cannot get financing at home often can raise capital from a foreign partner who wants the company's product. This financing can include seed capital for a concept-stage company. Coupled with the fact that more U.S. companies are doing business abroad every year via foreign partners, the trend clearly suggests that a U.S. company lacking foreign markets may not compete as well in the future as a company that has expanded abroad.

Section 3
Glossary

Countertrade: the exchange of one commodity or product for another between two or more countries or foreign companies.

Eurodollars: U.S. currency deposited in banks outside the United States that is used in international transactions. A Eurodollar is only one of the many Eurocurrencies, which are not limited to currencies of European countries.

Export-Import Bank (Eximbank): a bank established in 1934 by Congress to assist U.S. trade overseas. It borrows from the U.S. Treasury to finance exports and imports, extend credit directly to foreign borrowers and provide such things as export guarantees, discounts loans and insurance against unstable conditions.

Export License: official permission by the U.S. Department of Commerce to make, use or sell U.S. products or technologies overseas. Required by all companies doing business in a foreign country.

Foreign Corporation: a company chartered in a state other than the state in which it does business (also an out-of-state corporation), or a company chartered in a foreign country (also called an "alien corporation").

Foreign Direct Investment: can be an investment in a U.S. company by a foreign company, or a joint venture between U.S. and foreign companies.

Foreign Exchange: currency, notes, checks, electronic data, bills of exchange or anything used to make payments between countries.

Forfeiting: the sale of a foreign buyer's obligation, usually in the form of a promissory note guaranteed by the buyer's bank and without recourse to the exporter. These obligations are sold to European investors for medium-term debt of over $1 million.

Free Trade Lone: specified areas throughout the world in which export products can be inspected, sorted, labeled, assembled, repackaged or manufactured without import taxes. Export products can be shipped without paying U.S. duty taxes on the imported content, or they can be distributed to other points in the U.S. under favorable terms.

Letter of Credit: a financial instrument issued by a bank that guarantees the payment of a company's draft up to a certain maximum for a specified amount of time. This document is used often in international trade.

Petrodollars: dollars that are paid to oil-exporting countries and deposited in U.S. banks. They are a key component in the world economy and in the ability of borrowing countries to repay loans to U.S. banks.

Pre-export Financing: includes unsecured and secured short-term commercial credit, term-loan commercial credit, export revolving line of credit program (through the SBA), working capital guarantees and letters of credit.

Post-export Financing: includes insured receivable financing, bankers' acceptances and forfeiting.

Sponsor: usually a general partner who organizes and sells a limited partnership (also called a promoter). In stocks, the sponsor is a big trader, e.g., an institution whose favorable opinion of the stock stimulates demand from other investors.

CHAPTER 9

Licensing Agreements

DESCRIPTION

A licensing agreement is a very flexible contract typically between two like parties (i.e., corporation to corporation or limited partnership to limited partnership) whereby one company may sell rights to the control of its technology to the other company, which then can produce, market or distribute the technology according to the terms of the contract.

Most licensing agreements are between an emerging company with a proprietary technology or product that needs financing and sales assistance to develop and market the technology, and a larger company with a compatible technology and/or a sales network already in place.

The two key features of a licensing agreement, which controls only the technology or product involved, are (1) the development stage or age cycle of the technology and (2) the nature of the legal rights that control the technology patent, trademark, copyright or contract, which determines the income potential for the licensee.

PROFILE OF A SUCCESSFUL LICENSING AGREEMENT

A licensing agreement can by structured for almost any entrepreneur who has (1) a technology that can be easily defined,

113

(2) a proprietary technology that can be protected by patent, trademark or copyright, (3) other financing sources to supplement the licensing agreement, (4) strong potential markets for end-users of the technology or (5) a technology monopoly attractive to domestic or foreign end-users.

Companies that have raised capital and expanded their markets with licensing agreements include:

Interpreter, Inc.
Jack Henry & Associates, Inc.
Vertical Software Systems, Inc.

RESULTS OF A LICENSING AGREEMENT

Entrepreneurs who develop a licensing agreement with other companies can expect (1) to raise modest amounts of capital in order to complete research and development on the technology, hire necessary labor, and utilize additional equipment and/or facilities, (2) to give up only specified rights to the technology in exchange for capital and assistance, (3) to avoid filing require ments unless the licensed technology will be produced or sold overseas, requiring an export license from the U.S. Department of Commerce, (4) to expand and develop new markets at a lower cost and more quickly with outside support from the licensee and (5) to develop second-, third- and fourth-generation spin-offs of the technology with a shorter R&D stage.

WHEN TO CREATE A LICENSING AGREEMENT

A licensing agreement should be created when (1) the cost of start-up or R&D financing is high in relation to the benefits derived, (2) the company is incorporated or structured as a distinct corporate entity such as a limited partnership, (3) the technology to be licensed is well-defined and protected, (4) management wants to access new markets quickly and enlarge market share due to the competitive or economic environment or (5) the company wants the maximum flexibility for future operations offered by a licensing agreement.

There was a 40 percent increase in total foreign investment in U.S. companies to a record high of 307 offshore purchases in 1988, which represents 13.6 percent of the year's total transactions—up 11 percent from the year before.

Foreign Buyers
Number of Transactions by Country 1979–1988

Country of Buyers	1979	1980	1981	1982	1983	1984	1985	1986	1987	1988	Ten Year Cumulative
United Kingdom	60	50	80	54	41	48	78	89	78	114	692
Canada	50	57	62	36	28	36	25	64	28	37	423
Japan	11	9	9	4	6	6	9	16	15	35	120
West Germany	37	14	14	6	2	4	12	19	15	29	152
France	18	20	14	12	7	7	4	6	19	25	132
Switzerland	16	7	6	7	7	7	10	6	9	15	90
Australia	5	2	7	2	6	5	10	12	17	10	76
Netherlands	11	6	8	5	7	5	17	9	9	9	86
Italy	1	1	4	1	5	1	4	5	6	7	35
Sweden	4	8	7	4	3	8	7	11	9	6	67
Hong Kong	2	2	2	4		1	1	3	3	3	21
Denmark						1	2			3	6
Spain	2	2	1	2		1			1	3	12
Ireland			1	21	1	1		2	2	2	11
Argentina	2	1	1							2	7
Venezuela	1				1			1		1	4
New Zealand				1	1	1		2		1	6
Indonesia										1	1
Belgium	2					3		2		1	9
Brazil	4		1	1	1			3	1	1	11
Israel	1		2			1		2		1	9
South Africa			2					5	6	1	19
Greece			1			1					2
Libya				1	1						1
Luxembourg	1										1
South Korea				1	1			1			2
Malaysia			1								2
Singapore				2							3
Mexico	1	1	2	3							7
Bahrain											1
Panama				1							1

Foreign Buyers (continued)

Country of Buyers	1979	1980	1981	1982	1983	1984	1985	1986	1987	1988	Ten Year Cumulative
Bermuda					1						5
Puerto Rico			1		1						2
Kuwait		1	1	1	1	2					6
Saudi Arabia	1	3									4
Philippines	2		1	1			1				5
Taiwan			1								1
Colombia		1		1		1					3
Thailand				1							1
Norway		1			1	5	2		1		10
Jamaica	1										1
Bahamas		1			1						2
Trinidad					1						1
Finland	2	1			5	2	4	1			15
Undisclosed	1	2	2	2				2	1		10
Totals	236	187	234	154	125	151	197	264	220	307	2,075

Source: *Mergerstat Review.*

THE HOW-TO TIMETABLE

Six Months before the Effective Licensing Agreement

1. Business Plan. Contingent on how developed the technology is, management should outline for potential licensees certain information including:

Analysis of the (proposed) technology and base technology available, and the equipment, facilities and personnel necessary to complete the R&D phase.

Feasibility of the technology based on a technical evaluation by an outside consulting firm.

Market analysis with potential demand, existing and potential markets, estimated revenues, estimated production costs and the competition.

Technology budget including the costs and specific work stages to be completed.

Investment analysis with projected cash flow, and other benefits and tax consequences of a licensing agreement.

2. *Third-Party Professionals.* Professional outside assistance should be retained from among specialists in the company's industry, including:

Legal: An attorney or law firm should be retained to develop documentation and contracts for the licensing agreement. They should be specialists in the appropriate field of technology and be familiar with licensing agreement trends.

Marketing: These specialists will develop a growth strategy for the company using the business plan to develop new markets, expand sales and spinoff.

Technological: An outside evaluation of the technology should be performed for inclusion in the business plan.

Three Months before the Effective Licensing Agreement

1. *Licensee Selection.* Management should identify and interview several potential licensees before selection. This stage may take up to six months, depending on the nature of the technology, the number of competitors, the delays inherent in a foreign licensing agreement and the market for new technologies. A good source of leads is usually the professional team of outside specialists retained to structure the deal.

2. *Licensee Analysis.* The company selected as licensee should be evaluated by legal counsel in terms of licensing agreement benefits. Some companies may prefer another structure like a joint venture (which can include a licensing agreement), an R&D partnership or a limited partnership.

3. *Licensor Analysis.* The professional team will work together to create a matrix analysis that defines the technology, "fractures" the technology markets from horizontal to vertical, breaks out benefits resulting from the deal and outlines operations aspects of the technology.

4. *Filing.* If the licensee is a foreign entity, management will have to apply early on for an export license through the U.S. Department of Commerce. The license is signed by both parties. If the technology represents the total assets of the licensor, SEC and state filing may be required of the licensee who, in effect, acquires a new company.

5. *Contracts.* Legal counsel will develop the necessary documentation, including:

Licensing Agreement: This document outlines the specific terms, conditions and rights of licensor and licensee regarding the technology, projected cash flow, and marketing, sales and distribution.

Technology Transfer Agreement: This document delineates what portion of the incomplete technology remains under company control and determines the compensation for the portion that may be sold.

Purchase Options: If the technology is eventually sold outright to the licensee, this document outlines strategies by which the company can buy back rights to the technology.

Optional: Other documents that may need to be prepared by appropriate outside professionals include (1) feasibility study, (2) tax opinion or (3) budget.

FILING REQUIREMENTS

Licensors and licensees are not subject to SEC or state reporting/disclosure requirements unless they are publicly held. (The majority are not.) However, if the licensee is a foreign company, the licensor will have to apply for an export license through the local office of the U.S. Department of Commerce. In addition, if the licensor's technology represents the total assets of the company, the licensee may be subject to certain additional SEC and/or state filing requirements, as applicable.

COSTS

The total cost of structuring a licensing agreement is highly negotiable, depending on the complexity of the agreement and the company, the product or technology to be licensed and the condition of corporate documents. Most licensing agreements cost between $15,000 and $100,000. To keep the cost down, it is vitally important for management to keep all corporate and financial documents up-to-date, and to hire professional third parties to represent management's interests.

If the licensee is a foreign corporation, travel expenses add to the cost of raising capital with a licensing agreement. The average cost of creating an agreement with a foreign entity is about $25,000 (including an average of two visits to the foreign country) unless the licensee is willing to negotiate in the United States. If the licensee is a foreign company, add about 50 percent to the cost of third-party professionals.

Four factors contributed to the increased level of foreign investment in U.S. companies in 1988: the stability of the U.S. dollar against foreign currencies, the trend toward production facilities in the U.S., earnings improvements in U.S. companies and the stock market crash of 1987.

Foreign Buyers Dollar Total by Country 1983–1988

Total Dollar Value (Base*)

Country of Buyer	1983	1984	1985	1986	1987	1988
United Kingdom	$1,024.5 (22)	$2,754.1 (31)	$3,401.3 (40)	$7,827.8 (72)	$23,519.3 (60)	$24,031.3 (79)
Canada	1,309.9 (16)	1,266.6 (19)	2,143.0 (6)	2,837.3 (33)	4,052.7 (12)	9,257.5 (16)
Japan	688.7 (4)	430.4 (3)	34.2 (3)	899.4 (10)	3,349.2 (6)	5,966.5 (22)
Italy	56.1 (1)		20.2 (1)	72.9 (3)	2,266.9 (4)	206.7 (3)
Australia	2,468.4 (3)	626.3 (4)	1,266.7 (5)	926.3 (6)	2,253.2 (11)	4,047.3 (6)
West Germany	44.0 (1)	214.5 (2)	1,243.0 (4)	4,303.3 (7)	1,260.2 (5)	2,857.6 (16)
Netherlands	48.8 (3)	5,605.4 (2)	1,871.3 (8)	3,491.7 (4)	1,116.0 (4)	178.7 (3)
Switzerland	107.7 (3)	2,904.6 (3)	221.9 (2)	291.0 (3)	802.0 (6)	2,158.9 (7)
Hong Kong				79.8 (2)	764.0 (2)	89.1 (2)
Sweden	8.3 (1)	137.6 (4)	22.0 (2)	827.6 (3)	432.8 (5)	743.6 (5)
France	15.0 (1)	236.8 (4)	135.7 (3)	2,332.5 (4)	374.4 (9)	4,200.0 (13)
Spain					82.0 (1)	452.0 (2)
South Africa					49.5 (1)	
Ireland	95.0 (1)		150.0 (1)	103.5 (1)	43.8 (2)	939.0 (2)
Venezuela				290.0 (1)		125.0 (1)
Belgium		46.0 (2)		116.5 (1)		16.3 (1)
Brazil				72.0 (1)		

Foreign Buyers (continued)

Total Dollar Value (Base[*])

Country of Buyer	1983	1984	1985	1986	1987	1988
South Korea				13.4 (1)		
Finland		3.7 (1)	108.3 (2)	12.3 (1)		32.0 (1)
New Zealand		36.0 (1)		10.2 (1)		8.13 (1)
Israel	10.0 (1)	8.0 (1)		2.6 (1)		
Bermuda	39.7 (1)		215.0 (1)	1.2 (1)		37.0 (2)
Singapore			50.0 (1)			116.0 (2)
Denmark		113.0 (1)	1.3 (1)			
Argentina						
Norway		45.0 (1)				
Philippines						
Bahamas		24.8 (1)				
Bahrain		70.0 (1)				
Colombia						
Greece		23.0 (1)				
Kuwait		340.0 (1)				
Malaysia		71.0 (1)				
Mexico						
Puerto Rico	11.4 (1)					
Saudi Arabia						
Trinidad		175.0 (1)				
Undisclosed						
Totals	$5,927.5(59)	$15,131.8(85)	$10,883.9(80)	$24,511.3(156)	$40,366.0 (128)	$55,462.8(184)

[*]Base: The number of transactions disclosing a purchase price.
Source: Mergerstat Review.

ADVANTAGES AND DISADVANTAGES

Advantages

1. The company can create flexibility for current and future operations by customizing almost any terms desired by either or both parties.

2. A licensing agreement provides relatively low-cost research and development or startup capital when compared to the varying amount of equity given up in venture capital, a limited partnership or a joint venture.

3. Virtually any small startup company can create a licensing agreement provided it has a defined and protected technology.

4. Undeveloped foreign markets are lucrative expansion opportunities for small U.S. companies that want to expand rapidly. Many foreign companies are eager to become licensees in order to acquire rights to technology their country may not have.

5. Internal company growth is achieved more quickly with access to facilities, labor, equipment and financing provided by the licensee.

6. A licensing agreement can make the company more effective in taking a larger market share from competitors, thus improving future company prospects.

Disadvantages

1. The company may convey too many rights to the licensee unless a technological evaluation is performed by an outside professional and the contract is structured by an attorney familiar with licensing agreements and the company's industry.

2. One of the most common errors committed by a licensor is not specifying performance benchmarks that should be required of the licensee.

3. If the technology is not fully defined, the licensor may lose protection for spin-offs, or special terms and rights.

TESTING THE WATERS

A technological analysis will usually yield the information necessary to determine whether or not a licensing agreement is more beneficial than a joint venture or some other form of doing business. Also, a licensing agreement is favored over other relationships when the other party, particularly a foreign entity who wants technology transfer to the host country, wants rights to the technology rather than part ownership in the company.

After a slump in 1987, American purchases of offshore businesses increased 6 percent to 151 in 1988. This rebound reflected a slight increase in total merger and acquisition activity, but also the weakness of the dollar against foreign currencies.

U.S. Acquisitions of Foreign Business— Number of Transactions 1980–1988

	Acquisitions of		Divestitures of		Total
	Controlling Interests	Minority Interests	Foreign-Based Units	U.S.-Based Units	Foreign Sellers
1980	62	15	18	7	102
1981	67	14	9	11	101
1982	69	15	22	15	121
1983	95	15	17	19	146
1984	81	16	28	22	147
1985	89	17	37	32	175
1986	93	8	36	43	180
1987	84	6	27	25	142
1988	64	8	46	33	151

Source: *Mergerstat Review.*

ALTERNATIVES TO A LICENSING AGREEMENT

1. *Leasing.* Two-year-old Megaphone Co. went to a specialist for a syndicated equipment-leasing package to produce a $1 million lease-line that cost only about one-tenth as much equity in the company as equivalent equity financing.

2. *State Venture Capital.* International CMOS Technology, Inc. raised more than $11 million in equity funding, a $52 million lease-line and $3 million in tax abatement from a group headed by

the Indiana Corporation for Innovation Development, created by
the Indiana state legislature in 1981 (see Chapter 1).

3. *Combinations.* Studio Software Corporation raised more
than $2 million in second-round financing from venture capital
firms, two corporate investors and individual investors.

4. *Franchising.* Franchisors raise additional financing by selling franchisees the right to sell their products and market their
name. Comprehensive Accounting raises $70,000 every time it sells
a franchise (see Chapter 5).

PITFALLS TO AVOID

Avoid the transfer of all rights to the technology or product in
favor of limited rights for a specified period of time or terms
that allow management to retain rights under certain circumstances.

The licensee should have a track record in the sale, marketing or distribution of the product or technology.

Management should guard against signing rights to a licensee who may keep the product or technology from the
marketplace to decrease competition.

CHAPTER 10

Foreign Venture Capital

DESCRIPTION

Foreign venture capital can be seed or expansion financing from overseas companies to support U.S. development of specific products or technologies. Most foreign venture capital is invested in exchange for royalties, a profit percentage, sales agreements, licensed technology or foreign manufacturing rights.

PROFILE OF A SUCCESSFUL FOREIGN VENTURE CAPITAL CANDIDATE

The opportunity to attract foreign investments to the company increases greatly if the firm is in an industry, or produces a product, that is of specific interest to a foreign country. Most foreign venture capitalists try to invest "intelligent money" or funds that will achieve several purposes. Foreign investors look for strategic partnerships, that is, (1) sound investments in young companies (although many countries, like Japan, prefer later-stage development companies) while there is still room to invest at the ground-floor level, (2) products or technologies needed overseas, (3) technologies that later can be exported in a process called "technology transfer," (4) future trade possibilities with the companies, (5) companies in which foreign investors can be more than passive participants and (6) firms that have been financed by American venture capital firms, so the foreign investors can learn more about the operation from those who have worked closely with it.

Examples of U.S. companies financed by foreign venture capital firms include:

Britton Lee, Inc.
Microrim, Inc.
Integrated Circuit Testing
Syntro Corporation

RESULTS OF FOREIGN VENTURE CAPITAL FINANCING

In many ways, foreign venture capital can be more lucrative in the long run than similar domestic financing. Along with a good return on investment, most foreign investors are interested primarily in future trade with U.S. companies. Therefore, the company has a long-term sales opportunity that may be hard to duplicate without some form of partnership with a foreign firm.

Another direct result of foreign financing can be a technology transfer arrangement, in which the company has a ready market not only for products and/or services, but also for expertise and technology. This results in additional revenue from consulting fees, equipment sales and/or licensing income.

As a rule, foreign venture capitalists are more passive investors than American investors are, and do not take an active part in the day-to-day operations of the company because of unfamiliarity with American entrepreneurial practices. This may change as foreign venture capitalists increase their level of investment and become more familiar with American culture. The Japanese, for example, tend to be more involved in their investments than French or German financiers.

Although most experts agree that a company with slow U.S. sales should not try to open foreign markets before domestic sales are stable, certain products and services that are obsolete in the United States create a strong potential for better earnings through initial trade in foreign markets. Many heavily capitalized U.S. manufacturing firms have revived their balance sheets with foreign sales in markets that still need U.S. industrial exports.

Because foreign venture capitalists frequently seek trading opportunities above all, company management usually doesn't have to give up as much equity to foreign investors.

WHEN TO OBTAIN FOREIGN VENTURE CAPITAL

The best time to attract foreign financing is when the company (1) has a new product or technology sought after by foreign markets, (2) wants to establish long-term, exclusive trading partners, (3) has saturated the domestic marketplace, (4) wants to sell proprietary technology with second- and third-generation markets in place or (5) wants to gain an edge over domestic competitors in a shrinking market.

Total Foreign Direct Investment Position by Country
(End of year totals for 1988)

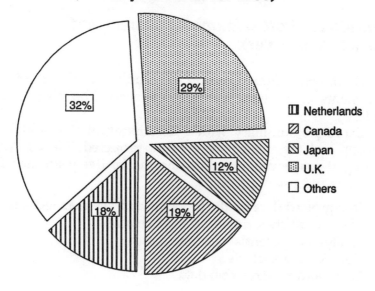

32% 29% 12% 19% 18%

☐ Netherlands
☑ Canada
☒ Japan
☷ U.K.
☐ Others

THE HOW-TO TIMETABLE

One Year before Financing (Startup Companies)

1. Market Research. Determine the need for the product or technology at a price that provides a significant return on investment for the company and its foreign investors. The U.S. Department of Commerce, through its local offices, is the best source for general information about foreign markets.

2. Product Protection. Patents, trademarks, copyrights and trade secret protection should be sought through third-party professionals before the company is structured and before a business relationship is established with foreign investors.

3. Professional Team. Third-party professionals including attorneys, accountants, advisors, strategists and financial planners should be retained for business formation, first-round and later-stage financing, estate planning and legal counseling.

4. Business Formation. Incorporation should be structured by the professional team before a contract is signed with foreign investors.

Nine Months before Financing (Startup and Mature Companies)

1. Business Plan. Develop a business plan that meets the requirements of domestic venture capitalists. The plan should include:

Executive summary with a description of the product, sales markets and the management team, projected financial data including annual revenue and net income for five years, and financing needs and use of proceeds.

Background data on the founders and key management
Market statistics, domestic and overseas
Analysis of potential customer base
Competitive analysis
Labor and material cost data

R&D data
Product/technology protection program
Regulatory information

In general, seed companies can provide all the necessary information for the initial business plan in 15 pages. However, companies that seek more than $1 million in financing and high-tech companies with complex products should provide more in-depth information including more detailed R&D data, a market analysis, and five-year sales and cost projections.

2. *Financial Projections.* Concept-stage and startup companies should develop sales estimates as a basis for later analysis. Data on manufacturing, administrative and sales costs, and cash-flow projections should be included. Mature companies also can include profit-and-loss statements, balance-sheet projections and a five-year cash-flow sheet. Most projections are based on:

Capital expenditures
Gross margin by product line/total
Sales increases by product line/unit or total dollar volume
Interest rates on debt and interest income on temporary investment of excess funds
Income tax rate
Accounts receivable collection
Accounts payable payment
Inventory turnover
Depreciation schedules and asset utility

3. *Financial Request.* This section states how much capital is requested and why it is needed and gives a use-of-proceeds analysis that demonstrates consistency with financial projections. Startup companies need to explain capitalization, enumerate shareholders and their company positions, how much stock they own and their share cost. Management of older companies should explain the capital structure and how venture capital funding will affect it. Also, simultaneous and future financing sources should be described, including immediate financing and/or staged financing as various corporate development goals are met. Both should include an analysis of the debt/equity capital mix in light of the company's ability to repay (debt) and/or grow (equity).

Six Months before Financing

Select the Fund. There are several categories of foreign venture capital firms that make investments in U.S. companies:

Foreign banks with offices in the United States and abroad, for example, Banque Nationale de Paris of France and Banque Indosuez

United States banks with offices abroad: Most U.S. bank holding companies in major cities have offices abroad and contacts with foreign investors who want to capitalize small U.S. companies, for example, Citicorp and Crocker Bank

Private or public foreign funds with U.S. offices, for example, Singacon Investments and Ing. C. Olivetti & Co.

Private or public U.S. venture capital firms with foreign backers, for example, TA Associates, and Oceanic Capital Corporation

Foreign investors should be selected carefully, preferably by referral from at least two parties. The venture capitalists should be matched to the capability and industry of the company, and should demonstrate at least a three-year track record of expertise in the company's business.

FILING REQUIREMENTS

Venture capital generally is first-round financing for a private company. For this reason, the company is not subject to federal or state disclosure/reporting requirements. Incorporation documentation must be filed with the state when a new business is created. Foreign trade and trade agreements are subject to the stringent regulations of the U.S. Department of Commerce. An export license is generally required, obtainable through any local Department of Commerce office.

COSTS

1. *Management Fee.* Most foreign firms charge a fee of 3 percent of the amount invested in the company.

2. Equity Stake. Some foreign venture capitalists buy the company's technology instead of investing to get a stake in the company. A straight venture capital investment, without technology transfer, requires from 20 to 50 percent of the equity.

3. Capital Gains. Like U.S. venture capitalists, foreign firms require 20 percent of the capital gains.

4. Return on Investment. For a straight investment of more than $1 million, up to about $4 million, investors look for at least a 30 percent return on investment. Adding technology transfer to the same agreement, investors seek 20 to 25 percent returns.

5. Out-of-Pocket. Preparation and production of the business plan, finder's fees, and legal and accounting fees usually total 4 to 6 percent of the amount invested. These fees are higher than domestic venture capital fees because of the increased complexity of doing business with a foreign firm.

The following distribution of foreign buyer transactions by the price paid value includes the average and the median purchase price. The price paid distribution of all acquisitions also is provided for comparative purposes.

Foreign Acquisitions of U.S. Companies
Price-Paid Distribution 1982–1988

Number (Percent of Base)

Price-Paid Value	1982	1983	1984	19985	1986	1987	1988
$5 million or less	14 (17%)	6 (10%)	6 (7%)	12 (15%)	12 (8%)	1 (1%)	10 (5%)
$5.1–25.0 million	23 (28%)	20 (34%)	27 (32%)	25 (31%)	52 (33%)	19 (15%)	43 (23%)
$25.1–99.9 million	29 (36%)	23 (39%)	29 (34%)	22 (27%)	41 (26%)	46 (36%)	54 (29%)
$100 million or more	15 (19%)	10 (17%)	23 (27%)	21 (27%)	51 (33%)	62 (48%)	77 (43%)
Base*	81	59	85	80	156	128	184
Average Purchase Price (millions)	$63.0	$100.5	$178.0	$136.0	$157.1	$315.4	$301.4
Median Purchase Price (millions)	$32.4	$36.5	$49.6	$35.3	$70.7	$96.6	$65.8

*Base: Number of transactions disclosing purchase price.
Source: *Mergerstat Review.*

Price-Paid Distribution of All Acquisitions

				Number (Percent of Base)			
Price-Paid Value	1982	1983	1984	1985	1986	1987	1988
$5 million or less	296 (32)	321 (30)	270 (25)	296 (23)	219 (15)	92 (10)	1091 (9)
$5.1–25.0 million	338 (36)	380 (35)	361 (33)	454 (34)	519 (35)	294 (30)	320 (28)
$25.1–99.9 million	180 (20)	238 (22)	253 (23)	300 (23)	384 (26)	285 (29)	359 (31)
$100 million or more	116 (12)	138 (13)	200 (19)	270 (20)	346 (24)	301 (31)	369 (32)
Base*	930	1,077	1,084	1,320	1,468	972	1,149
Average Purchase Price (millions)	$57.8	$67.9	$112.8	$136.2	$117.9	$168.4	215.1
Median Purchase Price (millions)	$10.5	$16.5	$20.1	$21.1	$24.9	$51.3	56.9

*Base: Number of transactions disclosing purchase price.
Source: *Mergerstat Review*.

Sources of Capital Committed to Independent Venture Funds, 1983–June 1987 (Percent)

	1983	1984	1985	1986	January–June 1987
Total (Billions of Dollars)	3.4	3.2	2.3	3.3	1.4
Share contributed by:					
Pension Funds	31	34	33	50	47
Foreign Sources	16	18	23	11	8
Corporations	12	14	12	11	17
Endowments	8	6	8	6	5
Individuals	21	15	13	12	11
Insurance Companies	12	13	11	10	12

Source: Capital Publishing Corporation, *Venture Capital Journal*, various issues.

ADVANTAGES AND DISADVANTAGES

Advantages

1. Management can profitably expand built-in sales markets with (generally) long-term trading relationships developed through foreign venture capitalists.

2. Long-term trading relationships can result in other lucrative exchanges: technology transfer in exchange for consulting fees, equipment sales, and licensing and rights fees.

3. A ready test market for new products and technologies is available to adequately financed candidates.

4. Most foreign venture capitalists require a smaller equity stake in the company than U.S. venture capital firms.

Disadvantages

1. Foreign venture capital can be a costly financing technique if the company is not thoroughly advised of the procedures, customs, regulatory requirements and expenses involved.

2. A company can lose U.S. sales if domestic marketing is not stabilized before overseas marketing is introduced.

3. If the long-term trade and technology transfer goals of foreign venture capitalists do not match company goals, the company may expand too quickly or unwisely and lose profits.

4. Management may lose control of the company, product or technology if third-party assistance from U.S. professionals is not factored into the foreign agreement.

TESTING THE WATERS

Foreign venture capital can be a viable financing source almost without regard to specific domestic market conditions. High interest rates and resulting loan restrictions for startup companies create a good foreign venture capital market for U.S. companies, as do a strong dollar and excessive tariff restrictions, since these limit foreign purchase of products and technology.

ALTERNATIVES TO FOREIGN VENTURE CAPITAL

1. Warrants. Camex, Inc. issued the Bank of Boston a five-year warrant to purchase 5,500 shares of its stock in exchange for waived loan restrictions that might have inhibited future financing opportunities for the company. Camex later did a $1.7 million private placement (see Chapter 25).

2. Networking. Venture Capital Network, Inc. in New Hampshire helps entrepreneurs find investors and develop business plans. Officials in St. Paul, Minnesota, worked with a local law firm to raise $50,000 and attract national professional expertise for Summit Brewery (see Chapter 9).

3. Combinations. Computer Telephone Corporation put together private investor funding and a private investment firm guarantee on a bank loan, in exchange for a total 34 percent equity in the company.

SOURCES

Information about foreign venture capital:

> Venture Capital Journal, Venture Economics, Inc., Wellesley, MA.
> Peat Marwick Main, New York, NY.
> Hambro International Venture Fund, New York, NY.

PITFALLS TO AVOID

If foreign venture capitalists require technology transfer as part of the financing agreement, management should avoid signing away all rights to the technology in favor of terms that limit the time period or the manufacture/use of the technology.

Management should make careful due-diligence analyses of the foreign firm's liquidity and its ability to finance future rounds if necessary or desirable.

Avoid a right-to-buy clause that the foreign venture capitalist can exercise if management is not able to achieve benchmark goals, particularly if equity ownership and technology transfer already are written into the agreement.

CHAPTER 11
Foreign Partnerships

DESCRIPTION

Foreign partnerships, in the forms of wholly owned operations, joint ventures, or contract manufacture or licensing, are trade structures comprised of U.S. companies and foreign companies or quasi-government agencies that assist the transfer of goods, technology, expertise, equipment or services from the United States to a foreign country. A foreign partnership can be solely an export relationship, or it can permit some or all aspects of design/production/distribution to be executed overseas.

Secondary, indirect forms of foreign partnership include:

Export Management Company (EMC). An EMC acts as the export department for groups of U.S. manufacturers, to provide market research, distribution, exhibition, shipping, financing, legal, regulatory, marketing and customs services abroad.

Trading Company. A trading company acts as a commissioned agent that buys products for its own inventory or handles products on consignment for sales abroad. Trading companies can be U.S.- or foreign-owned.

Export Broker. Such a firm that buys directly from U.S. manufacturers to resell overseas. It controls the merchandise at purchase, but assumes the marketing and credit risks.

Piggyback Sales. Large U.S. or foreign firms distribute for small companies that are not competitive abroad. It is an economical marketing method for small companies that do not have the credit, contacts or distribution network for overseas sales.

Foreign Distributor. Equivalent to a manufacturers' representative in the U.S., this agent buys the export products at a discount, acquires title and markets the line(s). A distributor usually works on a commission basis, assumes no risk or responsibility, and is under contract for a specific time period.

Direct Sales. A direct sales company utilizes direct mail or advertising in foreign countries. The company assumes all responsibility for the sales process, costs and risks.

PROFILE OF A SUCCESSFUL FOREIGN PARTNERSHIP

The highest export returns are reported by companies that (1) exhibit a long-term commitment to foreign trade (the average contract life is 10 years), (2) have at least a two-year history of quarter-by-quarter profitable growth in U.S. sales, (3) have a highly differentiated and noncost-competitive product, (4) can afford the extra, and hidden, costs of foreign trade by adding a 50 percent price margin over the domestic unit price, yet remain competitive, and (5) can document the demand for its product overseas. Successful foreign partnerships include:

Societe Togolaise de Siderurgie S.A. (American)
T.A. Pelsue Co.
Television Technology Corporation
Climax Molybdenum Co. (AMAX, Inc.)

RESULTS OF A FOREIGN PARTNERSHIP

There are distinct results from foreign partnerships, in general. Favorable results can include (1) import/export tax incentives, (2) expanded customer base and potential market, (3) potential long-term investors, (4) long-term trade possibilities, (5) long-term technology transfer for increased income, (6) in some cases, additional capital and (7) in some cases, duty-free imports/exports.

Negative results from a foreign partnership can be almost as numerous as there are nations to trade with. By hiring a professional foreign-trade liaison, management can avoid (1) bad credit risks, (2) misunderstanding due to cultural differences, (3) increased foreign taxation and duties, (4) naive pricing errors, (5) fraudulent sales organizations that defraud the company of profits, (6) inappropriate or unprofitable company growth and (7) hidden export expenses.

The higher acquisition prices paid by offshore buyers of U.S. companies in 1988 generated a 37 percent increase, to $55.5 billion, in total value of all offshore acquisitions in which a purchase price was disclosed.

Foreign Acquisitions of U.S. Companies, 1972–1988

Year	Total Transactions	Transactions Valued at		Total Dollar Value Paid (billions of dollars)	Base*
		$100MM or more	$1,000MM or more		
1972	88	—	—	#	
1973	143	5	—	#	
1974	173	4	—	#	
1975	184	2	—	$1.6	84
1976	178	5	—	2.4	87
1977	162	3	—	3.1	92
1978	199	17	—	6.3	134
1979	236	11	—	5.8	142
1980	187	22	—	7.1	110
1981	234	24	4	18.8	126
1982	154	15	—	5.1	81
1983	125	10	1	5.9	59
1984	151	23	2	15.1	85
1985	197	21	3	10.9	80
1986	264	51	3	24.5	156
1987	220	62	10	40.4	128
1988	397	77	12	55.5	184
Totals	3,202	352	35	202.5	1,548

#Data not collected in that year.
*Base: Number of transactions disclosing purchase price.
Source: *Mergerstat Review.*

WHEN TO STRUCTURE A FOREIGN PARTNERSHIP

It is most advantageous to pursue a foreign partnership when (1) a foreign representative initiates interest in the company, (2) the company has a unique and noncost-competitive product, (3) the domestic market has been saturated or is in decline, (4) foreign trade is a logical next step in the company's financial plan or (5) management wants, and can fulfill, a long-term trade relationship.

THE HOW-TO TIMETABLE

One Year before Negotiating a Foreign Partnership

1. *Export License.* The first step is to inquire at a local office of the Department of Commerce about the potential for getting an export license. The United States has more stringent export policies than most other countries, so it is important to know early on if the product or technology can, in fact, be cleared for export.

2. *Survey Specific Foreign Markets.* International trade requires much the same initial market research that domestic trade does, only more of it. The key to success is understanding the specific marketplace, including:

Potential: Review general economic indicators such as size, economic growth of the host country, its stage of development, public policies, income and expenditure patterns of the local customer base, and related trade statistics.

Competition: Consider any United States or foreign competitors already in the targeted marketplace, their market share, size and depth, how they produce, market and distribute, and cost and profit comparisons.

Market Entry: Research restrictions in the form of quotas, non-tariff barriers and tariffs.

Regulatory Environment: Assess the political priorities of the host country, U.S. trade embargoes, political or economic instability, legal and currency restrictions, and patent protection differences.

Market: Investigate the country's infrastructure and laws regarding freight, transportation, packaging, storage, media, sales and distribution.

3. Survey Company Potential. Not all products that are successful in the U.S. will be successful overseas. Some of the success factors to consider are:

Product Standards: Safety, design, quality and technical specifications often must be met before the product can be sold overseas.

Pricing: Can the product be sold competitively with a margin high enough to cover the additional costs of exporting, including setup, administration, duties, foreign taxes and sales?

Product Function: Products often are used differently in a foreign country. Can they be easily modified for foreign use?

Expense: Can management afford the extra expense of setting up a foreign partnership, staffing it (if applicable), research and development on the product for adaptation to foreign requirements, travel, and third-party consulting on legal and tax matters?

Six Months before Negotiating a Foreign Partnership

1. Professional Liaison. Most international trade experts recommend hiring an individual or firm to act as a consultant to the company before it structures a foreign partnership or begins exporting. Several candidates should be interviewed from among three primary sources.

Government agencies offer startup and later-stage assistance, and in some cases financing, to U.S. companies. Examples are the local offices of the U.S. Department of Commerce, Small Business Administration (SBA), Overseas Private Investment Corporation (OPIC), Agency for International Develop ment and Export-Import Bank of the U.S. (national agencies); consulates and embassies, and state development agencies. Others include:

Private U.S. liaison/export firms
Foreign liaison/export firms

Others, including local Chambers of Commerce, international banks, on-line database newsletters and international transportation firms.

2. *Targeting the Market.* With input from private and governmental agencies as well as from professional advisers who specialize in foreign trade, management should select a host country and obtain as much information as possible about its trade practices.

3. *Partnership Structure.* Aided by the professional liaison and an experienced corporate attorney who is familiar with foreign partnership structures, management should next draw up preliminary plans for how the company will function overseas. Partnership structures as a rule will limit not only capital investment overseas, but also legal liability, government interference and some tax consequences. Assuming the company will not simply export from the United States the three primary partnership forms are:

Licensing Relationship with a Foreign Company or Quasi-Government Agency: This is the easy way to do business in a foreign country because it simply makes a technology, product, patent, design or trademark available to a foreign manufacturer. The company generally receives a royalty on each unit sold or an agreed-upon fee as compensation. Licensing requires less capital expenditure in terms of investment or management time than a joint venture or subsidiary does.

Joint Venture: Shared ownership of the operation and property rights with a foreign firm, typically local and private, is another way. Joint ventures are popular abroad for two reasons: (1) the host country can prevent U.S. domination of particular local industries by owner-investors and (2) joint ventures help support local technology and managerial development. Market entry is almost always easier with a local joint-venture partner who is familiar with local practices.

Contract Manufacture: This is a step before technology transfer (in which the company actually sells its process or design to a foreign company), which entails U.S. production on a contract basis for a foreign company, often resulting in more competitive pricing abroad.

Three Months before Negotiating a Foreign Partnership

1. Testing the Market. To determine whether or not the company is ready to trade overseas, there are several ways to pretest the market:

Trade Missions: Organized by private organizations like Colorado/China, and state and federal agencies like the Department of Commerce, these trips provide firsthand exposure to overseas markets.

Catalog and Video Exhibitions: Sales materials and/or videotapes of products in use are exhibited monthly in U.S. embassies and consulates by the Department of Commerce. This is the least expensive way to test the market.

Trade Fairs: Such meetings are organized by private firms and government agencies like the International Trade Association (ITA) through the Commercial Exhibits Program. Most U.S. trade fairs are listed in the Export Promotion Calendar, available from the Department of Commerce.

2. Finding a Foreign Partner. As a result of pre-testing the market through trade missions, catalog exhibitions and/or trade fairs, management should have leads from interested foreign entrepreneurs. These leads should be followed up with the assistance of an outside foreign liaison, who is retained by the company to advise management about language, customs, business practices and social protocol indigenous to the host country.

3. Visiting the Host Country. It should be noted that although foreign leads are easy to acquire, resulting visits to the host country should be planned carefully. Management's foreign liaison can set up appropriate travel and visit arrangements, and ensure that U.S. visitors to the host country have the right documentation to begin negotiations.

Negotiating a Foreign Partnership

Management's foreign liaison can be extremely helpful about negotiating customs in the host country. The primary pitfall for a U.S. entrepreneur is usually the time factor. Negotiations can take anywhere from one week to two years and three months is average. It may take more than one trip to the host country before contracts are signed. It is exceedingly important to have U.S. legal counsel review all documentation before it is signed.

In the analysis of the foreign acquisition of American firms, both foreign purchases of domestic companioes and purchases of foreign-based subsidiaries of U.S. corporations are included in the chart below.

Foreign Purchases

Year	U.S. Domestic Businesses	Foreign-Based Units of U.S. Companies	Total Foreign Buyers
1979	202	34	236
1980	159	28	187
1981	185	49	234
1982	117	37	154
1983	101	24	125
1984	129	22	151
1985	143	54	197
1986	228	36	264
1987	171	49	220
1988	265	42	307

Source: *Mergerstat Review.*

FILING REQUIREMENTS

If the U.S. partner is a public company, it is subject to the reporting/disclosure requirements of the SEC. Reporting documents include a quarterly financial report (Form 10-Q), annual financial report (Form 10-K), reports about current material events in the company (Form 8-K), proxy statements, annual report to the shareholders and other reports for audited financial statements. Also, public companies must meet state reporting/disclosure requirements, if any.

Private and public companies must qualify for a Department of Commerce export license before exporting products, expertise or technology, or doing business in a foreign country. In addition, U.S. companies may have to comply with the reporting requirements of the host country.

COSTS

The first key to estimating the total cost of operating a foreign partnership is control: the less control a company has over its foreign operation, the less sales will cost. The least expensive option is to give up control over product and let an ETC (export trade company) sell it. The most expensive option is to retain total control over a wholly owned subsidiary in the host country.

The second key to cost is location. Currently, Sidney, Australia, and Frankfort, Germany, are low-cost locations; London and Tokyo are high-cost locations.

Other significant costs include:

1. *Sales Representative.* The cost of using a foreign sales representative or distributor varies widely depending on the industry and the nature of the services performed by the distributor. Agents who take more control over the product and have liability can cost between 30 and 40 percent of sales. Agents who only sell the product and perform few other services charge between 5 and 7 percent of sales.

2. *Foreign Presence.* Small companies that maintain a wholly owned subsidiary in the host country, for example, will pay up to $100,000 annually in costs, on average.

3. *Consultant.* A third-party professional who helps management arrange a joint venture or partnership often charges between $1,000 and $2,500 per day for such services as translation, marketing and prenegotiating assistance. The average cost to the company ranges between $5,000 and $10,000. The rule of thumb is whatever the market will bear.

ADVANTAGES AND DISADVANTAGES

Advantages

1. Foreign partnerships can enlarge the potential market and increase the customer base, resulting in higher revenues and earnings, and a larger market share among competitors.

2. Most foreign partnerships contract over a 10-year time period for stable revenues and earnings, and simplified financial planning.

3. Existing and obsolete products often can be modified for international trade, reducing R&D costs and extending product life cycle.

4. Tax and financial consequences can be beneficial if accounting and legal professionals are consulted during the planning stage.

Disadvantages

1. Foreign trade can be an expensive way to increase sales unless the partnership is carefully planned, the company is financially stable and the product or technology is eagerly demanded by a foreign market.

2. A foreign partnership can be expensive unless management consults specialized professionals who can structure a favorable contract.

3. If the company is financially unstable and tries to revive with a foreign partnership, it may collapse under the expense and time involved in building a successful foreign operation.

4. There is little case law that backs joint ventures and other partnerships in some foreign countries.

TESTING THE WATERS

The time to consider a foreign partnership is when (1) the company has become financially stable and can afford the various costs of international trade, (2) the product or technology is sought by a foreign company, (3) management has appropriate outside counsel to help structure the deal, including a foreign liaison familiar with the host country, a specialist attorney and accountant, and contacts with U.S. trade organizations and (4) the political and economic climates of the host country and the United States favor foreign trade.

ALTERNATIVES TO A FOREIGN PARTNERSHIP

1. Wholly Owned. Subsidiaries. Acquiring or developing wholly owned facilities abroad can be cost competitive and insures control of the operation. Two options are to establish a branch of a U.S. corporation or a subsidiary of the U.S. company that incorporates in the host country. Tax consequences of both should determine the viability of this alternative.

2. Foreign Sales Distributors. Such a representative purchases the goods at a discount, acquires title and markets them. The distributor also provides contacts and many services that the company can't perform as economically. Cadnetix Corporation exports CAD/CAM technology directly to England and Germany, and uses a foreign sales distributor for exports to Sweden and Japan.

3. Free-Trade Zones. More than 100 free ports, trade zones and other customs-privileged facilities exist in 40 countries in which companies pay no duty on items exported and, in some cases, no import duties either.

SOURCES

Information about foreign partnering:

"U.S. Exports," U.S. Census Bureau, Washington, D.C.

"Trade Opportunities Weekly," U.S. Department of Commerce, Washington, D.C.

"International Trade Information Service (ITIS)," Data Resources, Inc., Washington, D.C.

"International Financial Statistics (IFS)," International Monetary Fund, Washington, D.C.

Foreign Partnership

	Good Deal	*Bad Deal*
1. Rights to the technology	Company retains the right to use and sell	Foreign partner gains all rights to the technology
2. Overseas facility	At least some U.S. ownership and management	No U.S. ownership or management
3. Buyout terms	U.S. right of first refusal at predetermined market value	No U.S. right of first refusal; competitive bid
4 Foreign sales	Local sales force in host country; local distributor	Any form of nonlocal sales results in higher costs
5 Tax benefits	Equitably shared; U.S. partner retains some foreign tax benefits	Foreign partner retains all foreign tax benefits
6 Wages	Host country rates	U.S. rates
7 Tariffs	Free-trade zone or GATT trading	Host-country tariff rates
8 Payment from overseas	Cash in advance; letter of credit	Open account, time draft or sight draft

CHAPTER 12

Going Public Overseas (London Exchange)

DESCRIPTION

There are two securities markets within The (London) Stock Exchange, both of which are accessible by foreign (U.S.) companies: (1) the listed securities market, which is the traditional public market, and (2) the unlisted securities market (USM), which is amenable to small or less mature public companies and has less stringent reporting requirements.

In addition, (1) a U.S. company can sell a private placement to UK financial institutions through a UK merchant bank or broker (called a private placing in the London markets), (2) a UK-incorporated company can conduct certain transactions in securities that are not traded on the listed or unlisted markets and (3) a U.S. company can take over a UK company already listed or traded on the unlisted securities market in order to trade on The Stock Exchange (called a reverse takeover).

An initial public offering (IPO) through a foreign stock exchange like The Stock Exchange is the process by which a privately held U.S. or other foreign company (1) sells previously issued or newly created shares of stock to the public in a foreign country for the first time, (2) discloses operations to the public, (3) registers with, and operates within the provisions and laws of, appropriate regulatory bodies in the United Kingdom and in the United States including the SEC (in some cases), The Stock Exchange (in London), and the Bank of England, if applicable.

U.S. management can use a sponsor (merchant bank)/stockbroker (underwriter) team to sell an IPO or private placement, or it can sell a self-underwriting to public or private UK markets.

PROFILE OF A SUCCESSFUL IPO CANDIDATE

The London capital markets have become increasingly attractive to foreign companies, particularly U.S. companies, because of their reduced costs and requirements. But certain criteria are applied to U.S. and other foreign companies that are unlike SEC requirements.

To qualify for admission to the listed securities market, The Stock Exchange requires that a U.S. company have (1) a market value of not less than £500,000 (approximately $667,000), (2) a market value of not less than £200,000 (approximately $267,000) in an individual class of security, (3) a five-year track record of operations, (4) a minimum 25 percent of any class of issued equity capital owned by public investors (not directors or substantial shareholders) and (5) no material number of options issued in relation to the securities.

To qualify for admission to the unlisted securities market, which has no minimum market value requirements for the company or its stock, The Stock Exchange requires that a U.S. company have (1) a three-year track record of operations, (2) a minimum 10 percent of any class of issued equity capital owned by public investors and (3) no material number of options issued in relation to the securities. U.S. companies that are traded on The Stock Exchange include:

InfraRed Associates, Inc.
CVD, Inc.
Pacer Systems, Inc.

RESULTS OF A FOREIGN INITIAL PUBLIC OFFERING

U.S. companies that go public via The Stock Exchange rather than via U.S. capital markets (1) gain access to public markets before undergoing the more stringent registration requirements of the SEC, (2) raise public capital at a lower cost than in U.S. markets, (3) increase awareness of the company overseas and (4) take advantage of certain tax deductions that may apply in foreign markets.

When a U.S. company sells an initial public offering overseas, IPO results are the same as a U.S. offering, including (1) eligibility for exchange listing, (2) disclosure of information about the company to public shareholders and to appropriate regulatory bodies (although SEC disclosure requirements are more extensive), (3) a broader capital base and (4) the unrestricted sale of shares among public investors.

WHEN TO SELL A FOREIGN INITIAL PUBLIC OFFERING

The best time to apply for trading privileges on The Stock Exchange is when (1) the company meets Exchange requirements, which differ from U.S. requirements, (2) the company is not mature enough for entry into the U.S. capital markets or is not ready to meet SEC registration requirements, (3) the U.S. market is not receptive to new issues, but the London market is or (4) the company meets all U.S. market requirements, but wants to reduce registration and cost constraints related to U.S. trading.

THE HOW-TO TIMETABLE

One Year Prior to Impact Day (Effective Date)

1. *Institutional Image.* Determine how the company is perceived in the European marketplace. Is the product appealing and modified for export sale, if necessary? How are the product, company and industry perceived in Europe? Is the company distinguishable from European or other competitors?

Major Form of Foreign Investment in U.S. Companies
(Corporate Stocks in Billions)

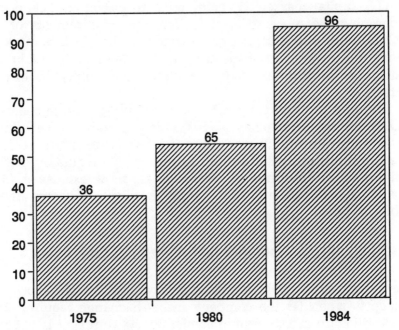

Source: Commerce Department.

2. Target Market. The company's institutional image must be sold effectively to European target markets who will buy shares after the offering. The longer a targeted marketing campaign has been in effect, the more responsive investors tend to be. Management should retain a UK public relations firm to market the company more effectively to the European market.

3. Reorganization. Many private companies are organized as partnerships or joint ventures. The legal structure may have to be modified prior to going public. An additional consideration when going public on the London exchange is whether the company should enter the market directly or indirectly through a UK holding company. Some companies have to recapitalize to have an appropriate capital structure for the public offering.

4. *Legal Review*. The Stock Exchange in London has specific requirements that must be addressed prior to going public. A review of the following, conducted by attorneys who are familiar with Exchange requirements, should begin well in advance of the initial public offering sale:

Corporate charter and bylaws
Shareholder or management loans
Debt outstanding
Employment contracts
Lease agreements
Stock option or purchase plans
Supply contracts and arrangements
Rights of first refusal
Export contracts

Six Months Prior to Impact Day

1. *Business Plan*. This document is used by the UK stockbroker (the underwriter) and merchant bankers to analyze the company and assess the probable outcome of the offering. It outlines the company's current condition and growth potential, including:

Plan summary
Business description
Market analysis
Product/service description
Marketing strategy
Manufacturing/service operation
Management and organization
Financial data
Capital needs/timetable

2. *Outside Professionals*. UK trading requires that certain third-party professionals be retained to help structure and sell the offering (unless the offering is self-underwritten). Each professional should be carefully interviewed and selected on the basis of expertise in the company's industry and in UK trading.

Sponsor: An "issuing house," which is a merchant bank or brokerage house, expedites the offering by reviewing the offering documents for accuracy and completeness, and by qualifying company directors for their corporate responsibilities within a publicly traded company.

Stockbroker: A member of The Stock Exchange formally submits the company's application to the exchange, acts as liaison between the company and the investment community, helps negotiate the issue price and assists in the sale of the securities.

Accountants: The due-diligence investigation of the company must be performed in order to compile a "long-form report" or "businessman's review," which is an unpublished document that aids the sponsor in qualifying the company for the London markets and in structuring the entry. The long-form report yields a short-form or accountants' report, which is included in the prospectus. The accountants usually act as tax advisers also, to clarify tax ramifications for a U.S. company going public on The Stock Exchange.

Solicitors (Legal Advisers): A local firm is retained to oversee production of the required legal documents and to ensure their compliance with UK law. Solicitors represent the sponsor's interest in the offering and work in tandem with the company's in-house counsel.

Receiving Banker: If the offering is a self-underwriting, called an "offer for sale" or a "prospectus issue," a receiving banker must handle the application for securities and the proceeds from the offering.

Printer: Production of the prospectus must be contracted for by the company.

In addition, the sponsor and/or stockbroker will hire other professionals, including:

Registrar, usually a bank department that keeps a list of security holders
Property appraiser
Industry specialist

Four Months Prior to Impact Day

   1. *Long-Form Report.* An outline of the company's current condition and future prospects (which cannot legally be included in the prospectus of a U.S. company) is prepared by the accountants for the sponsor's analysis.
   2. *Bank of England.* If the offering is to raise £3 million (approximately $4 million) or more, the company must apply to the Bank of England for assignment of "impact day," a date on which the issue can be announced publicly and secondary underwriting can begin.
   3. *Issue Documents.* The prospectus must be drafted for preliminary review by the Quotations Department of The Stock Exchange. On approval, the draft becomes the issue document, or prospectus.

One Month Prior to Impact Day

The solicitors will file appropriate documentation to the SEC, if necessary.

Impact Day

   1. The prospectus is signed by management and all third parties involved.
   2. Advertising about the offering begins.
   3. The underwriting agreement is signed by the sponsor.
   4. Secondary underwriting begins.
   5. The sponsor prices the issue. To avoid some of the pricing risks, many high-tech and other companies that are hard to establish a market price for choose to use a tender offer in which applications for securities are solicited at or above a minimum tender price. A "striking price" is set from the tenders received, which becomes the issue price.

FILING REQUIREMENTS

UK corporate law and The Stock Exchange requirements set the regulatory environment for going public on the London exchange. UK reporting requirements apply to those companies incorporated in Great Britain or to those with a place of business there. Foreign companies with shares traded on The Stock Exchange, but with no place of business in the United Kingdom are subject only to The Stock Exchange requirements and any regulations dictated by their country of incorporation. U.S. companies whose shares are traded on the London exchange should retain local solicitors to ensure compliance with local securities regulations, which include:

Six-month interim reports by mail or in the media
Annual audits
Material event notification to shareholders and regulatory
bodies

Other accounting requirements apply to foreign companies traded on The Stock Exchange. UK regulations differ in several important respects from U.S. requirements, and should be supervised by UK accountants to ensure compliance.

COSTS

It costs about the same to go public on The Stock Exchange and in the United States. A full discussion of the itemized costs of going public in the United States is found in Chapter 20.

ADVANTAGES AND DISADVANTAGES

Advantages

1. The company usually can access public capital markets in the UK earlier in the corporate life cycle as compared to the accessibility of U.S. capital markets.

2. European markets become more familiar with companies traded on the London exchange, sometimes resulting in increased sales and a more successful stock offering.

3. By going public in the United Kingdom, a U.S. company can build a track record to ensure a more successful offering in the United States when it is ready to trade on the American markets.

4. UK investors value a company on projected earnings, but projections must be met to retain the ongoing interest of investors.

Disadvantages

1. Unless careful consideration is given to the quality of third-party assistance, an IPO in the United Kingdom can be unsuccessful, premature or more expensive than a comparable U.S. offering.

2. Some companies that have gone public in European markets are perceived as thin new issues that could not succeed in U.S. markets.

3. If management is not prepared for the additional responsibilities of going public, a foreign offering can be an expensive and time-consuming additional burden that results in lower profits and inappropriate growth.

TESTING THE WATERS

The standard guideline for going public via an initial public offering applies to a foreign exchange IPO: it is influenced 70 percent by local market conditions, 20 percent by the potential of the industry in which the company competes and 10 percent by the merits of the company. Local advice should be sought to assess local (UK) market conditions, the industry as it exists overseas and the local perception of the company.

ALTERNATIVES TO GOING PUBLIC IN LONDON

1. *Domestic IPO.* Unless management is willing to take the time for adequate due diligence on the London markets, an IPO in the U.S. market may be more successful. Pasta & Cheese, Inc. went public in the United States at $6 a share in 1985 to raise almost $5 million during a soft initial public offering market (see Chapter 20).

   2. *Other London Exchange Techniques.* There are several other ways in which a U.S. company can trade in the United Kingdom, including:

>   Reverse takeover, in which a private company takes over a small public company (comparable to a shell company in the United States)
>
>   Private placing, in which the company offers shares to private capital markets
>
>   Registration in a marking name, in which a listed nonresident company does not maintain a separate UK register, so shareholders register their stock in a marking name for endorsement of the share certificate in blank, creating a bearer security
>
>   Trading within the UK through an agency or branch

SOURCES

Peat Marwick Main, New York, NY.
The Stock Exchange, London, England.

PITFALLS TO AVOID

Some foreign stock underwriters price shares on the basis of earnings projections that are printed in the prospectus. Avoid the temptation to project earnings unrealistically. If projections are not achieved, investor confidence is eroded and it becomes far more difficult to sell shares.

It can be less costly and less time-consuming to go public overseas. Be sure that the consequences of going public quickly match the goals and financial structure of the company.

The marketing practices allowed by overseas stock exchanges vary widely and generally are more lenient than U.S. standards. To remain competitive against local and other foreign stocks, it is advisable to hire local public relations representation.

Section 4
Short-Term Techniques

Section 4
Introduction

Four short-term techniques described in Section 4 can be appropriate strategies for a small public or private company in the under–$25 million category. In many ways, these strategies are simply sound cash management practices, but they are included because they generate immediate cash, rather than the cash savings that result from astute cash management.

If the company has a short-term cash lapse that can be covered by assured revenue at a future date, these techniques provide ready funds between long-term financings. But they should always be considered a supplement to standard debt, equity or combination financing packages.

The newest option in Section 4 is commercial paper issues, which can now be sold by small business owners as well as by large, bond-rated corporations. In fact, commercial paper issues flourish in foreign markets as well, supplementing barter and letters of credit as foreign trade techniques used by increasing numbers of sophisticated entrepreneurs. It has been estimated by the U.S. Department of Commerce that at least half of all foreign trade will be transacted through a form of barter known as countertrade by the end of this century. Visionary business owners who anticipate expansion to overseas markets should be conversant with these strategies to increase their competitive posture now and in the future.

Short-term techniques are used best by managers who know how to fine-tune the financial structure of the company by capitalizing on hidden assets and finding offbeat markets for them.

Section 4
Glossary

Accounts Receivable Financing: short-term financing for working capital, pledging accounts receivable as collateral. Accounts receivable turnover is the ratio of total credit sales to accounts receivable, indicated by how many times receivables have been collected during a given period of time.

Compensating Balance: the average balance a borrowing company must keep on account to hold credit available, as in revolving credit. A standard compensating balance for a line of credit is about 10 percent of the line, in addition to about 10 percent of the amount borrowed.

Direct Issuers: companies that sell commercial paper directly to investors, rather than indirectly through paper brokers.

Maturity Factoring: a method of financing in which the factor company handles the credit and collection functions, and remits to the seller company for the receivables sold each month on the average due date of the factored receivables.

Overadvance: a loan in advance of sales that allows management to build inventory prior to peak sales periods.

Performance Bond: a surety bond to protect against loss as a result of nonperformance. Performance bonds are often required of small companies that issue commercial paper.

Recourse Loan: a loan for which an undersigner or guarantor is liable for payment if the borrower defaults. A nonrecourse loan (usually in a limited partnership's direct participation program) signifies that the lender has no recourse to the assets of a limited partnership beyond those held by the limited partners who borrowed the money.

Revolving Credit: a contract between a company and a bank in which the bank makes loans up to a specific amount for one year or longer. As the company repays on the loan each month, an amount equal to the monthly payment can be borrowed again (also called open-end credit).

DESCRIPTION

Commercial paper is the short-term, revolving debt obligation of a company (or bank) borrowed for a term of from 2 to 270 days from individual or institutional investors. A commercial paper issue is a promissory note that is unsecured, discounted and usually not interest-bearing (although some issues now bear interest at the Safe Harbor rate under variable tax laws). This debt can be issued directly or through a commercial paper broker at a large brokerage firm.

Commercial paper maturities are flexible and rates are generally lower than bank rates. Small company issuers may be required to back the paper with a bank or insurance line of credit to offset the lack of a top credit rating.

A commercial paper issue is often considered a cash management technique, but a series of issues can be structured to save a considerable amount of the cost of raising money over time.

PROFILE OF A SUCCESSFUL ISSUER

Although the commercial paper market in the past was limited to large, blue-chip companies, small companies can now enter this market by pooling their issues to create a borrowing fund of up to

$100 million through a national brokerage house. To qualify, a company should have (1) at least $20 million in stockholders' equity, (2) a bank line of credit, (3) a debt-to-capitalization ratio of less than 40 percent, (4) three or more years of positive earnings, (5) internally generated cash flow equal to 100 percent of capital expenditures and (5) tangible assets.

Small business-issuers of commercial paper include:

Tri-State Auto Rentals, Inc.
Texas Automobile Dealers Association

RESULTS OF ISSUING COMMERCIAL PAPER

A small business can (1) access an untapped, multibillion-dollar market by pooling issues with other small companies who want to adjust their credit needs regularly to keep costs down, (2) negotiate a maturity of usually less than 45 days and other flexible terms, (3) borrow at rates 0.5 to 3 percent cheaper than the prime rate and (4) get a good credit rating more easily via the surety bond, dealer or letter of credit required by most brokerage pools.

WHEN TO ISSUE COMMERCIAL PAPER

The time to issue commercial paper is when (1) the company has short-term borrowing needs, (2) the interest or prime rate is high, (3) the company's credit rating potential is good or (4) the company can pool organizationally with other franchises, leasing operations or association members to create a small business paper fund.

THE HOW-TO TIMETABLE

One Month before Issuance

1. Guarantees. The best source for letter-of-credit or line-of-credit backing is a bank with which the company has had a startup or long-term relationship. Many insurance companies offer additional backing with the top rating guaranteed by a surety bond. Some surety bonds can be obtained only after the company has a bank line of credit.

Another source of guarantees is the brokerage firm which operates the pooled commercial paper fund. A prospectus, offering circular, audited income statements and/or pro formas will be required to demonstrate that the company meets qualifications, which vary by institution.

2. Pool. With a line of credit and/or surety bond backing, management can apply at several pooled funds operated by national brokerage firms. They will conduct due-diligence investigations of the company and assign it to an appropriate issuer pool, from which as little as $1 million can be borrowed for as short a period as overnight or over a weekend.

FILING REQUIREMENTS

Commercial paper issuers are not subject to federal or state reporting/disclosure requirements. Public companies are required to note the debt obligation in financial statements included in annual and quarterly reports.

COSTS

1. Interest. Most small companies pay about 1.5 percent above the current commercial paper rate to borrow, which results in a reduction of 0.5 to 3 percent below prime.

2. Surety Bond. An insurance company charges from 1/4 to 1 percent of the issue's value to lend a top rating to the issue.

3. Combined Dealer Fee. Most brokerage firms charge from 1 to 1.5 percent above the commercial paper rate for combined surety bond, dealer and letter-of-credit fees.

ADVANTAGES AND DISADVANTAGES

Advantages

1. Commercial paper can be sold in a very short period of time.

2. Commercial paper rates, even to small companies with no credit rating, are less than the prime or bank interest rate, resulting in a financial strategy that is less costly than bank borrowing.

3. Management can manipulate the issue to meet specific and variable credit needs.

Disadvantages

1. Unless management shops carefully for the required guarantees, fees can offset the interest savings between the commercial paper rate and the bank lending rate.

2. Short-term maturities may not fit the current repayment capability of the company.

3. The company needs a line of credit and/or surety bond to meet the guarantee requirements of the instrument.

TESTING THE WATERS

If the company can qualify for a commercial paper issue offered at 2 percent under current lending rates (or 1 to 1.5 percent over the current commercial paper rate), this strategy will result in a nominal savings in the cost of borrowing funds. Net costs for acquiring a line of credit and/or a surety bond should not reduce net savings (2 percent) by more than 1 percent.

ALTERNATIVES TO COMMERCIAL PAPER

1. Line of Credit. If the company doesn't want to pay the guarantee fees required to issue commercial paper, a line of credit can be as good a financing source as commercial paper. Scan-Optics, Inc. obtained line of credit agreements with two major banks for $2 million in unsecured borrowings and $1 million for lease-financing purposes (see Chapter 17).

2. *Factoring.* An easier way to raise short-term funds is to sell discounted accounts receivable to a factor, who then collects the asset plus a small commission based on the value of the asset (see Chapter 15).

3. *Letter of Credit.* Management can obtain a letter of credit based on a reliable account receivable, or on an account payable, in order to raise short-term cash, borrow more or obtain another letter of credit. Orion Manufacturing Corporation got a letter of credit from Penn Square to assure Philadelphia Gear Company of payment for oil pumps Orion had ordered (see Chapter 14).

SOURCES

Merrill Lynch's Capital Funding Corporation, New York City
E.F. Hutton's Corporate Paper, Inc., New York City

PITFALLS TO AVOID

It can be difficult to find a surety bond or guarantee that does not add significantly to the cost of issuing commercial paper. The guarantee and dealer fees should not total more than two percentage points.

Commercial paper should be considered only a short-term financing option that supplements strategic, long-term financings.

Commercial paper that is continually reissued can burden the debt/equity balance during the life of the issue, precluding other debt financing that may be more important to the future of the company.

CHAPTER 14

Letters of Credit

DESCRIPTION

As a financing tool, the letter of credit is a passive technique that requires no action on the part of the company except to ask for the instrument in specific situations that are enumerated below.

A letter of credit is a bank instrument that guarantees payment of the company's drafts up to a specific amount for a specific time period. It replaces the buyer's credit with bank credit, thus eliminating the seller's risk. A company can ask for a letter of credit from a customer (domestic or overseas) before manufacture or shipment, for example, to ensure payment. It becomes a financing strategy when the letter of credit, or guaranteed payment, is used to get (1) credit, (2) more favorable terms from suppliers or (3) accounts payable discounts by borrowing against the letter to pay early.

There are specialized letters of credit, including (1) performance letter of credit, which guarantees contract performance, (2) revolving letter of credit, which is issued for a specific, renewable amount over a specific time period to permit any number of drafts to be drawn against it up to the specified limit, (3) confirmed letter of credit, which is offered by a correspondent bank and backed by the issuing bank, and (4) traveler's letter of credit, which is issued for travelers who cash them at correspondent banks where the drafts are honored.

Although letters of credit have been used increasingly over the past decade, cash has been the leading form of payment in all transactions involving companies and their products since 1974, with the exception of 1983. Prior to 1974, stock was the favorite method of payment.

Payment Trends 1964–1988

		Number (perecent of deals disclosing payment form)			
Year	Total Number Disclosing Payment Form	Cash	Stock	Combination	Debt
1964	1,950	1,248 64%	702 36%		*
1965	2,125	1,436 68%	604 28%	85 4%	*
1966	2,359	1,438 61%	802 34%	119 5%	*
1967	2,975	1,077 36%	1,783 60%	115 4%	*
1968	4,462	1,314 29%	2,762 62%	386 9%	*
1969	5,181	1,667 32%	2,945 57%	569 11%	*
1970	3,523	1,023 29%	1,834 52%	575 16%	91 3%
1971	2,963	961 32%	1,441 49%	514 17%	47 2%
1972	3,328	1,120 34%	1,696 51%	475 14%	37 1%
1973	2,686	1,113 41%	1,172 44%	365 14%	36 1%
1974	1,672	805 48%	555 33%	259 16%	53 3%
1975	1,225	585 48%	325 27%	285 23%	30 2%
1976	1,255	656 52%	327 26%	250 20%	22 2%
1977	1,238	663 54%	322 26%	224 18%	29 2%
1978	1,182	539 46%	353 30%	273 23%	17 1%
1979	1,233	654 53%	323 26%	247 20%	9 1%
1980	1,121	522 47%	345 31%	237 21%	17 1%
1981	1,309	542 42%	448 34%	301 23%	18 1%
1982	1,083	405 38%	317 29%	338 31%	23 2%
1983	1,108	350 32%	387 35%	362 33%	9 —
1984	1,079	465 43%	281 26%	320 30%	13 1%
1985	1,468	742 51%	344 23%	377 26%	5 —
1986	1,303	545 42%	411 32%	345 26%	2 —
1987	724	298 41%	248 34%	176 24%	2 1%
1988	777	437 56%	166 21%	170 22%	4 1%
	49,329	20,605 42%	20,893 42%	7,369 15%	465 1%

*A separate tally of debt payments began in 1970. Prior to 1970, debt was included in cash payments.

Source: *Mergerstat Review.*

PROFILE OF A SUCCESSFUL LETTER OF CREDIT TRANSACTION

The company is most likely to obtain a letter of credit from a customer or the customer's bank when (1) company performance is projected from proven sales, (2) the company has a strong operating history and a good reputation, (3) buyer conditions are unstable (i.e., political unrest in the host country of a foreign buyer) or (4) guarantor banks are secure and/or have an existing relationship with the seller or the buyer.

Letters of credit are most easily obtained in a transaction with a foreign buyer, where the company's product is in demand and the importer has no choice but to use a letter of credit to get the product.

Companies that have used letters of credit in export trade:

Sports Accessories
Medical Light Sources
Daechter, Inc.

RESULTS OF A LETTER OF CREDIT TRANSACTION

With a letter of credit from a buyer, the company (1) has a high degree of protection against bad-debt risk (second only to cash in advance), (2) can expand more aggressively by exporting with legal assurance, (3) can negotiate more favorable credit terms from suppliers and lenders with an assignment of proceeds, (4) can transfer the rights inherent in the letter of credit in part or in full, to another party, to buy goods from a manufacturer, be the exporter of record and earn a profit without having to use money or (5) use the letter of credit as collateral for another letter of credit (a back-to-back transaction), if the company is very strong financially and has established a proven record in exporting.

WHEN TO SOLICIT A LETTER OF CREDIT

Under specific circumstances it is vitally important to obtain a letter of credit from a buyer. They are: (1) in a foreign trade or export transaction in which the buyer resides and/or does business in another country and the company has little or no recourse, (2) a domestic buyer is unknown or has an undesirable reputation, (3) the company needs to borrow or order goods against the instrument to complete the transaction, (4) when the buyer can't get cash in advance from a foreign buyer or (5) when payment delays threaten company cash flow.

THE HOW-TO TIMETABLE

The key to obtaining a letter of credit for payment, guarantee or cash flow purposes is to establish a sound banking relationship early in the development of the company. It is very difficult for management to get a letter of credit without a well-established banking relationship.

Three Months before Letter of Credit Issuance

1. *Review.* In-house accounting and legal counsel should review the financial condition of the company and update certain documents including:

Balance sheet
Profit and loss statement
Accounts receivable and payable documents
All documentation related to the company's current ratio including liquidity, short- and long-term debt, turnover and profit

2. *Proposal.* Management should prepare a five- to ten-page proposal outlining:

Need for credit
Length of time needed

Use of credit
Repayment schedule
Available collateral

3. *Tax Returns.* Private companies should be prepared to produce tax returns for the past three years.

One Month before Letter of Credit Issuance

1. *Selection.* Management should interview several banks (the international department, as a rule) to compare terms.
2. *Appointment.* The bank selected should be queried about additional credit documentation that may be required.

FILING REQUIREMENTS

A letter of credit is not subject to federal or state registration/disclosure requirements. A public company must footnote the transaction in financial statements contained in the annual report.

COSTS

Domestic and export letters of credit cost about 2 percentage points per year (2 percent of the dollar value of the letter of credit). That rate increases or decreases slightly depending on the bank's perception of the risk involved in the transaction or within the company.

ADVANTAGES AND DISADVANTAGES

Advantages to the Recipient/Seller Company

1. A letter of credit offers maximum protection in transactions with a foreign or unstable buyer (second only to cash in advance).

2. The company can borrow or buy goods against the letter of credit, with a document called an "assignment of proceeds"' in order to complete the transaction.

3. A letter of credit can be used as collateral for another letter of credit if the company is financially strong and has a proven track record in exporting.

4. The effect of delayed payment is eliminated with the guaranteed payment aspect of a letter of credit.

Disadvantages

1. The requirement to use a letter of credit may make the company less competitive if the buyer can import elsewhere without it.

2. If the company needs cash or goods upfront to complete the transaction, cash in advance from the buyer is a better option.

TESTING THE WATERS

The only guideline on whether or not to ask for a letter of credit from a foreign or domestic buyer is management's assessment of risk to the company.

If the company cannot afford a bad debt risk-nonpayment or delayed payment, then a letter of credit should be required, especially in a no-recourse transaction.

ALTERNATIVES TO A LETTER OF CREDIT

1. *Short-Term Borrowing.* To cover a cash-flow interruption that precludes completing an order, short-term borrowing may be the best alternative if the company has an existing bank relationship or line of credit. Profit Systems, Inc. obtained a multimillion-dollar line of credit in 1985 to cover unforeseen expenses related to industry deregulation, new laws and cost increases (see Chapter 17).

2. *Factoring.* Another short-term financing strategy is factoring, in which the company sells a reliable account(s) receivable to raise immediate cash. Ford/Higgins Ltd. factored excess inventory to raise short-term financing for further development of its computer products (see Chapter 15).

3. *Commercial Paper.* Competitive brokerage firms allow small companies and individuals to pool small amounts for short- or long-term commercial paper/CD investing (see Chapter 13).

SOURCES

Any state or federally chartered bank is a potential source for a letter of credit.

Foreign letters of credit can be obtained from the international department of any bank.

PITFALLS TO AVOID

A letter of credit should be guaranteed by a financial institution that is recognizable and stable; foreign financial institutions should be scrutinized carefully.

Management shouldn't pay a fee of more than 3 percent of the value of the letter of credit.

The correspondent bank that guarantees a confirmed letter of credit should be as stable and recognizable as the lead bank that backs the correspondent.

CHAPTER 15

Factoring

DESCRIPTION

Factoring is a technique for raising short-term capital to cover a temporary cash flow lapse by selling one or more reliable accounts receivable at a discount with or without recourse to a private factoring company (factor) that acts as principal. Factoring functions as an asset-based accounts receivable credit line that allows the company to finance specific operations with sporadic additional capital—for example, to buy seasonal inventory in advance.

There are two kinds of factoring. (1) Discount factoring remits funds to the seller before the average maturity date, based on the invoice amount of the account receivable, less cash discounts and estimated claim allowances. The company pays the factor an interest rate based on daily balances plus 2 to 5 percent above bank prime. (2) Maturity factoring means the factor executes the credit and collection function, and remits to the company based on the receivables sold monthly on the average due date of the factored receivables. Management also can obtain advance loans from the factor based on anticipated sales to build up cyclical inventory.

Company owners can use factors in many ways, selecting the factor services that best fit their particular corporate needs. A factor can be used to protect the company against customer credit losses. When receivables are sold on a nonrecourse basis, the factor assumes the risk. In exchange, the owner defers to the factor for a determination of the risk level.

Factors also can lend money to owners, using current or fixed assets like inventory, equipment and real estate as collateral. Other owners use factors for complete credit administration, including advice on customer risk, receivables collection and receivables accounting.

No longer considered a last-ditch financial strategy to use when the company is in trouble, factoring is considered a sophisticated financial tool that speeds up cash flow and helps avoid the problems that slow-paying customers can create for fast-growing companies. Generally, factors work with companies generating a minimum of $2 million in annual sales, but not always: some companies use a factor as soon as they begin operations, others wait until they're more established or are in an expansion stage—especially when new customers are diverse and unknown, which creates a need for fast, reliable credit information.

PROFILE OF A SUCCESSFUL FACTOR CANDIDATE

A nonretail company that meets one or more of the following requirements is the best factor candidate: (1) the company sustains an unforeseeable reversal (e.g., a large customer goes bankrupt), (2) inventory must be purchased well before sales (as for foreign imports), (3) the company's product permits markups to cover factoring costs, (4) the company is in the first (startup) phase of the business cycle, in a good sales niche, with satisfied customers, too early growth and no financial backing, (5) the company is in the last business cycle or (6) accounts receivable are unencumbered and prompt.

Although there are factors who buy assets from retail companies, they usually charge more because of demand volatility in the retail sector and higher bad-debt risks. Companies in the following sectors tend to benefit from lower interest rates and more beneficial terms than retail companies: distribution, wholesale, manufacturing and services.

RESULTS OF FACTORING

(1) The company can weather a temporary cash-flow shortage. (2) Because factoring involves outright purchase, a debt-free factor transaction sometimes improves the company's debt-to-equity ratio and adds cash to the bottom line (unless the factor price is less than the value of the asset factored). (3) Unit price markups can offset the cost of factoring, enabling the company to raise short-term capital at no cost. (4) Also no long-term negative implications appear on the balance sheet.

WHEN TO FACTOR

The time to factor is when (1) the company has one or more reliable accounts receivable to sell, (2) short-term borrowing rates are more than 5 percent above prime, (3) the company will lose substantial future sales because of its inability to buy inventory during a cash shortage, (4) the company wants to retain slow-paying customers (by selling prompt accounts receivable), (5) factoring can be used as a beneficial supplement to other forms of longer-term financing, (6) the balance sheet looks good, but the company can't get bank or other credit and (7) Certificate of Deposit rates are low (factoring is backed primarily by private investors who shop good rates).

THE HOW-TO TIMETABLE

One Month before Factoring

(1) Apply to a factor for credit. Typically a factor will get a commercial credit rating on the company and/or owner, and will require proof that accounts receivable are unencumbered. If the credit rating is favorable, (2) the factor will require that Uniform Commercial Code documents be filled out (factors currently are not regulated, so they operate under the UCC).

Factoring the Asset

1. The company must sign over title to an account receivable, which the factor will collect when due. Most factors require the company to buy back the asset if it is uncollectible by the factor (a recourse debt). Nonrecourse debt, which is rarely available, is an account receivable that is not collected when due, but doesn't have to be purchased back by the company.

2. The interest rate plus points if applicable, discounted sales price of the asset, recourse terms, and corporate/personal guarantees are negotiated before the company receives the funds.

FILING REQUIREMENTS

Public companies that factor must note the event in financial statements and other documents that relate to the sale of assets.

COSTS

1. *Discounted Factoring.* The company pays from 2 to 5 percent above bank prime rate based on daily balances until the purchased account(s) receivable is paid. The value of the account(s) receivable may be discounted. Late fees range between 5 and 10 percent; 7 percent is average.

2. *Maturity Factoring.* The company pays from 0.75 to 3 percent in commissions for the factor to handle credit and collection functions. Commissions are based on bad-debt risk and handling expense. Late fees range between 5 and 10 percent; 7 percent is average.

The use of factoring as a financing strategy by small business often is a reflection of the regional economy in which the company operates, including the number and velocity of merger/acquisition transactions.

Regional Ranking

Number of Sellers (Rank)

	1984	1985	1986	1987	1988	Five-Year Total
Middle Atlantic	320 (2)	454 (1)	439 (2)	426 (2)	501 (1)	2,140 (1)
Midwest	258 (3)	399 (2)	483 (1)	443 (1)	414 (2)	1,997 (2)
Southwest	334 (1)	350 (3)	357 (3)	339 (3)	370 (3)	1,750 (3)
Southeast	172 (4)	212 (4)	281 (4)	233 (4)	271 (4)	1,169 (4)
New England	116 (6)	139 (6)	170 (5)	120 (6)	168 (5)	713 (5)
South Central	166 (5)	147 (5)	151 (6)	136 (5)	164 (6)	764 (6)
Northwest	38 (7)	51 (7)	53 (7)	54 (7)	51 (7)	247 (7)
Alaska & Hawaii	2 (8)	3 (8)	3 (8)	2 (8)	15 (8)	25 (8)
Totals	1,406	1,755	1,937	1,753	1,954	8,805

Number of Buyers (Rank)

	1985	1986	1987	1988	Four-Year Total
Middle Atlantic	467 (1)	537 (1)	535 (1)	579 (1)	2,118 (1)
Midwest	441 (2)	511 (2)	399 (2)	375 (2)	1,726 (2)
Southwest	285 (3)	303 (3)	242 (3)	261 (3)	1,091 (3)
Southeast	177 (4)	224 (4)	175 (4)	170 (4)	746 (4)
New England	133 (5)	190 (5)	137 (5)	152 (5)	612 (5)
South Central	120 (6)	119 (6)	112 (6)	117 (6)	468 (6)
Northwest	29 (7)	33 (7)	31 (7)	32 (7)	125 (7)
Alaska & Hawaii	1 (8)	0 (8)	2 (8)	7 (8)	10 (8)
Totals	1,653	1,917	1,633	1,693	6,896

Middle Atlantic: New York, Pennsylvania, New Jersey, Delaware, Maryland, West Virginia, Virginia, Washington, D.C., Kentucky.

Midwest: North Dakota, South Dakota, Nebraska, Kansas, Minnesota, Iowa, Missouri, Wisconsin, Illinois, Michigan, Indiana, Ohio.

Southwest: California, Nevada, Utah, Colorado, Arizona, New Mexico.

South Central: Texas, Oklahoma, Arkansas, Louisiana.

Southeast: Florida, Mississippi, Alabama, Georgia, South Carolina, North Carolina, Tennessee.

New England: Maine, New Hampshire, Vermont, Massachusetts, Rhode Island, Connecticut.

Northwest: Washington, Oregon, Idaho, Montana, Wyoming.

Source: *Mergerstat Review.*

ADVANTAGES AND DISADVANTAGES

Advantages

1. Management adds cash to the bottom line and improves the debt-to-equity ratio.

2. Factoring adds no long-term negative implications to the balance sheet.

3. Advance inventories can be purchased despite cash flow shortages.

4. The cost of money is low or nonexistent if the unit sales price of other products can be marked up.

5. Slow-paying customers can be carried at little or no charge.

6. High-growth startup companies can finance growth on a current basis.

7. A seed company can, in effect, "borrow" money with no credit rating.

8. Temporary reversals need not have a negative effect.

9. Many factors require no minimum volume or dollar amount contracts. Factoring can be a one-time-only strategy, although infrequent factoring results in higher rates and/or deeper discounts on the asset.

Disadvantages

1. The company and/or its owner must have a good credit rating, or be prepared for less favorable contract terms.

2. Factors require that accounts receivable be unencumbered.

3. Some factors require a recourse contract in which the company must buy back the account(s) receivable if the factor cannot collect.

4. A bad credit rating can result in additional factor fees (and an interest rate) that total more than 5 percent above prime rate.

5. Unless the company can mark up the sales price of its products, the cost of short-term money can be high.

6. Factoring should be considered only a stop-gap technique, as a supplement to other forms of long-term financing.

7. Factoring can reduce revenue, earnings or accounts receivable unless there is a matching increase in cash.

TESTING THE WATERS

The best guide to factoring is the company's ability to borrow from a bank. If the company has good credit and strong cash flow, a bank is more willing to lend short-term funds. If the company is a good bank borrowing candidate, it can benefit more from factoring if favorable rates are available. Some companies use factoring to stave off the effects of falling sales, but this strategy for raising short-term funds can be expensive if sales do not increase over time. Unless favorable factor rates and volume discounts are available, bank borrowing is less costly.

ALTERNATIVES TO FACTORING

1. Line of Credit. If the company has a bank relationship and good credit, a line of credit usually is a less costly way to raise short-term funds. During its first year of operation, Croce Advertising determined that a secured line of credit from Colorado National Bank was the least costly way to raise short-term capital and bridge cash-flow volatility during the company's startup phase (see Chapter 17).

2. Commercial Paper. Although commercial paper and CDs typically trade in $100,000 increments, brokerage houses like Merrill Lynch and E.F. Hutton in New York City pool smaller issues for 2 to 270 days (see Chapter 13).

3. Letter of Credit. Wyse Technology arranged for a letter of credit from a Taiwanese bank when the company entered into a contract to construct a new manufacturing facility in Taiwan R.O.C. (see Chapter 14).

Two other measures of the economy in which a factored company operates are the average P/E ratio paid and the average percent premium paid over market price, as shown in the following tables.

Industry Sectors—Average P/E Paid 1982–1988

Industry Sector	Average P/E Paid (Base)						
	1982	1983	1984	1985	1986	1987	1988
Argricultural Production	10.0 (2)	13.7 (2)	10.1 (1)	—	5.7 (1)	7.4 (1)	—
Manufacturing	14.1 (81)	16.6 (68)	19.0 (92)	15.9 (110)	22.9 (131)	26.4 (89)	22.6 (168)
Natural Resources	10.7 (14)	13.8 (19)	19.1 (23)	15.1 (15)	49.7 (2)	27.7 (3)	24.2 (7)
Transportation	8.2 (5)	14.1 (2)	11.2 (4)	27.3 (9)	17.5 (11)	15.6 (4)	16.4 (15)
Comm. & Broadcasting	31.3 (1)	36.3 (2)	35.2 (2)	22.4 (8)	46.1 (1)	23.0 (3)	29.4 (8)
Utilities	13.0 (3)	14.2 (3)	11.4 (1)	15.6 (6)	23.3 (4)	26.2 (7)	14.4 (2)
Wholesale & Distribution	8.8 (4)	11.7 (5)	17.8 (8)	14.7 (15)	24.0 (1)	19.0 (3)	24.4 (10)
Retail	16.9 (11)	13.5 (7)	16.4 (23)	17.9 (22)	22.8 (18)	24.0 (26)	23.3 (25)
Financial Services	11.9 (37)	15.9 (45)	13.4 (35)	14.2 (177)	18.9 (134)	15.4 (42)	15.0 (55)
Other Services	15.9 (23)	19.5 (25)	21.1 (39)	29.4 (52)	30.4 (50)	24.9 (33)	24.1 (55)
Real Estate	18.7 (2)	8.5 (4)	8.7 (5)	9.4 (3)	22.7 (1)	—	12.4 (3)
Conglomerate	13.3 (10)	20.5 (7)	18.0 (13)	20.5 (10)	22.2 (10)	23.7 (5)	21.9 (11)
All-Industry Averages	13.9 (193)	16.7 (189)	17.2 (246)	18.0 (427)	22.2 (364)	23.3 (216)	21.6 (359)

Source: *Mergerstat Review.*

Average Percent Premiums Paid Over Market 1982–1988

Industry Sector	*Average P/E Paid (Base)*						
	1982	*1983*	*1984*	*1985*	*1986*	*1987*	*1988*
Argricultural Production	33.0 (2)	19.4 (3)	14.0 (1)	12.5 (1)	26.3 (1)	74.4 (1)	—
Manufacturing	48.2 (72)	32.9 (56)	36.8 (77)	31.9 (124)	35.6 (146)	35.4 (106)	45.0 (189)
Natural Resources	53.1 (16)	38.3 (23)	28.2 (22)	45.8 (22)	75.1 (9)	35.8 (9)	25.5 (9)
Transportation	66.8 (3)	23.5 (1)	40.3 (3)	50.6 (10)	34.4 (17)	29.1 (8)	40.6 (20)
Comm. & Broadcasting	52.9 (1)	69.4 (2)	19.0 (2)	49.6 (8)	54.9 (4)	18.3 (8)	31.7 (11)
Utilities	68.2 (2)	60.7 (2)	153.3 (1)	45.5 (3)	30.1 (4)	42.5 (6)	25.8 (6)
Wholesale & Distribution	47.0 (2)	32.9 (4)	34.2 (5)	35.4 (15)	36.1 (2)	22.7 (3)	48.0 (9)
Retail	50.3 (12)	43.1 (5)	35.9 (23)	31.7 (28)	45.4 (17)	50.7 (26)	37.9 (28)
Financial Services	43.6 (35)	46.6 (41)	39.8 (21)	34.1 (59)	43.9 (60)	42.8 (36)	31.2 (61)
Other Services	49.0 (19)	43.4 (22)	35.3 (32)	47.2 (47)	34.6 (60)	50.6 (31)	51.1 (59)
Real Estate	17.1 (2)	—	—	41.6 (5)	25.0 (1)	—	25.8 (6)
Conglomerate	46.7 (10)	31.8 (9)	35.0 (12)	23.1 (9)	28.1 (12)	37.3 (3)	47.6 (12)
All-Industry Averages	47.4 (176)	37.7 (168)	37.9 (199)	37.1 (331)	38.2 (333)	38.3 (237)	44.9 (410)

Factoring

	Good Deal	*Bad Deal*
1. Asset discount rate	Less than 20 percent	Greater than 20 percent
2. Recourse	No; company has to buy back uncollected account	Yes
3. Late fees	Less than 7 percent	Greater than 10 percent
4. Maturity factoring commissions	Less than 3 percent	Greater than 3 percent
5. Encumbered assets	No; results in higher costs	Yes
6. Contract terms	Allow one-time only or monthly account, although more costly	Long-term contract only
7. Retail companies	No; higher retail risks result in higher interest and commissions	Yes

SOURCES

Cash Management Services, Denver, CO.
Walter Heller & Co., St. Louis, MO.

CHAPTER 16

Bartering

Description

Barter is the exchange of services or tangible products without using money. The barter credit system is a commonplace trade practice during high inflation when product values are overrated, and when a company has unusable inventory it wants to barter for a product it can turn around for additional capital. About 500 national barter exchanges organize the marketplace for companies that have products or services to exchange, which created a $29 billion industry by 1985.

 Countertrade is the term used for barter in international trade, a strategy that is used extensively when a foreign country has high inflation or a soft currency. Much of the export/import activity between the United States and less developed countries (LDCs) is countertrade, which became a $500 billion industry by 1985 and is expected to comprise one-half of all world trade by the year 2000.

PROFILE OF A SUCCESSFUL BARTER

Nearly any company, from the size of General Electric to the smallest merchant or one-person shop, can barter successfully. The only prerequisite is an inventory of products that management can't sell to raise cash, or services that management has not traded for products that can be sold for cash. In domestic barter, the inventory usually includes (1) a seasonal, cyclical or trend product that has become obsolete, (2) damaged goods that must be discounted for sale or (3) services that can be traded out for hard assets, which in turn are sold for cash. Other domestic barter transactions occur between a seller company with a unique or sluggish inventory that sells to a company with more appropriate distribution channels or access to unusual markets for the product.

In countertrade, most U.S. companies that export to LDCs require salable assets in exchange for their product or service in order to guarantee payment. U.S. exporters who prefer countertrade should have (1) an export license from the U.S. Department of Commerce, (2) a banker who can evaluate the complexities involved in setting up an equitable barter and (3) distribution channels and the marketing capability to sell what the import country offers as barter. In most cases, the U.S. export company should accept in trade products that are related to the company's industry.

Companies that have bartered successfully for cash include:

Megabyte, Inc.
Western Job Lot Distributors
Ackerman's Restaurant, Inc.

RESULTS OF BARTERING

The primary result of a successful trade is extra capital the company would not otherwise have been able to raise without trading for a salable product. In other words, if management can trade off dead inventory to a company that has a market for it, in exchange for a product the company can sell more easily, new capital is obtained from previously useless inventory.

An alternative way to raise capital is to negotiate a straight swap of idle inventory in exchange for a product or service the company needs, without the use of cash or credit, by using a barter exchange organization. By using a barter broker or organization, the company eliminates the need for some additional financing to acquire what it needs.

WHEN TO BARTER

Bartering works best when the company (1) has inventory it cannot sell, (2) exports to a less developed country or a country with high inflation and/or a soft currency or (3) has a unique distribution channel or market for an inventory that another company can't sell.

THE HOW-TO TIMETABLE

1. *Domestic Barter.* Management can broker its own barter by finding another company with a desirable product that wants

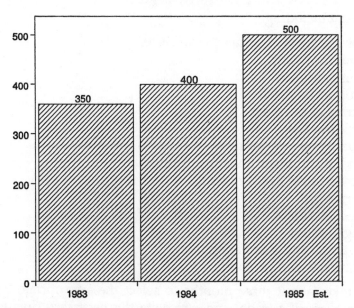

*Excluding countertrade, large corporate swaps and international barter firms and media barter house transactions.

Source: International Reciprocal Trade Association and industy analysts.

what management has to sell. This process can be costly in terms of the time it takes to locate another trader and match inventories. The easiest way is to contact a barter broker or organization that computerizes potential traders and inventories throughout the United States and worldwide. A transaction through a barter organization takes about one month to complete.

The best barter source is the International Reciprocal Trade Association in Alexandria, Virginia, which lists barter exchanges in every part of the country and describes how they operate, fees, terms and trade credits.

2. *Countertrade.* Participation in foreign barter can be a complex, but highly lucrative process. A United States export company that trades overseas, particularly in an economically unstable country and/or with an unstable company, should select an international banker before initiating the trade process. The banker should be a specialist in foreign trade, countertrade and relations with the import country. Once a banker has been selected, several important issues will have to be negotiated for the countertrade agreement including:

Specific form of countertrade barter
Counter-purchase
Compensation
Product buyback
Terms of payment
Risk transfer
Quality and performance standards
Bridge and other financing techniques
Government agency credit
Forfeiting
Blocked funds
Legal issues
National and international law
Contracts and protocol

It takes about three months to select the appropriate banker, analyze a specific trade, and complete the necessary documentation and filing requirements for overseas countertrade.

FILING REQUIREMENTS

A company that exports to a foreign country, or imports goods as compensation, is required to file for an export license from the U.S. Department of Commerce before initiating the trade.

In addition, all income from barter transactions is considered taxable and must be reported to the Internal Revenue Service, including unused tax credits from a barter organization or trade association.

COSTS

1. Barter Organizations. In exchange for providing the company with computerized information about traders, inventories and markets, a barter organization will charge from $50 to $800 in initial fees and about 10 percent of the barter value in monthly service fees, depending on the size and scope of the barter exchange and the value of the transaction. Annual renewals range from $25 to $200.

2. Brokers. Barter middlemen who develop an individual trade between a seller and one or more buyers usually charge $75 to $500 depending on the market and the exchange requirements in each organization.

3. Countertrade. A bank that analyzes a foreign trade and develops the contracts between a U.S. export company and a foreign country or company will charge about 10 percent of the value of the transaction.

ADVANTAGES AND DISADVANTAGES

Advantages

1. A straight swap increases liquidity by eliminating the need for additional capital required to buy certain products and/or services.

2. Idle or obsolete assets that are not earning money can be sold quickly to raise financing otherwise unavailable and to reduce storage costs.

3. Countertrade and some domestic barter may open up new markets for the company as well as guarantee payment from an economically unstable country or company.

4. New barter sales, which can average 5 to 15 percent of the company's total revenues, can be developed with no additional marketing or overhead costs.

Disadvantages

1. Seasonal or damaged goods that are bartered for inventory the company can sell may be discounted by barter organizations or individual brokers.

2. All barter transactions produce taxable income, including unused trade credits, and must be reported to the Internal Revenue Service.

3. Some barter organizations are undercapitalized and/or fly-by-night organizations that offer the company worthless trade credits. References should be requested of barter organizations or brokers before the company initiates a trade.

4. Markets may be limited for the company's inventory or only a limited inventory may be offered in exchange for the company's bartered products.

TESTING THE WATERS

Depending on the nature of the company's product, inventory that has been on the shelf for more than one year should be evaluated as potential barter. Such inventory should be considered assets that have income-earning capability at some point in time.

ALTERNATIVES TO BARTER

1. *Liquidation.* If the company is not interested in trying to sell swapped inventory, liquidation at a discounted price may be the easiest alternative. Firms like $64 million Close-Out Merchandise Buyers Co. in Minneapolis are 24-hour-a-day operations that sell seasonal, damaged or unusual inventories and financial products on a massive scale. W.T. Grant, the variety store chain, sold more than $25 million of distressed merchandise through C.O.M.B. when the chain went into liquidation (see Chapter 27).

2. *Asset-Based Borrowing.* Most community banks loan up to $100,000 on assets, while loans of $1 million or more are handled by large money center banks. Agencies like the Farmers Home Administration or the Economic Development Administration also make loans based on assets (see Chapter 17).

3. *Leasing.* If company equipment is frequently idle, leasing the equipment can generate short-term cash. Sigma Research, Inc. developed noncancellable leases for its ultrasonic and optical testing equipment worth $204,000. The equipment is amortized on a straight-line basis over the lease term.

SOURCES

International Reciprocal Trade Association, Alexandria, VA.
Business Exchange, Inc., North Hollywood, CA.
Attwood Richards, New York, NY.

PITFALLS TO AVOID

Regional or local barter organizations often cannot offer the company goods or services it can use or sell profitably.

International barter, or countertrade, can be an extremely risky transaction when the foreign buyer or seller is unknown.

Although barter organizations enable management to sell inventory quickly, the goods may be heavily discounted. Management should have a professional appraisal of the inventory to maximize profits.

Techniques with Debt

Section 5
Introduction

Five debt financing techniques, plus variations on convertible debt ("hybrid" securities), described in Section 5 can be profitable strategies for a small business in the under–$25 million category. All five techniques can be used by public or private companies. Public debt issues are omitted because they are confined to large companies with $100 million plus in annual revenue that raise in excess in $20 million on the basis of a bond rating from Moody's or Standard & Poor's.

Like equity financing, debt has a place in the capital structure of every small business. Optimal use of and benefits from a debt issue must be evaluated in terms of the company's capital structure, development stage and over all debt ratios (how much borrowing reserve remains).

Debt financing today is a good strategy for creditworthy companies and for managements who want to privatize, using Uncle Sam's lenient tax subsidies. But because government, corporate and consumer debt levels are at record highs, there is increasing concern that lower inflation and price depreciation, or at least the slowing of price appreciation, will prevent companies from repaying debt obligations. Investors in small companies, in particular, are burdened with this perception.

For these reasons, debt strategies should be carefully examined by management to avoid strapping future earnings and flexibility. For the small business with favorable ratios in the two best fundamental indicators, long-term debt as a percentage of long-term capital and the number of times interest charges are earned, debt techniques can offset the vagaries of the markets and the economy.

The pivotal factors in debt financing are a track record of stability in revenues and earnings, and cash flow to cover interest payments and principal. If the company is stable and has a strong cash balance, debt can be used effectively at appropriate development stages. Interest costs will be lower, and financial and protective covenants will be less restrictive.

In contrast, if the company cannot show stability and cash flow, interest will be higher, and the financial and protective covenants will be more restrictive.

To attract lenders, whether from a bank, the company's own management or outside investors, management should keep its maximum debt ratio below the maximum it can borrow, allowing a reserve for future issues. A company at its maximum debt level is considered to have poor credit. Privately owned companies can have a higher debt ratio and be more flexible than public companies, since management and lenders usually have a far more intimate picture of the company's capabilities and are not dependent on earnings projections for an indication of ability to repay debt.

If the company does not have a credit rating, or if management wants to attract lower-cost capital, a strategy that emphasizes equity should be considered. A gradually paced issue will prevent undesirable dilution all at once, and will prove to potential lenders and investors that management is capable of reaching improvement goals.

Bear Hug: an unsolicited proposal to the target company addressed directly to the board of directors or to management, which calls for a specific buyout price and a response within a certain time period. It forces the target to disclose the offer publicly and enter into negotiations with the bidder.

Bond: a discounted or interest-bearing corporate or government security that requires the issuer to pay bondholders a specified amount of money at intervals as interest, and to repay the principal amount of the loan at maturity.

Bridge Financing: a short-term swing loan used between long-term financings.

Call: the right to redeem bonds before maturity as specified in the bond prospectus.

CAT: Certificate of Accrual on Treasury Securities is a U.S. Treasury issue that is sold at a discount from face value. It pays no interest, but returns the face value at maturity. It is also called a "zero-coupon" security.

Convertibles: usually preferred stocks or bonds that are exchangeable in the future for a determinable number of common shares at a preset or formulated price.

Coupon: the interest rate on a debt security to be paid by the issuing company until maturity as an annual percentage of face value.

Credit: can be a bond, loan, charge-account obligation or an open account balance with a commercial firm. Unused bank letters of credit and other standby commitments, also fall into this category.

Crown Jewel: the company's most valuable asset or line of business.

Current Yield: annual bond interest divided by market price.

Debenture: general unsecured debt obligation backed by the borrower; usually subordinated.

Dividend: an amount of earnings determined by the board of directors that is paid quarterly to shareholders contingent on the class of security and paid in money, stock or scrip.

Exchange Offer: made directly to the target company's shareholders to solicit the exchange of their shares for the bidder's securities. No shareholder vote is required.

Face Value: the value of a bond, note or other security as shown on the instrument. Average face value for a corporate bond is $1,000; for a municipal bond, $5,000; for a government bond, $10,000.

Fairness Letter: a written opinion from an investment banker that evaluates the fairness of a proposed reorganization for company shareholders. Without a fairness letter, most proposals fall through.

Greenmail: a corporate repurchase of a block of stock at a premium price, to avoid the threat of a hostile takeover attempt by the seller.

Interest Coverage (fixed-charge coverage): the ratio of profit before payment of interest and income taxes to interest on bonds and other long-term debt. Interest coverage indicates how many times interest charges have been earned before taxes are paid. This is a key debt ratio in leveraged buyouts and debt issues.

Lock-Up: a merger agreement provision that gives the proposed acquiring company advantages over other potential acquirers, e.g., an option to buy a sizable block of the target company's 144 (insider) shares.

Maturity: the date on which the principal amount of the bond or other debt instrument is due and payable.

Mezzanine: a level of company development just prior to going public, when venture capitalists like to invest for least risk and greatest appreciation as a result of the initial public offering.

Pac-Man Defense: the attempt to prevent a hostile takeover by launching a counter-tender offer for the would-be acquirer.

Par: the nominal or face value of a security, usually applied to preferred stock and bonds. The interest paid on bond issues is based on a percentage of the bond's par value.

Poison Pill: a stock issued by the target company to its stockholders with special provisions that would make takeover costly for the bidder, e.g., the right to purchase the acquirer's stock at a below-market price.

Prime Rate: the interest rate banks charge their most creditworthy customers, determined by market forces including the bank's cost of funds and the rate borrowers will live with.

Rate of Return: (1) in corporate finance, the return on equity or on invested capital; (2) in common stock, the dividend yield (annual dividend divided by purchase price) or total return rate (dividend plus capital appreciation) and (3) in bonds and preferred stock, the current yield (coupon or contractual dividend rate divided by purchase price).

Scorched Earth Defense: an attempt by a target company to make itself less attractive to potential takeovers, e.g., by selling off desirable assets, making costly cash acquisitions or creating antitrust obstacles.

Security: a stock, which signifies ownership of the company, or a bond, which signifies that the bondholder is a creditor to the company.

Senior Security: a stock or bond that has prior claim and is paid first upon liquidation. Debt that includes notes, bonds and debentures is senior to stock.

Sinking Fund: funds accumulated in a separate account to be used to redeem debt securities or preferred stock issues.

Spin-Off: a reorganization in which existing operations are distributed to shareholders in the form of a separate, public company.

Spread: the difference in dollars or percentage between the current market price of a target company's stock and its expected value on completion of a proposed reorganization.

Subscription: an agreement to buy newly issued securities. Subscription price is the price at which shareholders can purchase common shares in a rights offering or at which subscription warrants can be exercised.

Tender Offer: friendly or unfriendly solicitation of shares, usually at a premium above market price, for cash, securities or both; can be an attempt to get control of the company.

TIGR: Treasury Investors Growth Receipt is a form of U.S. government-backed zero-coupon security. The principal of the bond and its coupon are sold separately at a deep discount from face value.

Yield: return on investors' capital. Current yield is the coupon rate of interest divided by purchase price. Yield to maturity is the rate of return on a bond, including the total of annual interest payments, redemption value, purchase price and the balance of time until maturity.

Zero-Coupon Bond: a government or corporate bond that makes no interest payments. These securities are sold at a deep discount from face value.

CHAPTER 17
Borrowing

DESCRIPTION

Corporate borrowing from a financial institution or sophisticated investors provides the use of a specified amount of capital, to be repaid within a certain time period along with interest in the form of cash and/or stock, warrants, royalties or licensing fees. If the company is liquidated before the loan is repaid, lenders are paid off before stockholders receive distributions from the liquidation of the company. Investors in such debt instruments as commercial paper and bonds are considered lenders with the same rights and powers as a bank.

There are six primary ways to borrow.

Long-Term. A standard loan matures after at least one year. Repayment must be made at a set interest rate usually tied to the prime or U.S. Treasury bill rate. Long-term loans can be obtained from banks, special or institutional investment funds, or government agencies like the Small Business Administration (SBA). They can be used for everything from first-round financing as a personal loan to fourth-round financing for a mature company.

Short-Term/Mezzanine/Bridge Financing. This is a tailored loan that matures within two years. It is repaid at a higher interest rate than long-term borrowing, and also is tied to the prime or U.S. Treasury bill rate. Bridge financing can be obtained from banks, individual investors, venture capitalists and combination funds that specialize in bridge financing. This capital is second through fourth-round financing for a later-stage company to support it from initial product sales through going public or acquisition.

Line of Credit. A bank's contractual or noncontractual commitment makes available a negotiable amount of financing contingent on the company's or management's creditworthiness for varying periods of renewable time, usually one year. The interest rate is generally about two points above the prime or U.S. Treasury bill rate, depending on the stability and prospects of the company, It is common for banks to require that at least 10 percent of the line of credit value be retained in a bank account as a compensating balance. New sources for lines of credit include the Small Business Administration and other private organizations that promote exporting. A collateralized line of credit can be initial financing for a startup company, or supplementary capital for a later-stage company.

Letter of Credit. A specialized way to borrow against a receivable, primarily it guarantees the payment of a customer's draft up to a stated amount for a specific time period, allowing a buyer to use the bank's credit and eliminating the seller's risk. It is used primarily, but not exclusively in foreign trade (see Chapter 14).

Guaranteed Loan. This is often a self-guarantee of part or all of an entrepreneur's bank loan in exchange for cash, equity or other compensation. A guaranteed loan is particularly useful for startup companies that have good credit and collateral. Public and private venture capital firms, as well as private investors, are the most common sources of loan guarantees.

Asset-Based Loans. Hidden company assets can yield additional capital if they are collateralized for short-term borrowing, including real estate, receivables, inventory and equipment. Most financial institutions and some private firms are asset lenders.

Another primary debt technique is a special lending category to fund a leveraged buyout. A leveraged buyout is the friendly or unfriendly purchase of a company's assets, using borrowed funds. The typical strategy is a management buyout of all the company's outstanding stock, using as little of its own capital as possible.

A standard buyout or acquisition is the purchase of a company without substantial use of borrowed capital. Tax-free buyouts are outlined in Chapter 7.

In a leveraged buyout, company assets are used as collateral for a loan taken out by managemnt purchasers and repaid out of company cash flow or the sale of assets. Management also can borrow using its own assets as collateral.

Other leveraged buyout techniques are used to acquire a company less expensively without significant direct cost to the owner, or tax-free, using statutory reorganizations as described in the Internal Revenue Code. In exchange for stock, assets and/or cash, a company is acquired for on- or off-balance-sheet assets, or earning power or income sources that can be borrowed against or divested later to raise capital.

PROFILE OF A SUCCESSFUL BORROWER

Borrowing terms vary widely among banks, contingent on the current interest rate, the cost at which banks can borrow from the Federal Reserve, the condition of the company and/or its industry, and the creditworthiness of management. In general, borrowers who receive the lowest negotiated interest rate and the most consideration for future financing are companies that (1) have at least a two-year operating history, (2) are earning a profit or will soon, (3) have stable, professional management, (4) enjoy a unique or leading niche in the company's industry, (5) have an adequate and growing market share in the industry, (6) have strong monthly cash flow or the promise of it and (7) can obtain short- or long-term financing from other sources to supplement current borrowing if the need arises.

Corporate borrowers who have successfully financed their operations with bank backing include:

Cheryl's Cookies, Inc. (guaranteed loan)
Dimensional Medicine, Inc. (bridge financing)
Integrity Solutions, Inc. (line of credit)

Historically, most successful leveraged buyouts have been large public or private companies with over $100 million in revenues and at least 10 percent earnings per share increases annually. In the past few years, however, LBO techniques have been adapted for companies that report as little $100,000 or $200,000 annual revenue. A major shift among these small "sons of LBOs" has taken place, from an emphasis on earnings-per-share improvement to cash-generating power that can deleverage or pay off the debt that made the buyout possible.

The best leveraged buyout candidate among companies with at least $20 million in revenues is a private firm with hard assets to loan against in a strong or growth industry. The best LBO can be justified at about 12 times cash flow, so historical cash flow is strong, usually at least twice fixed-charge coverage on the proposed buyout debt. Professional management is committed to entrepreneurial principles because it acquires an equity stake as a result of the buyout. Generally, the farther down the organization chart an equity stake is offered, the more widespread commitment there is to company goals.

In addition, the company should have pretax profits of at least $1 million, low capital requirements and immunity to cyclical volatility. One year after the buyout, the capital structure should be no more than 50 percent debt.

Service companies must have a strong niche in the marketplace, top quality managment and the same cash-flow generating potential as industrial companies. Increases in earnings per share are still important as an indication of growth and strength, but they're no longer the pivotal criterion.

Small leveraged buyouts include:

Bridgeport Brass Corporation
Ray-O-Vac Corporation
Conair Corporation
Expediter Systems

RESULTS OF BORROWING

Standard borrowing results in (1) long-term financing with at least a one-year maturity, (2) a future financing source if the loan is repaid on time, (3) management assistance for startup firms, (4) no loss of equity in the company if loan compensation is paid in the form of cash interest on the loan and (5) a good credit rating and/or more favorable interest rate on future financing, if the loan is repaid on time.

Bridge financing provides some of the above benefits, plus others if the company pays the lender compensation in the form of equity or warrants: (1) an enlarged investor base, (2) more working capital when compensation is not paid in cash interest, and (3) higher valuation of the company because of less long-term debt financing.

Loan guarantees may result in (1) leveraging of the entrepreneur's net worth, (2) earned income from the capital that is securing the loan while it secures the loan, (3) loss of up to 35 percent equity in the company in exchange for the guarantee or (4) other compensation requirements including warrants on the stock, a percentage of future revenues or profits, and/or upfront fees.

Total 1988 LBOs by Quarter

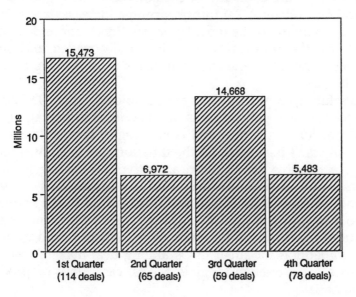

Source: Standard & Poor's Compustat Services, Inc.

Small, successful leveraged buyouts result in (1) more commitment by management in the long term because of its equity stake in performance, (2) increased productivity, (3) recapitalization of the company at up to 12 times cash flow, (4) revitalization of a mature company, (5) improvement in market position against competitors because of increased capitalization, (6) a less expensive source of capital with potentially higher returns (technically, higher returns can be gained by leveraging further), (7) conversion to privately held status or (8) increased profits for public shareholders who can sell their shares to the buyer at a premium because of arbitrageurs or bidding competitors who boost the stock price.

WHEN TO BORROW

The best time to borrow is when (1) the interest and Federal fund rates are low, (2) the company or management has a good credit history and/or collateral, (3) future earnings increases are achievable, (4) the company or its industry is positioned for and capable of growth, (5) the company's stock is heavily traded and share price is increasing or (6) the company has a sales backlog or sales contracts in hand.

Successful leveraged buyouts are completed when (1) interest rates are low so cash-generation is not as crucial to paying off the leveraged portion of the deal and borrowing to recapitalize a mature company isn't beneficial, (2) the inflation rate is high so rising prices make tangible assets more attractive, (3) management or employees (ESOP buyouts are described in Chapter 26) who want to own and/or control the company, (4) the owner doesn't want to sell out to a larger company or conglomerate, (5) the owner wants to cash out of the company for estate or retirement purposes or (6) there is competition for small LBOs among deal-makers who bid up the price for attractive tangible assets, cash flow or product growth potential.

THE HOW-TO TIMETABLE

Six Months before Borrowing

1. *Optional Assistance.* Interview several third-party professionals, who can help management develop a business plan, including CPA firms, attorneys, financial consultants or investment bankers, and who are specialists in the company's industry.

2. *Consulting.* Select a professional individual or organization to either develop the plan or review it before submission to a lender.

3. *Corporate Goals.* Management should evaluate the future direction of the company by projecting several what-if buyout scenarios. Options include continuation of current policies after employee or management buyout, a combination deal in which part of the company is bought out by investors and part is bought out by venture capitalists, or a sale to the highest bidder.

4. *Evaluation.* The founder of a small company may negotiate directly with a managment or employee group who wants to buy the company, based on legal and accounting reviews of operations. Large companies generally will contact an investment banker who evaluates the business and suggests potential buyers. Evaluation in either case is based on:

Current capital structure of the company
Cash flow projections
Tangible asset valuation
Historical financial statements dating back at least five years
Market analysis, including the competition, market share, growth potential and pricing
Level of productivity
Condition of the industry

5. *Marketing.* If the company is not sold to an in-house buying group, there will be one or more bids by outside buyers who at least begin the negotiation process. Public companies must disclose the information publicly and to shareholders, possibly en-

couraging additional bidders. The negotiation process with an outside buyer can be delayed or halted at any time due to incompatibility, antitrust issues or a bidding war. SEC or FTC approval of the buyout may be delayed for various reasons.

Three Months before Borrowing

The business plan is a company's most important contribution to the borrowing process. It must be thorough, sequential and accurate enough to assist the lender in making an initial decision about the company's current condition and growth potential. For this reason, the business plan should make a favorable impression when it is first submitted by including:

Plan summary
Business description
Market analysis
Product/service description
Marketing strategy
Manufacturing/service operation details
Management and organization information
Financial data
Capital needs timetable

Most business plans are between 10 and 30 pages in length, depending on the complexity of the product, company and industry.

1. If a public or private company is sold to employees through an ESOP, an outside ESOP specialist firm or association should be retained to structure what is, in effect, a trust fund for transfer of ownership. The ESOP specialist will satisfy the necessary legal, accounting and filing (for public companies only) requirements.

2. If a private compny is sold to outside investors or upper-level executive, management will review the offers made by potential buyers and select the best deal.

3. If a public company is sold to outside investors, or if there is a bidding war for purchase of a controlling number of shares to take over the company, there can be months of offers and

counteroffers made to managment and/or public shareholders before a bid is accepted.

If a public company goes private via an ESOP that transfers ownership to employees, current managment may or may not remain in place after the buyout contingent on the terms of the plan.

FILING REQUIREMENTS

Private companies are not subject to registration with the SEC or to federal and state reporting/disclosure requirements upon borrowing bank or other funds. Public companies must disclose the event to stockholders in a quarterly financial report (Form 10-Q) and in an annual financial report (Form 10-K).

If either entity in a leveraged buyout is a public company, it will be subject to federal and state reporting/disclosure requirements, including those of the SEC and the FTC. Reporting documents include a quarterly financial report (Form 10-Q), annual financial report (Form 10-K), annual report to shareholders, proxy statements, reports about current material events in the company (Form 8-K), and other reports for audited financial statements, the sale of control shares and tender offers. In addition, a public company must meet any reporting/disclosure requirements of the state in which it does business. State requirements vary.

Private companies in a leveraged buyout, or those that become privately held as a result of a buyout, are governed by simplified federal and state reporting/disclosure requirements.

COSTS

1. *Interest.* Rates vary widely, depending on the current prime or U.S. Treasury bill rate and the credit standing of the company or its management.

2. *Fees.* Some loan guarantors require an upfront loan fee, usually up to 2 percent of the loan amount.

3. *Equity.* Loan guarantors and other lenders may require some percentage of equity ownership of the company, particularly

if the company is a startup or it does not have a good credit rating.

   4. Warrants. Many owners persuade reluctant lenders to advance capital by offering warrants for future purchase of company stock at a specified price. The current and future costs of warrants are variable (see Chapter 25).

   5. Percentage of Revenues or Profits, Royalties, Fees. Some lenders will offset their risk in an early-stage company by accepting a variable percentage of future income in one of several forms as loan compensation.

   6. Discounts. Asset-based loans generally require discounts on the assets collateralized, ranging from 5 to 50 percent depending on the marketability of the asset.

   If management buys out the company, related costs are borne by the acquiring group. If employees buy the company, costs are borne by management and employees are described in Chapter 26.

   1. Legal. Attorneys who specialize in small leveraged buyouts charge from $50,000 to $100,000 for legal review, corporate evaluation, filing and contract development. Generally, the smaller the dollar amount of the buyout, the larger the fee as a percentage of the company's market value.

   2. Accounting. An evaluation of the tax and other consequences of the buyout costs between $30,000 and $100,000.

   3. Printing. If required, printing of the prospectus and proxy statement costs between $10,000 and $50,000 plus.

   4. Interest. Most buyouts are leveraged for up to 90 percent of the purchase price. The interest rate will vary, depending on the source of the debt, market rates, condition of the company and reputation of the acquirers.

ADVANTAGES AND DISADVANTAGES

Advantages

   1. Some loans carry a long maturity, allowing more time to repay.

2. Standard loans do not require management to give up income or an equity percentage of the company as loan compensation.

3. Borrowers can obtain professional management help from many lenders, including banks and venture capitalists.

4. Borrowers who repay on time acquire a good credit rating with which to attract future debt financing.

5. Companies with a good credit rating find additional financing markets when they need second-, third- and fourth-round financing.

6. Short-term loans can yield funds quickly without collection and/or additional paperwork.

7. In the long-term, borrowing is less costly than public debt techniques that encompass ongoing, annual costs.

For a leveraged buyout:

1. A publicly held company can become privately owned.

2. Management can increase its stake in the firm, which usually results in increased productivity and better returns to equity owners and investors.

3. The financial risk inherent in leverage can be offset by sould investors who seek strong cash flow, thus further minimizing the cost of raising capital.

4. The long-term effect of a leveraged buyout can be highly beneficial, especially to mature companies: greater recapitalization, improved competitive positioning and longer company life span.

5. Public shareholders almost always make healthy profits when a buyer bids for their outstanding shares.

6. New owners can borrow against company assets or cash flow in order to raise capital.

Disadvantages

1. In the short-term, borrowing can be a more expensive source of capital than a private placement, R&D partnership or franchising.

2. Loan guarantees and some bridge financing may require management to give up a percentage of equity ownership, future income or current cash in the form of upfront fees.

3. Borrowing may be limited to an amount far less than the company needs to finance current and/or future operations.

4. Short-term loans carry a higher interest cost and more hidden expenses (i.e., discounted asset value) than long-term loans.

In a leveraged buyout:

1. A leveraged buyout can easily fail if the debt-to-equity ratio—often more than 12:1—creates high interest payments that cannot be met by cash flow or the sale of assets.

2. A fluctuating or high interest rate can endanger the company's credit or bond rating.

3. Some managements propose a leveraged buyout only for short-term personal profit, which can threaten the existence of the company itself.

4. Debt repayment depends on the sale of assets or corporate profits. If sales fall and profit margins narrow for any of several economic reasons, repayment can become difficult.

5. Industry competition and volatility can undercut the company's performance in unforeseen ways, endangering operations.

6. Secured by assets, a leveraged buyout can be a good deal for lenders, but it can mean bankruptcy for unsecured workers and suppliers who can't collect when the company is dismantled.

TESTING THE WATERS

The best guide to borrowing remains: "Those who don't need it, get it." Most successful borrowers are those companies that already have a good credit rating, collateral, current and future income, and growth potential. Above all, they have other sources of capital.

The most accurate reading on the potential success of a leveraged buyout is the fixed-charge coverage ratio: if it is below one, the buyout probably would not succeed; if it is about two, the buyout looks strong. Another guideline is the payout period: if debt can be repaid based on historical cash flow in five to seven years, the buyout is probably solid. Payouts that take 10 or even 12 years mean the buyout may be questionable. Also, the buyout looks favorable if debt is about half of total capitalization one year after the buyout.

ALTERNATIVES TO BORROWING

1. Private Equity. Calgene, Inc. sold equity stakes of less than 10 percent each to two major research and development customers as a less expensive way to raise capital (see Chapter 23).

2. Combinations. Vixen Motor Co. used a combination of limited partnerships, state pension plan investment and capital advanced by the state of Michigan to raise more than $13 million for expansion capital.

3. Licensing Agreement. Vertex Peripherals negotiated a licensing agreement with the Bull Groupe, France's biggest computer manufacturer, that led to a $500,000 investment by Bull (see Section 1).

SOURCES

Golenberg Capital Associates, Cleveland, OH.
C.M. Capital Corporation (subsidiary of Carl Marks & Co.), New York, NY.
Thomas H. Lee & Co., Boston, MA.
Unirock Management Corporation, Denver, CO.

Borrowing

	Good Deal	*Bad Deal*
1. Interest rate	Current prime + 2% or less, depending on risk	More than 2% above prime, depending on risk
2. Warrants as equity kicker	None, or less than 5% of stock	Greater than 5% of stock
3. Maturity	180 days or less for lower interest	Greater than 180 days at higher interest
4. Receivable financing	Line of credit for lower interest	Long-term loan for higher interest
5. Future financing potential	Line of credit, letter of credit and bond financing	Short- or long-term working-capital loans only
6. Advisory services	Managment assistance, growth counseling and additional capital sources	None

CHAPTER 18

Private Placement of Bonds

DESCRIPTION

A private placement of bonds (long-term securities) is a direct sale by the company to one or more investors who typically are life insurance companies, pension funds, bond funds and similar financial institutions. A private bond placement also is called "corporate debt financing." In general, privately placed bonds are unsecured senior notes with fixed interest rates and maturities in the 12- to 18-year range.

PROFILE OF A SUCCESSFUL PRIVATE BOND PLACEMENT

More than any other financing technique, bond issues are sold by a company that surpasses industry norms and has strong fundamental value. This candidate is a small- to medium-size company with annual revenues between $5 million and $200 million that does not have access to the public debt market because of its relatively small size. For the most part, successful debt financing is obtained when the company has been in business at least five years and has an operating history by which to determine a fair market rating for the bond. Lenders prefer Baa and A ratings.

In contrast to other sources of capital, the debt market looks for stability rather than high levels of earnings. The company should show at least three years of sustained growth, even if growth is slight, and predictable future earnings contingent on: (1) age and size of the firm, (2) industry and economic conditions, (3) product line limitations and (4) marketing niche within the industry.

The company needs to document strong internal cash resources and a favorable capital structure, including the ability to obtain additional financing from other sources. Indices of cash-flow relationships and current assets should equal or surpass industry standards for (1) current ratio, (2) net current assets and (3) inventory and receivables turnover.

Depending on the nature of the industry or company, asset protection must be evident in such ratios as total long-term debt/net plant and net tangible assets/total long-term debt. Also, stated values should mirror real values in book value compared with market value of tangible assets, impact of long-term leases, and goodwill on debt and net tangible assets.

In general, the lower the company's total long-term capitalization (long-term debt plus equity) relative to industry norms, the stronger the likelihood of obtaining corporate debt financing.

The last key requirement is indenture provisions that will impact the company's ability to repay on schedule in case of liquidation: who has senior debt and gets paid before new, debtholders are paid.

Examples of successful private debt issuers:

Natural Horizons, Inc.
Ohmeda, Inc.
Summit Brewery

RESULTS OF A PRIVATE BOND PLACEMENT

When capital markets are tight, small companies often must compete for private funds with large firms. Most small firms raise between $2 million and $5 million, and few raise $1 million or less. Larger issues are usually syndicated among several lenders. Most small issues for under $10 million are completed without the assistance of an agent or investment banker.

Maturity ranges from 12 to 18 years, but many lenders will consider maturities between seven and 12 years, or over 18 years. Most repayment terms are tailored to the specific needs of the company and/or industry and to cash-flow trends. When interest rates are high, lenders may allow only up to 30 percent optional prepayment without penalty (called "doubling-up"); the reverse is true when rates are low, to allow the borrowing company to reduce the average life of a loan. Also available to the company are provisions for optional prepayment under certain circumstances (called "divorce clauses") and optional prepayment with a penalty. When rates are high, borrowers are prohibited from retiring the bond for an average of five to ten years with outside, lower-interest financing (a "no financial refunding" provision).

The most important long-range results of a private bond issue are indicated in the offering circular as protective covenants. They vary greatly depending on the deal concluded between the company and the lender, but usually cover five areas: (1) working capital or a minimum current ratio requirement, (2) short-term debt limitations, (3) long-term debt limitations in addition to senior and subordinated debt, (4) restricted payments in dividends, repurchase of stock or other stock payments, and (5) limitations on lease obligations beyond two to five years.

WHEN TO DO A PRIVATE BOND PLACEMENT

When capital markets are flexible and/or interest rates are low, management can structure a more beneficial private bond placement. More favorable treatment by lenders also is possible when the company has developed strong fundamentals and/or total debt ratios are low.

Total Debt Financing
(in Millions)

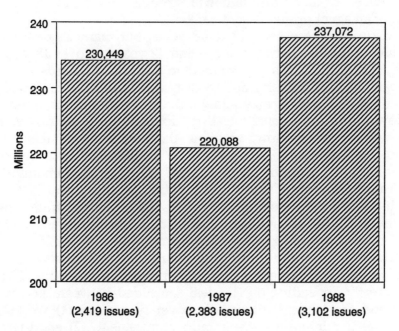

Source: *Investment Dealer's Digest.*

THE HOW-TO TIMETABLE
One Year before the Offering

If the offering exceeds $10 million or management is unfamiliar
with the private placement market and its myriad options, it is
recommended that an agent expedite the offering in order to coordinate the lender syndicate that will have to be formed to place
and sell the offering. An agent can be an investment banker,
money market bank group, accountant, consultant or attorney. The
agent will:

Determine amount, rate, terms and timing
Help establish the protective covenants and interest rate
Prepare the offering circular or memorandum
Present the proposed offering to appropriate investors

Before selecting an agent, many should be researched to match closely the specialties of the agent with the nature of the company's business. References should be checked carefully and several should be personally interviewed, based on:

Experience of the agent firm with private placements
Personnel experience and style
Firm services and strategy
Attitude toward private bond placements
Fee: negotiable based on the company's credit standing (weak credit requires more effort), the size and nature of the financing (large and/or complicated issues require more work) and market conditions (when capital is scarce or interest rates are high).

Nine Months before the Offering

An offering circular should be prepared for prospective lenders. This document is imperative to their analysis of the company's current position and prospects for successfully completing the repayment schedule. The offering circular should include:

1. Cover Page. Detail the proposed financing with amount, purpose and timing; proposed interest rate, covenants, final maturity, repayment schedule and average life; and type of financing and description of the security (secured, unsecured, subordinated, convertible debt or debt with warrants).

2. Company Summary. Give date and state of incorporation, lines of business, names and locations of divisions and subsidiaries, recent financial results, and management plans and expectations.

3. Capitalization. Review existing and pro forma capitalization, all long-term debt and lease obligations, short-term borrowing with monthly usage for two years, liabilities, guarantees, equity ownership (for private companies), where stock is traded, the number of outstanding shares and stockholders, and percentage ownership of officers, directors and major stockholders.

4. Products. Report the historical and projected growth in the markets served, sales and pretax profits by major product for five years, new product plans, and the research and development program.

5. *Marketing.* Outline how products are sold, distributed and priced, customer base, sales volume concentration, and sales contracts.

6. *Competition.* List by name, with market share of each and market position or niche in the industry.

7. *Manufacturing.* Cover location, nature, size, capacity and utilization of facilities, ownership or leasehold description, capital expenditures for five years, costs and methods, source, availability and cost of raw materials, and company status under federal, OSHA, state and local environmental regulations.

8. *Management.* Summarize the organization chart plus biographies on key management, salary and bonus arrangements, company directors and their outside affiliations, size and nature of the labor force, and wage and benefit plans with their financial aspects.

9. *Risk.* Assess historical impact, protective measures and major pending litigation.

10. *Historical/Financial Data.* Provide audited income statements, balance sheets, and sources and uses of funds for the past five years, abrupt changes in financial statistics, acquisitions and their rationale over the past five years, financial policies, management information systems, operating/capital budgeting and long-range planning procedures, and comparisons with major competitors by sales volume, margins, returns, capitalization and related ratios.

11. *Exhibits.* Include annual reports and consolidated financial statements for the past five years, current year interim reports, most recent 10-K and, proxy statement if applicable, recent prospectuses, existing loan and lease agreements, and current year operating budget.

12. *Forecasts.* Predict planned changes, use of proceeds, income statement, balance sheet, and sources and uses of funds statement forecasts for the next five years broken down by major divisions with detailed assumptions plus future capital requirements and use of proceeds.

Three Months before the Offering

1. Develop a list of potentially matched lenders for the company or agent to contact by telephone initially. If the lender is interested, a memorandum will be requested.

2. The second step is a face-to-face meeting between management (and its agent) and the lender to answer questions about the memorandum. While the lender sizes up the company, the company should be sizing up the lender for long-term financing possibilities.

3. After the meeting, lenders will complete their credit analyses, and those who are seriously interested will open final negotiations with management or the agent to determine the rate and terms. Final negotiations may require further meetings. (If the offering is large or complicated, final negotiations may take up to six months to complete.)

4. When the lender's loan committee approves the financing, negotiations on the loan agreement and closing documents can begin, involving meetings with management, an insurance company investment analyst, attorney and special counsel, and in-house or special legal counsel from the company.

The loan agreement typically has three sections, all of which must be carefully negotiated by management or its agent:

1. *Financial Covenants.* Cover loan repayment schedule, optional prepayments without penalty, restrictions on refinancing, optional prepayment under certain circumstances and optional prepayments with penalty.

2. *Protective Covenants.* Detail working capital minimums, short-term debt limits, long-term debt limits; lease obligation limits, and dividend payment restrictions, repurchase of stock or other stock payments.

3. *Interest Rate.* Within market conditions, a company's credit rating determines the interest rate it must pay. Most lenders use their own methodology for determining credit rating, and prefer at least a Baa or Ba rating. Interest rates in the private market often are 1/4 to 1/2 percent higher than public market rates, as compensation for the illiquidity of the unregistered

securities. If management does not use an agent, the lender's credit rating should be confirmed with similar companies, bankers or an investment banker.

If the company has a weak credit rating or if the stock market is highly competitive, lenders may require an incentive in addition to a relatively high interest rate in order to offset risk. The incentive is usually an equity stake in the company, called an "equity kicker," in one of three forms:

Convertible Debt: All or part of the principal loan amount is convertible into the common stock of the company at up to 15 percent higher than market price. Such debt is almost always subordinated.

Debt with Warrants: A call is held on an amount of the company's stock at a specified price up to 15 percent in excess of current market price. Such terms usually favor the lender; this debt may or may not be subordinated.

Contingent Interest: Terms require management to make interest payments over and above the coupon rate up to a maximum that are tied to net income, net operating income or sales. This strategy is not frequently used.

Straight Debt Financing

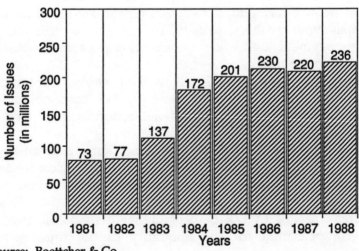

Source: Boettcher & Co.

FILING REQUIREMENTS

Most private bond issuers rely on Regulation D to provide the protection for the exemptions under which they sell their offerings. If certain guidelines provided by case law are followed to characterize the offering, Section 4 (2) of the 1933 Securities Act exempts private placements of securities (stocks and bonds) from registration with the SEC. The following guidelines must characterize the offering:

> Lenders are solicited only through direct communication, not advertising.
>
> The agent or issuing company believes each investor is sophisticated.
>
> The company gives the lender an opportunity to verify information provided.
>
> There are no more than 35 purchasers of the offering in any six-month period (with certain important exceptions).
>
> The company and its agent must make a reasonable effort to assure that lenders are not buying the securities for redistribution.

While private placements can be exempt from SEC registration, they must meet the requirements of individual state antifraud and sale of securities statutes.

COSTS

1. Agent. Most agents charge a minimum $25,000 to $50,000 contingent on completion of the financing, with a portion billed upfront to cover the time and cost of preparing the memorandum. Typically, fees are larger for small issues. A $2.5 million issue costs about 2 percent of the amount borrowed.

2. Lender. Lenders will charge a per-annum fee (commitment fee) of 1/4 to 1/2 percent on forward commitments, in which the lender agrees to deliver funds at a future date.

3. *Printing.* The offering circular or memorandum will cost between $5,000 and $50,000.

4. *Third-Parties.* The company must pay the legal and accounting fees of its own and the lender's outside counsel. These combined fees usually range between $20,000 and $100,000, contingent on the complexity of the issue or the company, and how up-to-date the financial and legal affairs of the company are.

ADVANTAGES AND DISADVANTAGES
Advantages

1. If a small company has strong fundamentals, debt financing costs much less than most other forms of financing, especially if the offering is self underwritten or interest rates are low.

2. It is easier to get future financing from a debt financing source than to go a second time to a venture capitalist or the equity market.

3. The repayment schedule often doesn't begin for a year or two (called the "blind-spot period").

4. Bond issues with an equity kicker often can be sold in less time than it takes to raise capital from more traditional sources.

Disadvantages

1. High interest rates can make a bond issue expensive for the company over the long-term.

2. A company with a weak credit rating may give up more control of the company to get debt financing than a company with a strong credit rating.

3. Financial and protective covenants in the loan agreement have to be negotiated carefully to avoid restrictive limitations on the company's financial future.

4. Long- and short-term debt ratios must be at least standard for the company's industry in order to structure an issue with terms that are favorable to the company.

TESTING THE WATERS

The best time to do a private bond placement is when (1) interest rates are low, (2) the company's total debt ratio is less than 1:1, and (3) the company can justify, and borrow, at least $10 million (to pay the least amount, 1/4 to 1/2 percent, in agent commissions).

ALTERNATIVES TO A PRIVATE BOND PLACEMENT

1. *Public Bond Issue.* Large companies can borrow $20 million or more.

2. *R&D Partnership.* If the partnership bears the risk of loss, an R&D arrangement can affect aftertax earnings much more favorably. Telentry Systems, Inc. raised $22.2 million with an R&D partnership that offered an equity kicker. About 95 percent of the financing was backed by a package of insurance and a bank line of credit (see Chapter 4).

3. *Short-Term Borrowing.* Innovations like interest-rate swaps allow companies to move at will among floating-rate securities. The swap market grew to about $125 billion in 1984. Although many small businesses are not financially sophisticated, they can benefit by duplicating the borrowing trends of megasized companies who play commercial paper, for example, Lockheed Corporation boosted short-term debt by 124 percent, while reducing long-term debt by 84 percent (see Chapter 17).

4. *Do-It-Yourself.* Gelato Modo, Inc. raised $200,000 from 30 investors in six weeks with a private placement of equity. Net capitalization of the iced-dessert company topped $1 million two years later with only four outlets (see Chapter 21).

SOURCES

Most national, regional and local brokerage firms place and sell private bond issues.

Three Alternative Methods of Financing Sale of Securities:

| | | | Amount of Financing | Interest and Dividend Cost | After 50% Tax |
	Rate	Price	First of Year	Before Taxes	Rate
30-Yr. Bonds	7%	$100	$8,000,000	$560,000	$280,000
Preferred	7%	100	8,000,000	560,000	560,000
Common (4 million shares)	$1.20 Dividend	20	8,000,000		480,000

PITFALLS TO AVOID

Financial covenants should be negotiated to allow management to prepay without penalty, particularly if the interest rate is high. Protective covenants should be negotiated to allow management to increase short- and long-term borrowing as growth increases during the life of the bond.

An equity kicker tied to the bond should be avoided unless there are specific advantages to adding it.

Bonds

	Good Deal	*Bad Deal*
1. Required prepayments	When rates are low, lengthen average life	Shorten average life when rates are low
2. Optional Prepayments without penalty	Greater than 30 percent can be prepaid when rates are high	Less than 20 percent can be prepaid when rates are high
3. Refinancing restriction	Not mandatory Available for future financing from other sources	Mandatory when rates are high
4. Total prepayment	Up to 10 percent variation in forecast accuracy	Not available
5. Working capital covenant	Should increase with growth; eliminate only every 18 months	Less than 10 percent variation
6. Allowable short-term debt		No allowance for short-term debt when needed
7. Allowable long-term debt (leases, mortgage, etc.)	Increases with growth of company	None, or increases by dollar or percent amount

CHAPTER 19

Convertible Deben-
tures/Hybrid Securities

DESCRIPTION

A standard debenture is a general debt obligation, usually subordinated, that is backed only by the reputation of the issuing company, i.e., it is an unsecured bond. As an interest-bearing security,
it obligates the company to pay investors a specific amount of
money at intervals, and to repay the principal amount of the loan
at maturity. Bondholders, in this case, have no corporate ownership privileges as stockholders do.

Convertible debentures can be issued by private or public
companies, and they may be issued as a private placement. They
are also known as hybrid securities, with both equity and debt
features.

A convertible debenture is a bond (also called a "senior
security") that can be exchanged at a future date for a specified
number of common shares at a preset price. This corporate
security can be issued by a small company when management
wants to give an equity kicker to investors as inducement to buy
the offering. It provides higher income than common stock and
greater appreciation than common bonds. Large companies often
issue a convertible debenture for tax reasons or to create a more
appealing debt issue until greater returns are achieved.

All or part of the principal loan amount is convertible into common stock at up to 15 percent higher than market price.

Federal regulators have cleared the way for investment banks and businesses to issue several new forms of hybrid securities.

One new financial instrument is an over-the-counter debt vehicle that resembles a futures contract with options. This new security is considered to be a category of debt security or bank deposit called a hybrid, whose interest rates rise and fall with the prices of commodities, like oil, or stock indices. These securities generally are sold by local, regional and national investment banking houses.

Used by organizations like the Student Loan Marketing Association primarily to hedge risk, futures are agreements to buy or sell a commodity for delivery at some date in the future. The value changes as commodity prices change.

In the same way, an option gives the buyer the right to buy or sell a commodity at a set price within a certain time period. The value of the option fluctuates with the price of the underlying commodity.

Another new hybrid security available to business owners is an unbundled stock unit, which consists of a 30-year bond, preferred stock and a stock appreciation certificate. The stock unit, which is offered by investment banking houses, can be traded whole or broken into three parts.

This security is most viable for a larger company as an alternative to the heavy borrowing associated with stock buybacks that compel the company to sell off major assets, suffer a lowering of its debt rating and/or cut spending on items like R&D or marketing.

- The bond would carry an interest coupon equivalent to the current dividend rate of the stock and would mature at a premium to the current stock price.
- The preferred stock would entitle the holder to any increases in dividend payments compared with the current dividend over the next 30 years.

- The stock appreciation certificate would entitle the holder to any capital gain on the stock in 30 years that exceeds the premium allotted to the bondholder.

PROFILE OF A SUCCESSFUL CONVERTIBLE DEBENTURE ISSUER

A small company most likely to make optimal use of a convertible debenture (1) is undercapitalized, with a rated or unrated bond; (2) is growing, but earnings or the price/earnings ratios are down, (3) has off-balance-sheet assets or an unusual tax potential like a tax loss carryforward, (4) can afford to stage dilution levels, (5) can sell out an offering, but needs a sweetener to induce reluctant investors or (6) needs to refund existing debt to strengthen its capital structure.

A large company issues convertible debentures (1) to take advantage of certain tax benefits or (2) to raise capital with debt until higher returns are achievable.

Convertible debenture issuers include:

Lynne Rienner Publishers, Inc.
Snugli, Inc.
Gish Biomedical, Inc.

RESULTS OF A CONVERTIBLE DEBENTURE OFFERING

By selling a convertible debenture, management can (1) attract investors who may not have financed the company without the inducement of an equity kicker, (2) raise from $100,000 to $50 million in development or expansion capital, (3) keep capital ratios in balance despite extensive financing, but without selling a large number of additional common shares, (4) strengthen the capital structure by refunding existing debt, (5) preserve control for current shareholders by temporarily delaying the addition of new stockholders, (6) reduce the cost of raising money by selling more costly securities (common stock) later when earnings increase, (7) slow down the dilution of earnings per share with a later conversion and (8) raise capital despite unfavorable market conditions.

WHEN TO SELL A CONVERTIBLE DEBENTURE OFFERING

The best time to offer a convertible debenture is when (1) interest rates are down and the stock market is strong (the conversion feature provides a lower rate of interest), (2) carefully staged financing is necessary to prevent immediate dilution, a capital structure imbalance or an upfront increase in the cost of raising capital, (3) the company cannot sell a senior security at a reasonable price without a sweetener, or (4) the company's temporary balance sheet weakness is preventing management from competing effectively, especially in a growing industry.

THE HOW-TO TIMETABLE
One Year before a Convertible Debenture Offering

If the offering is to exceed $10 million, or management is unfamiliar with this corporate security, it is helpful to retain an agent to expedite the offering. An agent can be an attorney, investment banker, money market bank group, accountant or consultant. The agent will:

Determine amount, rate, terms and timing
Structure protective covenants and interest rate
Prepare the offering circular
Place the issue with appropriate investors

Before making a final selection of agent, management should research several firms to match the specialty of the agent with the nature of the business. References should be requested and interviews should cover:

Firm's experience with convertible debentures
Personnel experience, depth and style

Services available
Strategy

Fee, which can be relatively negotiable based on the company's credit standing (weak credit requires more effort), the size and nature of the financing (large and/or complicated issues require more attention) and market conditions (scarce capital and high interest rates require more work). The minimum is between $25,000 and $50,000.

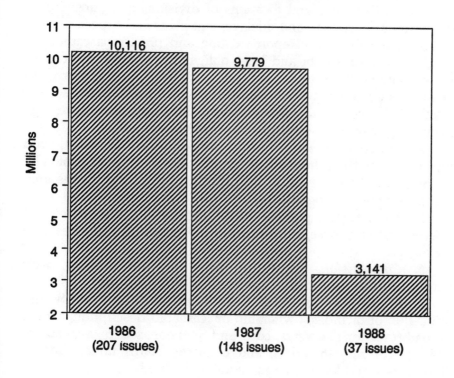

**Total Convertible
Debt Financing (in Millions)**

Source: *Investment Dealer's Digest.*

Nine Months before a Convertible Debenture Offering

An offering circular, or memorandum, should be prepared for prospective lender-investors. This document is their basis for evaluating the company's current position and prospects for successfully completing the repayment schedule. The memorandum is usually registered, and should include:

1. Cover Page. Outline the proposed financing including amount, purpose and timing, the proposed interest rate, covenants, final maturity, repayment schedule and average life, the type of financing and a description of the security (secured, unsecured, subordinated, convertible debt or debt with warrants).

2. Summary. Give the date and state of incorporation, lines of business with names and locations of divisions and subsidiaries, recent financial results, and management plans and expectations.

3. Capitalization. Report existing and pro forma capitalization, all long-term debt and lease obligations, short-term borrowing with monthly usage for two years, liabilities, guarantees, equity ownership (for private companies), where stock is traded, the number of outstanding shares and stockholders, and percentage ownership of officers, directors and major stockholders.

4. Products/Services. Discuss (by market) historical and projected growth in the markets served, sales and pretax profits by major product for five years, new product plans, and the research and development program.

5. Marketing. Explain how products are sold, distributed and priced, customer base, sales volume concentration and sales contracts.

6. Competition. Specify by name for the industry, with market share of each and company niche in the industry.

7. Manufacturing. Detail location, nature, size, capacity and utilization of facilities, ownership or leasehold description, capital expenditures for five years, costs and methods, source, availability and cost of raw materials, and company status under federal, OSHA, state and local environmental regulations.

8. Management. Summarize the organization chart plus biographies on key management, salary and bonus arrangements, company directors and their outside affiliations, size and nature of the labor force, and wage and benefit plans with their financial aspects.

9. Risk. Assess historical impact, protective measures and major pending litigation.

10. Historical/Financial Data. Review audited income statements, balance sheets, and sources and uses of funds for the past five years, abrupt changes in financial statistics, acquisitions and their rationale for the past five years, financial policies, management information systems, operating/capital budgeting, long-range planning procedures, comparisons with major competitors by sales volume, margins, returns, and capitalization, and related ratios.

11. Exhibits. Depict annual reports and consolidated financial statements for the past five years, current year interim reports, recent 10-K, proxy statement and recent prospectuses if applicable, existing loan and lease agreements, and the current year's operating budget.

12. Forecasts. Project planned changes, use of proceeds, income statement, balance sheet, and sources and uses of funds statement forecasts for the next five years broken down by major divisions with detailed assumptions included, future capital requirements and use of proceeds.

Three Months before a Convertible Debenture Offering

1. Contact List. The agent will develop a list of potential lenders. If the lender is interested in the deal, a memorandum will be requested.

2. Lender Meetings. The agent will arrange for interested lenders to meet management at the company, and to ask questions about the memorandum. While the lender sizes up the company, management should size up the lender as a long-term financing possibility.

3. Negotiation. After the meeting, lenders will complete their credit analyses. Those who are interested will open final negotiations with management or the agent to determine the rate and terms. Final negotiations may require further meetings. If the offering is large or complicated, they may take up to six months to complete.

4. Roundtable. When the lender's loan committee approves the financing, negotiations on the loan agreement and closing documents can begin, involving meetings with management, a lender investment analyst, attorney and special counsel, and in-house or outside legal counsel for the company.

The loan agreement typically has three sections, all of which must be carefully negotiated:

Financial Covenants: Specify conversion ratio (the key covenant in a convertible debenture), repayment schedule, optional prepayments without penalty, restrictions on refinancing, optional prepayment under certain circumstances and optional prepayments with penalty.

Protective Covenants: Set working capital minimums, short- and long-term debt limits, lease obligation limits, and restricted payments of dividends, repurchase of stock or other stock payments.

Interest Rate: Within market conditions, a company's credit rating determines the interest rate it must pay. Most lenders use their own methodology to establish a credit rating (at least a Baa or Ba rating is preferred). Interest rates in the public market often are 1/4 to 1/2 percent lower than private market rates, which must be higher to offset the illiquidity of unregistered shares. If management does not use an agent, it should confirm the lender's credit rating of the company with similar companies, bankers or an investment banker.

FILING REQUIREMENTS

Section 4(2) of the 1933 Securities Act exempts private placements of securities from full SEC registration if the Safe Harbor guidelines of Regulation D characterize the offering. If the company is public, it is subject to federal and state reporting/disclosure requirements. Reporting documents include a quarterly financial report (Form 10-Q), annual financial report (Form 10-K), proxy statements, annual report to shareholders, reports about current material events in the company (Form 8-K) and other reports for audited financial statements, the sale of control shares and tender offers.

COSTS

1. Agent. Most charge a minimum $25,000 to $50,000 contingent on completion of the financing, with a portion billed upfront to cover the time and cost of preparing the memorandum. Typically, fees are larger for small issues. A $2.5 million issue costs about 2 percent of the amount borrowed.

2. Lender. Expect a per-annum fee (commitment fee) of 1/4 to 1/2 percent on forward commitments, whereby the lender agrees to deliver funds at a future date.

3. Printing. The memorandum will cost between $5,000 and $50,000 to produce.

4. Third-Parties. The company must pay the legal fees of its own and the lender's special counsel, in addition to in-house counsel and accounting assistance. These fees range between a fraction of 1 percent to 5 percent of the amount borrowed.

ADVANTAGES AND DISADVANTAGES
Advantages

1. A convertible debenture offers a lower interest rate than the dividend on a convertible preferred, and interest results in income tax savings.

2. Debt financing is a less costly way to raise money than equity, especially if the interest rate is low.

3. Interest payments can be delayed.

4. The onset of the conversion feature can be delayed, preventing upfront dilution by a large number of new shareholders, or the conversion privilege can expire before maturity to encourage conversion at an early date, if desired.

5. A convertible debenture raises long-term debt and equity capital, which can be manipulated in infinite ways to achieve very specific capital and growth goals.

6. The conversion feature increases the marketability of the offering.

7. A convertible debenture can have a positive effect on the price of the common shares.

Disadvantages

1. The marketability of a small convertible debenture issue decreases if the security is not exchange-listed or interest rates are high.

2. The formulae for evaluating the security's return to both the company and investors are complex. A high interest rate, which usually discourages debt financing, must be balanced with both general market conditions and the company's share price compared to its proposed conversion price. Pricing, rate, terms and amount formulae must be carefully applied to avoid a negative impact on the company's short- and long-term capital structure.

3. A convertible debenture often is issued for very specific reasons, so the agent must be skilled in negotiating terms that support corporate goals.

4. This security may have a negative effect on the price of common stock.

5. Because two markets are involved in a convertible debenture, negative bond and equity market constraints can combine to depress the security more severely than a slump in either market alone would.

TESTING THE WATERS

A convertible debenture that provides new capital can be evaluated for effect by the principal applied to new shares of common stock: an offering that increases the stock 20 percent is a heavy offering, resulting in a 20 percent decrease in earnings per share from the added shares without allowing for any increase in earnings from the new capital; a 10 percent increase in shares is moderate; and a 5 percent increase is light. The key question is: what percentage can the company afford in terms of its current and future capital structure?

ALTERNATIVES TO A CONVERTIBLE DEBENTURE

1. Convertible Preferred. Encore Computer Corporation sold $22.6 million in convertible preferred stock at $4.50 a share to Schlumberger Ltd., Sperry Corporation and a few institutional investors. Later, the company got a $30 million revolving line of credit based on the offering (see Chapter 19).

2. Potential Customers. Charles River Data Systems, Inc. got $2 million from two corporate customers, Analog Devices Inc. and Medical Information Technology Corporation. In 1984, SORD Computer Corporation, now a potential reseller, invested about $2.5 million in the company.

SOURCES

Most national, regional and local brokerage firms underwrite convertible debenture issues.

PITFALLS TO AVOID

The conversion ratio should be negotiated so that it does not create a top-heavy equity ratio within the company.

Management should schedule conversion for a time when dilution of earnings per share can be most easily absorbed.

Small companies that offer an issue under $10 million have more difficulty selling convertible debt during periods of high interest rates.

Techniques with Stock

Section 6
Introduction

The 12 equity (stock) financing techniques described in Section 6 can be appropriate financing strategies for a small business in the under–$25 million category. Initial public offerings (IPOs) and self-underwritings of initial public offerings are sold only by private companies that want to go public. The other 10 techniques listed in Section 6 can be used by public and private companies. See the chart on pages 297–298 for an overview of public and private offerings.

Equity financing should be viewed as an expensive way to raise capital, because in exchange for financing from the sale of shares, management must give up some percentage of ownership, and control, of the company.

To make equity financing cost-effective, the company must be able to get a fair market price for the shares. In order to get the best possible share price, management must convince investors that the company has one or both of two things: (1) valuation that is equal to or more favorable than the competition, and/or (2) realistic earnings projections that reflect growth. The integrity of the valuation and projections is the pivotal factor in determining the price, cost and success of an equity offering.

A solid company with highly valued assets, for example, can sell higher-priced shares in both private and public markets because the shares represent ownership of something of value. The higher the share price relative to value, the lower the cost of giving up equity in the company.

249

Section 6
Glossary

All-or-None Selling: a best-efforts underwriting agreement in which the offering is completed only when the entire issue is sold.

Best Efforts: an underwriting agreement in which brokers use their best efforts to sell the offering as agents of the issuing company.

Bid/Asked Prices: bid price is the highest amount a buyer is willing to pay for a share of stock; asked price is the lowest amount at which a seller will sell a share.

Blue-Sky Lows: securities regulations that vary by state to protect investors against stock fraud.

Capitalization: total amount of securities (bonds and stocks) issued by a company, including all long- and short-term debt.

Cheap Stock: common shares issued to company directors, board members and other insiders before the public offering at a price discount; can also apply to other dilutive offerings of options and warrants.

Dealer: an individual or securities firm who buys stocks for the house account and sells to investors from that inventory.

Dilution: relative reduction of ownership or interest in the company by the sale of additional shares of stock, or the difference between the public offering price per share and the tangible book value per share just before the offering.

251

Due Diligence: investigation by underwriters, accountants or attorneys of the registration, income statements or other corporate documents to verify the information and ensure that no material facts are omitted.

Effective Date: the date when a registration statement becomes effective and the stock can be offered for sale.

Firm Commitment: an underwriting agreement which commits a brokerage firm to buy the entire offering for resale.

Insider Trading: trading by people with access to nonpublic information about the company, i.e., corporate officers, directors and public relations executives, among others.

Limited Offering: the sale of securities that are exempt from registration because of the limited size of the offering or because the number of buyers is limited.

Loyalty Shares: extra shares of stock offered gratis to IPO investors if they pledge to keep their shares for one year following the offering.

Market-Maker: a dealer who supports trading volume in a stock by making firm bid/asked prices in the shares; market-makers trade in the over-the-counter market only.

Managing Underwriter: the lead underwriter in an offering and the lead partner in the selling syndicate.

Offering Circular: document for a private offering that does not have to be fully registered with the SEC; it is also called a placement "memorandum."

Over-the-Counter (OTC) Market: a market of dealers for securities that are sold over the telephone between buyers and sellers in contrast to exchange listed stocks that are sold by auction.

Price/Earnings Ratio: the price of a common share divided by earnings per share.

Primary Offering: a company offering of unissued stock.

Quiet Period: the time between agreement with the underwriters to go public and 90 days after the effective date, during which only that information about the company or the offering that appears in the prospectus or its amendments can be made public.

Red Herring: a preliminary version of the prospectus used before the effective date for the due diligence meeting (as indicated in red ink on the cover page).

Registrar: an agency that issues certificates to stockholders and compares the number of new shares to the number of shares cancelled.

Registration: the SEC's procedure for filing information required by the 1933 Securities Act.

Restricted Stock: shares that have limited transferability and are usually issued in a private placement offering (also called "lettered stock" or "legend stock").

Rule 144: the exempt sale of insider, restricted or control stock in the public market without registration of the stock.

Safe Harbor Rule: an SEC provision that protects the company from legal action if it has made a good-faith effort to comply with SEC requirements.

Secondary Offering: an offering of previously unregistered stock made by existing stockholders.

Transfer Agent: an agency that officially records pertinent data about stockholders and transmits the shares between buyers and sellers.

CHAPTER 20
Initial Public Offering

DESCRIPTION

An initial public offering (IPO) is the process by which a privately held company (1) sells previously issued or newly created shares of stock to the public for the first time, (2) discloses operations to the public and (3) registers with and operates within the provisions and laws of the Securities and Exchange Commission (SEC), the National Association of Securities Dealers (NASD) and state regulatory bodies, if applicable.

PROFILE OF A SUCCESSFUL IPO CANDIDATE

The most promising IPO candidate is a small- to medium-sized emerging company. Annual revenues are at least $7.5 million—$10 million is better—and profit is about 10 percent of revenues. Company management is stable, with key-employee contracts in force for senior executives. Annual growth has averaged a minimum 10 percent for each of the past five years. The company has an appreciable and expanding percentage of market share in its industry and is free from significant foreign competition. Short- or long-term debt does not exceed 25 percent of total capitalization and increases are building in unit sales volume, pretax profit margin and return on shareholders' equity. The company does not need net proceeds for debt repayment.

Examples of successful initial offerings include:

PACE Membership Warehouse
Sun World Airlines
Price Warehouse
Western Health Plans

RESULTS OF AN INITIAL PUBLIC OFFERING

Following successful completion of an initial public offering, the company will be a registered public entity, subject to federal and state laws regarding public ownership. The company will be eligible upon qualification for NASDAQ listing or listing on the New York or American Stock Exchange. Publicly held shares of stock, called "float," can be freely bought and sold without restriction among public shareholders. Disclosure of information about the company will be required by the SEC and shareholders on a regular basis during the life of the corporation. Substantial amounts of capital can be raised from the public market at any time, either through an underwriter or through self-underwriting by company management/owners.

WHEN TO MAKE AN INITIAL PUBLIC OFFERING

It makes sense for a company to go public when (1) it needs access to a larger source of capital for a broader equity base and increased net asset value, (2) expansion demands public recognition, (3) operating history warrants the prestige of NASDAQ or exchange-listing, (4) the stock market is receptive to new offerings or (5) the company's industry is growing, deregulating rapidly or riding a broad economic movement.

THE HOW-TO TIMETABLE

One to Three Years Prior to the Effective Date

1. *Business Plan.* This document is a critical factor in the success of the offering, a first impression that should be complete

enough to interest investors and underwriters further. To enable investors and underwriters to make a thorough assessment of the company's current condition and growth potential, the business plan should include:

Plan summary
Business description
Market analysis
Product/service description
Marketing strategy
Manufacturing/service operation
Financial data
Capital needs/timetable

2. *Institutional Image.* Determine how the company is perceived in the marketplace. If the company sells within a small geographic region, should shares be offered regionally? Is the product appealing? What target markets are most likely to be attracted to the product, the company niche and the industry?

3. *Target Market.* After determining the appropriate institutional image of both company and product, that image, via information that is restricted to prospectus contents only, must be conveyed effectively to the company's target markets. The longer a targeted marketing campaign has been in effect, the more responsive the marketplace tends to be. Targeted marketing cannot be a mechanism for finding future investors, a disallowed practice that is construed as pump priming by the SEC.

4. *Reorganization.* Many private companies are organized as partnerships, joint ventures or other forms of cross-ownership. The legal structure of the company may have to be modified, therefore, prior to going public. Most companies have to recapitalize to have an appropriate capital structure for the public offering, and many split their stock forward or backward to fine tune the pricing level at which the initial public offering will be sold.

5. *Legal Review.* The SEC requires that public firms disclose all significant transactions between company-related associates. Although the company's private arrangements between officers and shareholders serve a private company well, they may not be perceived the same way by public shareholders or by the SEC. A legal

review of the following should take place before the initial offering
procedure begins:

Corporate charter and bylaws
Shareholder or management loans
Lease agreements
Debt outstanding
Stock option or purchase plans
Employment contracts
Supply contracts and arrangements
Rights of first refusal

Six Months to One Year Prior to the Effective Date

1. Company management can be supplemented and corporate vacancies filled with an eye toward the public responsibility office holders carry before and after the offering.

A number of professionals, some of them from outside the
company, should be involved in the offering to provide technical,
specialized assistance. They should be interviewed and selected
carefully. They include:

Attorneys/law firm with specialized securities training
Accountants with specialized securities training
Financial printer with specialized ability to produce SEC-regu-
lated documents
Underwriting securities firm with a track record in initial of-
ferings

Because the underwriter can make or break an initial offering,
it is important to select a firm with broad-based credentials such
as:

Good reputation in the market
Experience with initial offerings
Syndication/distribution network already in place, with 50 to
100 firms as secondary underwriters
Aftermarket support

Advisory services to support company management
   throughout the offering process
Research capability

2. After the primary underwriting firm is selected, the
underwriter's terms are negotiated, including the commission and
any stock options, warrants or nonaccountable, upfront expenses
the underwriter may require. (Upfront expenses are rarely sought
in offerings priced at more than $5 per share.)

Following are some of the offering terms that should be
negotiated before signing an underwriting contract:

Letter of intent
Type of underwriting, either firm commitment or best efforts
   (with or without an over-allotment option, or "green shoe")
Offering price and size
Underwriter's commission, or discount (usually 7–10 percent
   of the value of the offering), any nonaccountable upfront
   expenses or reimbursement for underwriter legal fees,
   geographic syndication costs and marketing
Right of first refusal on future offerings
Underwriter stock warrants (the number and terms of warrants sometimes are exchanged for lower commissions)

Six Months Prior to the Effective Date

A planning session is held by all company executives, corporate
attorneys and accountants, and the underwriting firm and its
counsel to discuss terms of the offering, determine the kind of offering it will be and assign specific responsibilities for preparation
of the registration statement. This statement consists of two parts:
Part I, which includes a prospectus, to be distributed to underwriters and prospective investors and Part II, which gives information required by the SEC and state regulators if applicable. The
contents of Parts I and II, which are required and determined by
the SEC, become part of the public record.

The prospectus should contain:

Outside Front Cover: Summarize all key offering facts.

Inside Front and Outside Back Covers: Include the table of contents, price data and an underwriter disclaimer on delivery requirements.

Prospectus Summary: Give a company overview, offering description, net proceeds and use of proceeds, and selected financial data.

Company Background: Provide detailed information and an overview of the firm's primary business.

Risk Factors: Assess risks inherent in the company, industry and market. (Risk factors appear only in the prospectuses of low-priced offerings under $5 per share.)

Use of Proceeds: Disclose the company's intended use of the net proceeds of the offering, including debt payment or acquisitions.

Dilution: Report in tabular form any material dilution of the prospective investors' equity interest caused by a disparity between the offering price and tangible book value of the share before the offering. (Dilution only appears if insider stock has been purchased in the last five years at a lower price than the offering price.)

Dividend Policy: Review the company's dividend history and current policy, if any. Any restriction or reinvestment of dividends must be disclosed.

Capitalization: Detail data on the company's equity capital and debt structure before and after the offering. The pro forma capital structure after the offering should be adjusted to reflect the securities issued and the intended use of proceeds.

Selected Financial Data: Show financial data for each of the previous five years, the interim period since the last year end and the comparative interim period of the preceding year.

Management Analysis: Analyze the financial condition and results of operations for the last three fiscal years, trends, cash flow, liquidity and capital resources, expected sources of capital and longer-range plans. This section is the most important disclosure to professional investment analysts.

Detailed Business Description

Properties of the Business

Legal Proceedings: Describe actions other than routine litigation.

Management and Security-Holder Backgrounds: Give biographical data, compensation, loans, transactions with promoters, shareholdings, and golden parachute arrangements.

Description of Registered Securities: Describe title, dividend rights, conversion and voting rights, liquidation rights and warrant terms.

Underwriting: Provide a description, a distribution plan, principal underwriters in the syndication, number of shares underwritten by each underwriter, method, material relations between the company and underwriters, compensation, board representation and indemnification.

Legal Review: Name attorneys, and report their opinions of the validity of the offering, any shareholdings, independent contractors to the underwriting, and procedure for obtaining Part II of the registration statement.

Financial Statements: Show the accountants' report as well as audited balance sheets up to the end of each of the last two fiscal years, audited statements of income, changes in financial position, shareholders' equity for each of the last three fiscal years, and some unaudited interim statements if applicable.

The following information should be included in Part II of the registration statement (but not included in the printed prospectus):

Expenses of issuance and distribution
Indemnification or insurance for liability of officers and directors acting on behalf of the company
Various financial statement schedules
Sales of unregistered securities in the last three years
Written consent of all experts who have certified or prepared any material included in Parts I and II
Exhibits, including all subsidiaries, underwriting agreement, charter and bylaws, and material contracts

It normally takes about two months to prepare Parts I and II of the registration statement. Allow another month for revisions and then signatures by all parties, including the company's board of directors. The completed document is filed with the SEC about 90 days after the first planning session.

Three Months Prior to the Effective Date

1. Once the registration statement has been filed with the SEC, a "road show" is staged by company management and primary underwriters who meet with prospective syndicate participants to describe the company and the offering, using a preliminary version of the prospectus called the "red herring." While the road show is in progress, the SEC's Division of Corporate Finance evaluates the registration statement, and will comment on its contents within one to three months. If the SEC requires revisions in the registration statement before issuing the go-ahead, final changes must be made before the company be-

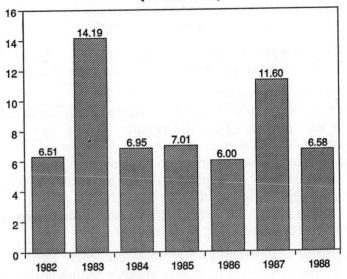

**Average Dollars Raised in IPOs
(in Millions)**

Source: *Going Public: The IPO Reporter.*

comes effective for selling shares. The National Association of Securities Dealers (NASD) clears the prospectus under Regulation S-K for compliance to fairness practices for underwriter compensation.

2. The time period up to 90 days after the effective date is called the "quiet period." Company and underwriter participants are not permitted to disclose information about the company that is not found in the prospectus or its amendments. During this time, attorneys will "blue sky" the offering to satisfy state securities regulations in all states in which the offering is sold. "Merit" states have approval power over the offering prospectus.

3. Shortly before the effective date, a due diligence meeting is held by all offering participants for the underwriting syndicate, enabling them to raise final questions about the offering or the company.

4. The night before, or the morning of, the effective date, final considerations are agreed to regarding: offering price, underwriter's commission and net proceeds. This data plus revisions to the registration statement are filed as a final amendment known as the "pricing amendment."

FILING REQUIREMENTS

All public companies are subject to the federal reporting/disclosure requirements of the SEC. Reporting documents include proxy statements, the annual report to shareholders, a quarterly financial report (Form 10-Q), annual financial report (Form 10-K), reports about current material events in the company (Form 8-K) and other reports for audited financial statements, the sale of control shares and tender offers.

In addition, public companies must meet any reporting/disclosure requirements of the states in which shares are offered (called the "blue sky" process). State requirements differ widely. The NASD must approve the underwriter's compensation portions of the prospectus prior to the effective date.

COSTS

1. *Underwriter's Commission.* This cost usually varies between 7 and 10 percent of the value of the offering, depending on the size and structure of the offering (best efforts or firm commitment), the stability of the company and industry, competition in the underwriting industry and market conditions. Generally, the smaller the offering, the higher the percentage of commission. Most commissions fall between $200,000 and $300,000 on offerings of between $2 million and $3 million. Small initial offerings range up to $10 million.

2. *Underwriter Reimbursements.* If the offering is small, the company has no track record or market conditions are not receptive to IPOs, many underwriters will ask that up to $50,000 in underwriter legal and filing expenses be paid by the company. In addition, many firms also ask for a minimum 2.5 percent of the value of the offering in upfront, nonaccountable expenses.

3. *Out-of-Pocket Expenses.* For an offering in the $5 million to $10 million range, expenses of $150,000 to $300,000 will be incurred for legal, accounting and marketing (road show and aftermarket program) fees.

4. *Printing Costs.* These costs range from $50,000 for a small offering to up to $200,000, including revisions and color photographs.

5. *Filing Fees.* SEC filing costs .02 percent of the maximum aggregate offering price. NASD filing costs $100 plus .01 percent of the maximum aggregate offering price, with a $5,100 maximum. State blue-sky filing fees range up to $15,000. Registrar and transfer agent fees are between $5,000 and $10,000.

6. *Public Relations.* Many companies hire a financial consulting firm to help market institutional image and provide information to the financial press once the quiet period is over. These firms can be paid by project or by monthly retainer, which ranges from $3,000 to $10,000 per month.

7. *Ongoing.* Add one-third to one-half the initial cost of going public for annual legal, accounting, compliance, filing and mailing fees.

ADVANTAGES AND DISADVANTAGES

Advantages

1. The primary benefit is the net proceeds of the offering, which average from $1 million to $10 million. These funds can be used for anything from paying off long-term debt to working capital to acquisition of capital equipment for growth.

2. By going public, the company has a broader equity base and larger net asset value. It is thus easier to raise future equity capital and borrow additional funds because of the improved debt-to-equity ratio.

3. Stock exchange or NASDAQ listing is possible if the company meets exchange qualifications. This means corporate image is enhanced, the company will receive more attention from the media, and key employees can be attracted with stock options and purchase plans.

4. After two years, management estates are more liquid because the shares can be sold publicly, creating a market value and a public market for the sale of control shares.

Disadvantages

1. The management of a private company will lose some or all control over the company depending on share value and how many shares are sold to the public. Future acquisitions and offerings may dilute the stock, hence control, even further.

2. Going public is one of the most expensive ways to raise capital. Costs can range, on average, more than $100,000 above other financing techniques.

3. Public shareholders are now management partners, entitled to share all information about the business and its management, including remuneration at all levels and the company's competitive position. Management will be held accountable to public shareholders for everything on the financial statements and for other results of its management of the company.

4. Controlling or insider shareholders in management are not free to sell shares at will. Stringent SEC regulations determine when and how insider shares can be sold.

5. Going public precludes management from raising capital from several other sources.

TESTING THE WATERS

The best guideline to judge whether or not the time is right to go public is a reverse of the 70/20/10 rule. Common wisdom says an initial offering will be influenced 70 percent by the merit of the company, 20 percent by the potential of the industry and 10 percent by broad market conditions. Put those percentages in reverse order for a more accurate reading of success probability: 70 percent for market conditions, 20 percent for the potential of the industry and 10 percent for the merit of the company.

ALTERNATIVES TO GOING PUBLIC

1. Venture Capital. Many funds specialize in less mature firms, even startups. BioStar Medical Products, Inc. raised $1 million from the Rockies Fund, a later-stage venture capital firm (see Chapter 1).

2. Limited Partnership or Joint Venture, Domestic or Foreign. The terms of these financing methods are negotiable and more control/ownership is retained. Rather than go public in a depressed market, the Briar Rose in Boulder, Colorado, raised $200,000 from a group of 12 private investors (see Section 1).

3. Self-Underwriting. To reduce costs and attain exchange listing as a public company, management can first do a self-underwriting. Century Park Pictures Corporation in Minneapolis raised $2.5 million with a self-underwriting that took only three months (see Chapter 21).

4. Combinations. Sigma Circuits, Inc. dropped out of the IPO process after spending over $300,000 on the preliminaries. The company opted instead to use an additional bank credit line and cash flow.

Initial Public Offerings: Summary Table

	Good Deal	*Bad Deal*
1. Underwriter commission	Less than 9 percent	Greater than 10 percent
2. Advance underwriter expenses	None	Greater than 2 percent
3. Share price	Realistically, greater than $5	Less than $1 stocks considered penny stocks
4. Underwriter warrants	None or priced at current market price	Priced at 90 percent or less of current market price
5. Equity give-up	Less than 30 percent	Greater than 30 percent
6. Underwriter commitment	Firm	Best efforts, all or none
7. Price/earnings ratio	10+	5 or less
8. Number of OTC market-makers	5+	Less than 5
9. Professional fees	Paid in cash	Paid in stock

The IPO Universe

Senior companies: 34.7% (revenues $10,000,000+)
Startups: 46.5% (revenues 0–$400,000)
Mid-range companies:
   10.9% (revenues $400,000–$2,500,000)
   2.0% (revenues $2,500,001–$5 million)
   5.9% (revenues $5,000,001–$10 million)

Source: *Going Public: The IPO Reporter.*

CORPORATE FUNDAMENTALS

Criteria by which experts value a company and compare it to competitors:

Revenues; net sales
Net earnings
Pretax income
Operating income
Pretax profit margin
Retained earnings
Cash balances; working capital
Dividends
Cost of sales
Stockholders' equity: net earnings less dividends
Return on stockholders' equity (ROE): net profit after taxes divided by stockholders' equity
Return on investment (ROI): net profit after taxes divided by initial investment Current ratio: current assets divided by current liabilities
Debt-to-equity ratio: long-term debt divided by stockholders equity
Price/earnings multiple: price/share divided by earnings/share
Unit sales volume

SOURCES

Most national, regional and local brokerage firms underwrite initial public offerings.
Going Public: The IPO Reporter, Philadelphia, PA.
Crocker Bank's San Francisco-based Corporate Finance Group offers the "National IPO Advisory Service." For a $50,000 fee, it will find a lead underwriter, negotiate spreads and per-share price, and suggest use-of-proceeds financing.

CHAPTER 21

Self-Underwritings

DESCRIPTION

A self-underwriting is the process by which a private company goes public without the assistance of a brokerage firm acting as an underwriter to (1) sell previously issued or newly created shares of stock to the public for the first time, (2) disclose operations to the public, (3) register with, and operate within the provisions and laws of, the Securities and Exchange Commission (SEC), National Association of Securities Dealers (NASD) and state regulatory bodies, if applicable.

A self-underwriting also can be completed to raise debt or equity capital from selected private investors under exemptions of Regulation D of the 1933 Securities Act. A private (exempt) self-underwriting does not alter private ownership of the company.

It should be noted that many states prohibit company management from self-underwriting an initial public offering, although the federal Safe Harbor Rule grants management that right if strict compliance requirements are met.

PROFILE OF A SUCCESSFUL SELF-UNDERWRITING CANDIDATE

The strongest case for going public with a self-underwriting is a small, later-stage, tightly run company that can show better value than the competition. The company should be in an industry that is gathering strength in domestic and foreign sales, with some protection from foreign competition.

Annual revenues should be about $10 million, with profits about 10 percent of revenues. Although this guideline is often relaxed for standard IPOs, self-underwritings are judged by more stringent standards. Stability and operating history also are weighted more heavily in self-underwritings. Key management contracts for senior executives should extend over two years at least, and operating history ideally should extend over a five-year period.

The company should show a minimum 10 percent growth annually for the past five years. Projections should show an increasing market share of the industry for several succeeding years and an increasing position against competitors.

The company does not need net proceeds to pay off debt. The debt-to-equity ratio, whether current or long term, should not exceed one-to-one; debt of 25 percent of total capitalization is better. Many financial institutions will not extend credit to companies in which debt exceeds capitalization by two or three times. If the company's value warrants, shares should be priced above the $2 level—closer to $5 is better—to avoid falling into the penny stock category. A self-underwriting candidate should be qualified to raise capital from other sources.

Because of the drastic drop in confidence in the IPO market the past several years, and the increasing difficulty of completing a self-underwriting, management must demonstrate strong financial sales/distribution capability within the organization in order to sell shares against a cautious, dwindling IPO market and 35,000 other listed and unlisted stocks. Successful self-underwriting examples include:

International Broadcasting Corporation
First Federal Savings & Loan Association of Colorado Springs
Mesa Medical, Inc.
Hughes Steel & Tube Ltd.

RESULTS OF A SELF-UNDERWRITING

The results of a self-underwriting are the same as the results of an initial public offering completed by a brokerage firm underwriter. The difference is that company management or a contracted broker/dealer completes the offering instead of a brokerage firm acting as underwriter.

Following successful completion of a self-underwriting, the company will be a registered public entity, subject to federal and state laws regarding public ownership. The firm will be eligible upon qualification for NASDAQ listing or New York Stock Exchange listing. Publicly held shares of stock, called "float"' can be freely bought and sold without · restriction among public shareholders. Disclosure of information about the company will be required by the SEC and shareholders on a regular basis during the life of the corporation. Substantial amounts of capital can be raised from the public market at any time in secondary offerings either through an underwriter or through self-underwriting by company management.

WHEN TO DO A SELF-UNDERWRITING

The best time for a company to consider a self-underwriting is when (1) it has a superior financial sales and distribution network in place within the organization to sell shares independently and support the aftermarket, (2) it needs access to a larger source of capital for a broader equity base and increased net asset value, (3) expansion demands public recognition, (4) operating history warrants the prestige of NASDAQ or exchange listing, (5) the stock market is receptive to new offerings, (6) the company's industry is growing or deregulating rapidly, or riding a broad economic movement, (7) the industry shows improvement on a standard market index like the SPOC or (8) the company offers bankable solutions to potential problems of the future.

Sources of Business Financing, 1987[1]
(Billions of Dollars)

	All Business	Small Business
Total Assets[2]	9,124	4,252
Total Debt[2]	3,776	1,943
Total Net Worth[2]	5,347	2,310
Other Debt and Net Worth Estimates[3]		
Trade Credit[4]	579	194
Commercial and Industrial Loans by Banks[5]	570	280
Commercial Mortgages	601	539[6]
Finance Company Receivables from Businesses	208	NA
Venture Capital Pool	29	29
Initial Public Offerings of Common Stock[7]	47	26

NA = Not available.

[1] All estimates are stock estimates valued at the end of 1987, unless otherwise noted. Small business includes all noncorporate business and small corporations with assets under $10 million.

[2] Estimates by the Federal Reserve Board for nonfarm, nonfinancial corporations and nonfarm, noncorporate businesses. Total assets and net worth for small corporations were estimated by applying 19.7 percent and 16 percent respectively to that of all corporations. Debt is treated as a residual.

[3] These estimates are obtained from sources using different methodologies. They are not strictly comparable and should not be summed for a total.

[4] Totals estimated by the Federal Reserve Board. Trade debts for small corporations were estimated by applying 25 percent to total trade debt of all nonfinancial corporations.

[5] Total commercial and industrial loans outstanding of banks other than large weekly reporting banks are used as a proxy for loans to small businesses.

[6] For nonfarm, noncorporate business only.

[7] The total estimated cumulative value of initial public offerings of common stock for the period 1976–1987.

Source: Board of Governors of the Federal Reserve System, *Balance Sheets for the U.S. Economy 1974–1987* (Washington, D.C.: Board of Governors of the Federal Reserve System, October 1988); U.S. Securities and Exchange Commission, Directorate of Economic and Policy Analysis, *Small Business Financing Trends* (Washington, D.C.: U.S. Securities and Exchange Commission, September 1988).

THE HOW-TO TIMETABLE

One to Three Years before the Self-Underwriting

1. Business Plan. This is a primary success factor in any offering, but particularly in a self-underwriting. It is the first impression an investor has of the company, and it should be complete and accurate enough to interest potential investors and sales support further. To enable investors and sales support to make a thorough assessment of the company's current condition and growth potential, the business plan should include:

Plan summary
Business description
Market analysis
Product/service description
Market strategy
Manufacturing/service operation
Management and organization
Financial data
Capital needs/timetable

2. Institutional Image. As in an initial public offering (IPO) underwritten by a brokerage house, determine how the company is perceived in the marketplace. If the company sells within a small geographic region, should shares be offered only regionally? Is the product appealing? What kind of target markets are most likely to be attracted to the product, the company niche and the industry?

3. Target Market. Special emphasis must be given to the marketplace, financial media and sales support in a self-underwriting. The company must act as its own underwriter to organize and execute the sale of its shares and the critical aftermarket support. Therefore, a delivery system for promoting the company's institutional image must be in place and be used effectively to create awareness in the marketplace.

The longer a marketing campaign has been in effect, the more responsive the marketplace tends to be. Once an offering is planned, management can publicize only company information that is contained in the prospectus or its amendments.

4. *Reorganization.* Many private companies are organized as partnerships, joint ventures or other forms of cross-ownership. The legal structure of the company may have to be modified, therefore, prior to going public. Most companies have to recapitalize to develop an appropriate capital structure for the public offering, or split the stock forward or backward to adjust the pricing level at which the self-underwriting will be sold.

5. *Legal Review.* The SEC requires that public firms disclose all significant transactions between company-related associates. Although the company's private transactions between officers and shareholders serve a private company well, they may not be perceived the same way by public shareholders or the SEC. It is important for self-underwriting companies to have competent legal advice well in advance of the offering to replace the additional legal review that underwriters normally require. A legal review of the following should occur before the self-underwriting procedure begins:

> Corporate charter and bylaws
> Shareholder or management loans
> Lease agreements
> Debt outstanding
> Stock option or purchase plans
> Employment contracts
> Supply contracts and arrangements
> Rights of first refusal

Six Months to One Year before the Self-Underwriting

Third-Party Professionals. A number of professionals, some of them from outside the company, should be involved in a self-underwriting to provide technical or specialized assistance. They should be interviewed and selected carefully.

Company management should be expanded if necessary, based on the capability to perform job functions as well as on willingness to accept accountability to public shareholders and regulatory bodies before and after the self-underwriting.

Attorneys with specialized securities training, preferably in self-underwriting, should be retained to support in-house counsel. This is critical for self-underwriting companies that will not have legal review by an underwriter.

Accountants with specialized securities training also should be retained to support in-house expertise.

A financial printer with the specialized ability to produce SEC-related documents should be hired.

Sophisticated public relations or financial consulting promotion specialists who identify and target potential markets should be retained well in advance of the quiet period. Promotion of the company's institutional image and viability as a public concern, by prospectus information only, is critical to a successful offering.

Underwriter support should be sought although self-underwriting is orchestrated without a brokerage firm as primary underwriter. Management can contract for a registered broker/dealer to provide sales support. Some states do not allow self-underwriting unless a registered broker/dealer is selling the shares.

Six Months before the Self-Underwriting

1. An initial planning session is held by all company executives, corporate attorneys and accountants, and financial consultants or public relations experts (if applicable) to discuss the terms of the offering, determine the kind of offering it will be and assign specific responsibilities for preparation of the registration statement. At this time, the offering price and size are discussed, as well as how to supplement corporate sales efforts during the offering period. If a broker/dealer is brought in to help sell shares, the commission structure (usually 7 percent to 10 percent of the maximum aggregate offering price), expenses and other terms are decided.

Responsibility for producing Part I of the registration statement is assigned. Part I consists of a prospectus, which is distributed to prospective investors and participating brokers, if any.

Part II includes information that must be provided to the SEC, and state regulators if applicable. Parts I and II, which are required and determined by the S-1 and S-18 rules, become part of the public record, including:

Outside Front Cover: Summarize all key offering facts.

Inside Front and Outside Back Cover: Include the table of contents, price data and information about how the company will expedite the offering.

Prospectus Summary: Give a company overview, offering description, net proceeds and their use, and selected financial data.

Company Background: Provide detailed information and an overview of the firm's primary business.

Risk Factors: Assess risks in the company, industry and market; these appear only in the prospectus of a low-priced offering.

Use of Proceeds: Disclose the company's intended use of the net proceeds of the offering, including debt payment or acquisitions.

Dilution: Report, in tabular form, any material dilution of the prospective investors' equity interest caused by a disparity between the offering price and tangible book value of the share before the offering. This information appears only if insider stock has been purchased in the last five years at a price lower than the offering price.

Dividend Policy: Review the company's dividend history and current policy. Any restriction or reinvestment of dividends must be disclosed.

Capitalization: Detail data on the company's equity capital and debt structure, before and after the offering. The pro forma capital structure after the offering should be adjusted to reflect the securities issued and the intended use of proceeds.

Selected Financial Data: Show financial data for each of the previous five years, the interim period since the last year-end and the comparative interim period of the preceding year.

Management Analysis: Explain the financial condition and results of operations for the last three fiscal years, trends, cash flow, liquidity and capital resources, expected sources of capital and longer-range plans. Management analysis is the key disclosure analyzed by investment professionals.

Detailed Business Description

Properties of the Business

Legal Proceedings: Describe actions other than routine litigation.

Management and Security-Holder Backgrounds: Give biographical data, compensation, loans, transactions with promoters, shareholdings, and golden parachute arrangements.

Description of Registered Securities: Describe title, dividend rights, conversion and voting rights, liquidation rights and warrant terms.

Self-Underwriting Terms: Give a description, distribution plan, syndication participants, number of shares underwritten by each underwriter, method, material relations between the company and syndicators, compensation if any, board representation and indemnification.

Legal review: Name attorneys and report their legal opinions on the validity of the offering, any shareholdings, independent contractors to the underwriting and how to obtain Part II of the registration statement.

2. Financial Statements. Provide the accounting report as well as audited balance sheets up to the end of each of the past two fiscal years, audited statements of income, changes in financial position and shareholders' equity for each of the past three fiscal years, and some unaudited interim statements if applicable.

The following information should be included in Part II of the registration statement (but not included in the printed prospectus):

Expenses of issuance and distribution

Indemnification or insurance for liability of officers and directors acting on behalf of the company

Various financial statement schedules

Sales of unregistered securities in the past three years

Written consent of all experts who have certified or prepared any material in Parts I and II

Exhibits, including subsidiaries, syndication agreements, charter and bylaws, and material contracts

It normally takes about two months to prepare Parts I and II of the registration statement. Allow another month to revise and obtain signatures from all parties including the board of directors. The completed document is filed with the SEC about 90 days after the first planning session.

Three Months before the Self-Underwriting

1. Once the registration statement has been filed with the SEC, a "road show" is staged by company management, who meet with prospective syndicate participants to promote the company and the offering. Promotion at this point must be by invitation only; by law, a company cannot promote by general solicitation orpublic advertising until after the "quiet period." The promotion literature is a preliminary version of the prospectus called the "red herring." While the road show is in progress, the SEC's Division of Corporate Finance is evaluating the registration statement, and will comment on its contents within two or three months. If the SEC requires revisions in the registration statement, final changes are made before the company becomes effective—or legally allowed to sell shares.

2. During the time up to 90 days after the effective date—the quiet period—company executives and syndication participants can disclose publicly only those facts contained in the prospectus or its amendments. During this time, corporate attorneys will blue sky the offering to satisfy securities regulations in all states in which the offering is to be sold. Merit states must approve the prospectus.

3. Shortly before the effective date, a due diligence meeting is held by all offering organizers for the underwriting syndicate, if any, enabling them to raise final questions about the offering or the company.

4. The night before, or the morning of, the effective date, final considerations are set by management: offering price, commissions (if any) and net proceeds. This data plus revisions to the registration statement are filed with the SEC as a final amendment known as the "pricing amendment."

Among larger companies, pending or completed acquisitions of publicly traded companies reached 462 in 1988, an increase of 62 percent from 286 the year before. There was an 82 percent increase in total value, from $85.9 billion in 1987 to $156.1 billion in 1988 among those companies that disclosed the purchase price.

Acquisitions of Publicly Traded Companies*
1974–1988

Year	Total Transactions	Transactions valued at $100MM or More	Transactions valued at $1,000MM or More	Total Dollar Value Paid (millions of dollars)	Base**
1974	68	#	—	#	
1975	130	#	1	#	
1976	163	#	—	#	
1977	193	#	—	#	
1978	260	61	1	#	
1979	248	57	2	#	
1980	173	54	3	#	
1981	168	62	10	$56,569.4	156
1982	180	65	6	31,501.8	176
1983	190	73	8	39,471.4	181
1984	211	95	15	82,731.0	204
1985	336	134	28	116,675.5	321
1986	386	150	18	89,866.2	352
1987	286	128	22	85,924.9	267
1988	462	172	29	156,112.9	436

= Data not collected that year.
*Purchase of a controlling interest.
**Base: the number of transactions disclosing a purchase price.

Source: *Mergerstat Review.*

FILING REQUIREMENTS

All public companies are subject to the federal reporting/disclosure requirements of the SEC, whether the offering is sold by an underwriter or by company management. Reporting documents include proxy statements, the annual report to shareholders, quarterly financial report (Form 10-Q), annual financial report (Form 10-K), reports about current material events in the company (Form 8-K) and other reports for audited financial statements, the sale of control shares and tender offers.

In addition, public companies must meet any reporting/disclosure requirements of the states in which shares are offered (the blue sky process). State requirements differ widely.

The NASD must approve underwriter compensation prior to the effective date, if applicable to secondary underwriters who form the selling syndicate.

COSTS

1. Many companies expedite a self-underwriting with the assistance of a broker/dealer that contracts independently to help sell shares. Broker commissions vary according to the size and structure of the offering, stability of the company and industry, competition in the brokerage industry and market conditions. Usually the commission is between 7 percent and 10 percent of the maximum aggregate price of the offering. Most commissions fall between $200,000 and $300,000 on offerings of between $2 million and $3 million. Like standard IPOs, small self-underwritings range up to $10 million.

2. For a $2 million self-underwriting, legal, accounting and marketing out-of-pocket expenses to third-party professionals may cost between $20,000 and $30,000, depending on the preparedness of the company in structure and legal status. Companies that need extensive legal or accounting assistance to organize the offering can spend much more.

3. Printing costs range from $50,000 for a small offering up to $200,000, including revisions and color photographs.

4. Filing fees are similar to those for an underwritten IPO. SEC filing costs .02 percent of the maximum aggregate offering price. NASD filing costs $100 plus .01 percent of the maximum aggregate offering price, with a $5,100 maximum. State blue sky filing fees vary up to $15,000. Registrar and transfer agent fees range between $5,000 and $10,000.

5. Self-underwritings gain the most benefit from a financial public relations consultant who can attract potential target markets with appropriate marketing materials. These firms are paid by project or by monthly retainer, which ranges from $3,000 to $10,000 per month.

6. The hidden cost of a self-underwriting is the number of hours spent by corporate executives who must complete all the tasks normally done by a primary underwriting firm. Depending on how highly executive time is valued, and how well-prepared the company is to begin a self-underwriting, the cost of labor in both time spent and lost opportunities can be quite high.

7. Add one-third to one-half the price of going public for the annual legal, accounting, compliance, mailing and hidden costs of remaining a public concern.

ADVANTAGES AND DISADVANTAGES

Advantages

1. The primary benefit is the net proceeds of the offering, which average from $1 million to $10 million. These funds can be used for anything from acquisition of capital equipment for growth to research and development.

2. By going public, the company has a broader equity base and larger net asset value. It is thus easier to borrow additional funds because of the enhanced debt-to-equity ratio.

3. Companies that do a self-underwriting save from $200,000 to $300,000 in underwriting expenses, on average, plus out-of-pocket expenses that start at 2.5 percent of the value of the offering.

4. Stock exchange or NASDAQ listing is possible if the company qualifies. This means corporate image is enhanced, the company will receive more attention from the media, and key employees are more easily retained with stock options and purchase plans.

5. After two years, management estates can become more liquid with the sale of insider shares and the existence of a public market for the control shares.

Disadvantages

1. Company management will lose some or all control over the firm depending on share value and how many shares are sold to the public. Future acquisitions and offerings may dilute the stock, hence control, even further.

2. A self-underwriting is the most time-consuming way to raise capital. All preparation, filing, sales and aftermarket support work must be completed by management in the absence of a primary underwriter.

3. Going public is the most expensive way to raise capital. Standard IPO costs can range, on average, more than $100,000 above other financing techniques because of underwriter commissions. The cost of man hours devoted to a self-underwriting can approach $100,000, which cancels out the cost savings.

4. Management must sell its shares against 35,000 other listed and unlisted stocks in the aftermarket. Without the support of a brokerage firm, management has to persuade market-makers to continue trading in order to have a market in the stock for future profits.

5. Public stockholders are now management partners, entitled to share all information about the business and its management, including remuneration at all levels and the company's competitive position. Management will be held accountable to public shareholders for everything on the financial statements, as well as for its administration of the company.

6. Control or insider shareholders in management are not free to sell shares at will. Stringent SEC regulations determine when and how insider shares can be sold.

7. The ongoing costs of remaining a public company are steep: one-third to one-half of the cost of the initial offering annually.

8. By going public, management will not have access to several other sources of financing.

TESTING THE WATERS

During normal market activity, an IPO is rated by the 70/20/10 rule: the potential of offerings is determined 70 percent by the mood of the market, 20 percent by industry popularity and only 10 percent by company value.

For self-underwritings, the rule changes drastically. The potential of the offering is determined almost equally by market conditions and by the company's sales capability. If the current market is not receptive to IPOs, sales ability takes on greater importance.

Many investors fear that a self-underwriting lacks brokerage support because no securities firm has agreed to underwrite the offering. A self-underwriting has to be sold against that preconception with salesmanship and a track record that are better than average.

ALTERNATIVES TO A SELF-UNDERWRITING

1. *Private Placement.* Freeman Productions, Inc. raised $100,000 to purchase audio and video production products and develop new products (see Chapter 23).

2. *Hire an Underwriter.* If the IPO market is slow, competition among underwriters often enables a company to negotiate both lower commissions and upfront costs. The key is to strike a balance between a firm small enough to want to negotiate and large enough to have sales clout (see Chapter 21).

3. *Debt Offering.* If the equity market is soft or if the company's debt/equity balance can support additional debt financing, management can turn to debt offerings, which cost far

less than equity offerings. Jones Intercable, Inc., which had used limited partnerships to finance growth, switched to a bond offering that netted nearly $30 million (see Chapter 19).

SOURCES

Going Public: The IPO Reporter, Philadelphia, PA.
Inc. magazine, New York, NY.

PITFALLS TO AVOID

Overpricing the shares adds to the difficulty of selling a self-underwriting. The per-share price should be evaluated carefully to conform to the balanced debt/equity needs of the company and to the perceived value of the stock in the marketplace.

The agreement with secondary underwriters who provide sales support should outline the specific amounts of stock they will sell and their commission rate.

The number of shares or warrants offered to self-underwriting participants should be monitored so that cumulative amounts of equity are not given away for services rendered. Participants in the self-underwriting should be paid from the proceeds.

CHAPTER 22

Preferred Stock

DESCRIPTION

Preferred stock is the third type of security, along with bonds and common stock, that is used to raise capital. It is a class of capital stock, junior to debt obligations which are always paid first, that can be issued by private or public companies. It pays dividends at a specific rate and has preference over common stock, but not debt, in dividend payment and asset liquidation. Like common stock, some preferred shares carry voting rights in the company, and sometimes special voting rights.

In addition to paying dividends, preferred issuers can contract to buy back an amount of preferred annually. The dollar amount held to buy the shares back may be fixed or variable. As the number of preferred shares in the marketplace dwindles, the value of those shares outstanding can increase, depending on how the stock is valued based on the interest rate.

Most companies are required under special terms of the sale to establish a sinking fund with which to guarantee orderly buybacks. Most preferred is cumulative, which means if dividends are passed (delayed), or not paid, they accumulate and must be paid before common dividends. There are several varieties of preferred stock, and each should be evaluated as part of a debt/common stock package as a means of raising capital.

Noncumulative Preferred: If dividends are passed, they are almost never paid.

Participating Preferred: Shareholders can profit from capital gains, as well as from declared dividends as common shareholders do.

Nonparticipating Preferred: The stock pays only the specified dividend.

Adjustable-Rate Preferred: An adjustable quarterly dividend is paid based on a variable Treasury bill or other money-market rate.

Convertible Preferred: This kind of preferred is exchangeable for a determinable number of common shares.

Nonconvertible Preferred: Less volatile, this stock resembles a fixed-income bond.

Prior-Preferred: Also called preference shares, this stock is senior to other issues of preferred and common stock in dividend payment and in claim on assets during liquidation.

PROFILE OF A SUCCESSFUL PREFERRED STOCK ISSUE

Most companies that are advised to issue preferred stock place it between debt and common stock in such a way that current and long-term debt ratios do not overwhelm equity security, and common stock is not devalued by excessive use of preferred or by potential capital problems.

Many investors in preferred stock are institutional buyers who look for strong issuers that can offer the security with terms that make it clearly senior to common stock in rights, but not restrictive enough to make the preferred subject to contractual debt obligations. Institutional buyers usually want preferred issued by a company that offers only one class of this security. They also look for issuers in sound enough financial condition to prevent the potential dissipation of assets and earnings.

Most preferred issuers have a five- to ten-year operating history, profits commensurate with or better than industry competitors and a debt ratio for long- or short-term obligations that do not exceed by one the value of assets.

The company should have solid internal resources and/or the potential to sell future preferred offerings that will finance the retirement of scheduled amounts of outstanding preferred. Strong cash flow and current assets relationships include current ratio, net current assets, and inventory and receivables turnover.

Noncyclical or nonseasonal companies with stable sales and earnings potential, and built-in growth potential of at least 10 percent annually, are strong candidates for preferred.

Successful preferred issuers include:

Koppers Co.
Dest Corporation
Goldome National
Encore Computer Corporation

RESULTS OF PREFERRED STOCK

Issuance of preferred results in supplementary capital raised without endangering borrowing reserve or financial insurance, increasing debt ratios, or devaluing the quality of the company's common stock. Preferred stock, which has no voting rights unless specified, can dilute the common if it is convertible or exchangeable.

The many classes of preferred can be tailored to the needs and suitability of the corporate capital structure and market desirability. Preferred backed by a sinking fund is usually easier to sell, because these shares resemble and are called "junior" or "baby" bonds for their safety provisions. But sinking fund provisions increase the future capital-raising burden because the cost of buy-back shares usually must be financed.

WHEN TO ISSUE PREFERRED STOCK

The time to issue preferred is when (1) the company is in strong financial condition, (2) debt ratios are nearing a comfortable limit, (3) preferred issuance does not endanger the quality of the company's common stock, (4) there is institutional interest in the company, (5) the company does not need large amounts of capital, and/or (6) interest rates are low.

THE HOW-TO TIMETABLE

Nine Months before the Offering

It is recommended that preferred stock offerings be evaluated, prepared and sold by an underwriter and professional team of specialists who are familiar with preferred offerings and the company's industry. The evaluation process on preferred is more complex than straight debt or common stock because this security must be carefully positioned within the company's total capital structure.

The underwriter will:

Determine amount, rate, terms and timing
Help establish the protective provisions and interest rate
Prepare the prospectus
Sell the offering to appropriate investors

Several underwriters should be interviewed before selection, based on:

Broker/dealer experience in preferred stock offerings
Individual broker experience and "style"
Services offered by the underwriter
Fee structure, including upfront and potential hidden costs

Six Months before the Offering

A planning session is held by all company executives, corporate attorneys and accountants, and representatives of the underwriting firm, to evaluate terms of the offering and assign specific responsibilities for preparation of the registration statement (for public companies) or offering circular (for private companies).

Part I of the registration statement is a prospectus which is distributed to underwriters and prospective investors; Part II is information that must be provided to the SEC and state regulators if applicable. Parts I and II, which are required and determined by the SEC, become part of the public record.

The prospectus should contain:

Outside Front Cover: Summarize all key offering facts.

Inside Front and Outside Back Cover: Include the table of contents, price data and an underwriter disclaimer on delivery requirements.

Prospectus Summary: Give a company overview, offering description, net proceeds and use of proceeds, selected financial data.

Company Background: Provide detailed information and an overview of the firm's primary business.

Risk Factors: Assess risks inherent in the company, industry and market; risk factors appear only the prospectus of a low-priced offering.

Dilution: Report, in tabular form, any material dilution of the investors' equity caused by a disparity between the offering price and tangible book value of the share before the offering. This information appears only if insider stock has been purchased in the past five years at a lower price than the offering price.

Use of Proceeds: Disclose the company's intended use of the net proceeds of the offering, including debt payment or acquisitions.

Dividend Policy: Review the company's dividend history and current policy, if any. The restriction or reinvestment of dividends must be disclosed.

Capitalization: Detail data on the company equity capital and debt structure, before and after the offering. The pro forma capital structure after the offering should be adjusted to reflect the securities issued and the intended use of proceeds.

Selected Financial Data: Show financial data for each of the previous five years, the interim period since the last year-end and the comparative interim period of the preceding year.

Management Analysis: Analyze the financial condition and results of operations for the past three fiscal years, trends, cash flow, liquidity and capital resources, expected sources of capital and longer-range plans. This section is the most important to professional investment analysts.

Detailed Business Description

Properties of the Business:

Legal Proceedings: Describe actions other than routine litigation.

Management and Security Holder Backgrounds: Give biographical data, compensation, loans, transactions with promoters, shareholdings and golden parachute arrangements.

Description of Registered Securities: Describe title, dividend rights, conversion and voting rights, liquidation rights and warrant terms.

Underwriting: Provide a description, a distribution plan, principal underwriters in the syndication, number of shares underwritten by each underwriter, method, material relations between the company and underwriters, compensation, board representation and indemnification.

Legal Review: Name attorneys and report their opinions on the validity of the offering, any shareholdings, independent contractors to the underwriting, and how to obtain Part II of the registration statement.

Financial Statements: Show the accounting report as well as audited balance sheets up to the end of each of the past two fiscal years, audited statements of income, changes in financial position, shareholders' equity for each of the past three fiscal years and some unaudited interim statements, if applicable.

The following information should appear in Part II of the registration statement (but do not include in the printed prospectus):

Expenses of issuance and distribution

Indemnification or insurance for liability of officers and directors acting on behalf of the company

Various financial statement schedules

Sales of unregistered securities in the last three years

Written consent of all experts who have certified or prepared any material included in Parts I and II

Exhibits, including all subsidiaries, underwriting agreement, charter and bylaws and material contracts

Generally, it takes about two months to prepare Parts I and II of the registration statement. Revisions will take another month and then signatures by all parties, including the company's board of directors, must be obtained. The completed document is filed with the SEC about 90 days after the first planning session.

Three Months before the Offering

1. Once the registration statement has been filed with the SEC, a "road show" is staged by management and the underwriter, who meet with syndication participants to describe the company and the offering with a preliminary version of the prospectus called the "red herring." During the road show, the SEC's Division of Corporate Finance evaluates the registration statement, and will comment on the contents two or three months later. The SEC may require revisions in the registration statement before permitting the offering to be sold.

2. The time prior to SEC comment is the quiet period. Company and underwriter participants cannot disclose information about the offering or the company that does not appear in the prospectus or its amendments. During this time, attorneys will "blue sky" the offering to satisfy securities regulations in all states in which the offering is to be sold.

3. Shortly before the effective date, a due-diligence meeting is held by all offering participants for the underwriting syndicate, enabling them to raise final questions about the offering or the company.

4. The night before, or the morning of, the effective date, when the offering can be sold, final considerations are agreed to regarding offering price, final buy-back terms, underwriter's commission and net proceeds. This data plus revisions to the registration statement are filed as a final amendment known as the "pricing amendment."

FILING REQUIREMENTS

All preferred issuers that are public companies are subject to reporting/disclosure requirements of the SEC. Reporting documents include a quarterly financial report (Form 10-Q), annual financial report (Form 10-K), proxy statements, annual report to shareholders, reports about current material events in the company (Form 8-K) and other reports for audited financial statements, the sale of control shares and tender offers.

In addition, public companies must meet any reporting/disclosure requirements of the states in which shares are offered (called the blue sky process). State requirements differ widely. The NASD has to approve the underwriter compensation provisions of the prospectus prior to the effective date.

Preferred stock issuers that are private companies must file registration and disclosure documents in accordance with the specific Regulation D exemption under which the offering is structured.

COSTS

A preferred stock offering by a public company costs about as much as an initial public offering, between 14 percent and 18 percent of the funds raised.

A complete discussion of public offering costs is found in Chapter 1. Ongoing annual costs will total from one-third to one-half the cost of the initial offering.

ADVANTAGES AND DISADVANTAGES

Advantages

1. Failure to meet offering terms will not result in bankruptcy.
2. The cost of raising capital is about 30 percent less when preferred is issued instead of secondary common stock.

3. Borrowing reserve and financial insurance are preserved.

4. Preferred carries no maturity unless investors require a sinking fund to guarantee the annual buy-back of a certain number of outstanding shares.

5. If the financial condition of the company is strong, the quality of the common shares is undiminished, nor are debt ratios altered by a preferred offering.

Disadvantages

1. In order to guarantee buy-back of a certain number of shares outstanding every year, the company may have to either establish a sinking fund from available cash, or reissue new shares of preferred to finance the buy-back.

2. If the offering terms are too restrictive in order to satisfy investors, the offering may limit future unsecured borrowing or other long-term debt financing.

3. The quality of common shares may diminish during bad economic times if too much preferred is issued.

4. Management must pay ongoing costs to keep the preferred offering in registration.

TESTING THE WATERS

The test of whether or not benefits will accrue from the preferred offering is found by evaluating the company's existing capital structure. If management wants to issue a security but more debt would adversely affect debt ratios, or more equity would dilute the common, preferred stock is a good compromise.

ALTERNATIVES TO PREFERRED STOCK

1. *Debt*: If debt ratios—debt-to-equity or current liabilities to current assets—are not too high, management may want to sell a debt issue. Many new or young companies are getting initial

capitalization from private convertible debt issues. Snugli, Inc. raised $250,000 in initial financing to manufacture and sell canvas child-carriers (see Chapter 17).

2. *Equity*: If management wants to avoid long-term obligations, a private or public equity issue can raise capital for startup or expansion. Venture Group, Inc. raised more than $2 million by selling 5 million shares at $.50 per share to establish its financial consulting practice (see Section 6).

SOURCES

Institutional Investor: Crane Publishing, Chicago, IL.

Most national, regional and local brokerage firms underwrite preferred stock offerings.

PITFALLS TO AVOID

Preferred stock should be issued sparingly in specific circumstances such as venture capital investments. If preferred is issued too often, it can devalue the common stock.

Avoid preferred stock that is so restrictive it becomes subject to contractual debt obligations. Most investors want preferred that is senior to common stock in rights.

Avoid the temptation to issue more than one class of preferred, which can contribute to the gradual dissipation of earnings and assets.

CHAPTER 23

Private Placements/ Exempt Offerings

DESCRIPTION

A private placement is an offering of equity or debt security, with or without the assistance of an agent, by a publicly or privately held company to a limited number of selected investors in order to raise capital. Shares are sold for investment not resale purposes. Private placement of debt securities is described in Chapter 8.

These offerings require simplified filing with the SEC, and may require filing with state regulatory bodies. Private placements are exempt from certain requirements of registration under the Securities Act of 1933; Regulation D describes the exemptions to SEC registration requirements and the conditions of exemption.

A private placement, also called a "limited" offering, "Reg D" offering or "unregistered" offering, is an umbrella term for several categories of issues: 504s, 505s, 506s (all Reg D offerings) and private placements [Section 4(6)].

Other issues also can fall under simplified filing exemptions, but these are public offerings: intrastate offerings or 147s (Rule 147) unregistered public offerings (Reg A) and S-18s [Simplified Registration Form S-18]. A comparison of private placements and simplified public offerings appears in the chart on pages 297–298.

PROFILE OF A SUCCESSFUL PRIVATE PLACEMENT CANDIDATE

The company is small, later-stage and has annual revenues of under $10 million. Operating history shows at least two years of profitability in the range of 5 to 10 percent of revenues. Company management is stable, with key-employee contracts in place for top-level executives. Annual growth has averaged at least 5 percent for each of the past two years, or the company is positioned to take advantage of growth conditions in a strong industry that is free from significant foreign competition. Short- or long-term debt does not exceed total capitalization and the company has other sources of capital, like a bank line of credit. The company shows increases, or the probability of increases, in market share, unit sales volume, pretax profit margin and return on shareholders' equity.

Examples of successful private placements include:

HealthMark, Inc.
Avtek Corporation
Parallel Computers, Inc.
Imagen Corporation
Microage, Inc.

RESULTS OF A PRIVATE PLACEMENT

Successful completion of any private placement will result in a specific amount of capital raised under simpler registration requirements, and with minimum disclosure and reporting to federal and/or state regulatory bodies. Limitations on the amount raised, depending on the kind of private placement offered, are covered later in this chapter.

Private placements maintain private ownership, and usually control, of the company. Confidentiality about the business of the company and its financial statements is maintained for the most part, and only a limited amount of registration data becomes part of the public record.

Because companies that sell private offerings have quasi-public status, resale of private shares is greatly restricted. Resale is permitted under special conditions by Rule 144 (insider or control shares are called "144 shares"). The company is excluded from stock-exchange listing.

WHEN TO MAKE A PRIVATE PLACEMENT OFFERING

A private placement should be offered when the company (1) wants to raise short-term capital or bridge financing, perhaps quickly, (2) doesn't want to go public, and/or prefers simplified registration and fewer disclosure/reporting requirements, (3) has a small pool of interested potential investors, (4) when the stock market is not receptive to initial public offerings or other financing techniques, (5) the company is in a strong growth mode, either realized or potential or (6) the company's industry is growing, deregulating rapidly or riding a broad economic movement or industry index like Value Line.

Competing with private placement and other stock offers are divestitures of large corporations which reflect the growing trend among buyers to pay higher prices for existing businesses rather than startups, and among sellers to divest major units.

Value of Divestitures 1982–1988

Number (Percent of Transactions Disclosing Price)

Price-Paid Value	1982	1983	1984	1985	1986	1987	1988
$5 million or less	82 (26)	108 (29)	69 (17)	104 (20)	76 (14)	29 (7)	30 (7)
$5.1–10.0 million	60 (19)	55 (15)	54 (13)	69 (13)	60 (11)	24 (6)	35 (8)
$10.1–15.0 million	32 (10)	30 (8)	32 (8)	50 (10)	45 (8)	27 (7)	21 (5)
$15.1–25.0 million	30 (9)	34 (9)	47 (12)	47 (9)	74 (14)	42 (11)	58 (13)
$25.1–50.0 million	37 (12)	57 (15)	65 (16)	70 (13)	76 (14)	72 (19)	79 (18)
$50.1–99.9 million	35 (11)	39 (10)	51 (13)	65 (12)	66 (12)	57 (15)	60 (13)
$100 million or more	41 (13)	53 (14)	83 (21)	120 (23)	146 (27)	137 (35)	162 (36)
Base*	317	376	401	525	543	388	445

*Base: Number of transactions disclosing a price.
Source: *Mergerstat Review.*

THE HOW-TO TIMETABLE

One Year before the Private Placement Offering

    1. *Business Plan.* A full discussion of business plan contents is found in Chapter 20.

    2. *Target Market.* The potential markets for company products should be identified and reached effectively with a marketing campaign promoting the company's institutional image and product. The longer a targeted marketing campaign has been in effect in advance of the offering, the more responsive the marketplace is likely to be.

    3. *Third-Party Professionals.* Outside professionals may need to provide technical or specialized assistance to in-house executives. Individuals and firms should be carefully screened and selected for expertise in private offerings; they include:

> Attorney/law firm
> Accountant/CPA firm
> Financial printer
> Investment banker to act as agent of the offering, if desired

Six Months before the Private Placement Offering

    1. *Legal Review.* Certain aspects of the company's business have a direct bearing on the type and amount of the private placement a company is eligible to offer. They should be reviewed before the offering is packaged, including:

> Corporate charter and bylaws
> Shareholder or management loans
> Lease agreements
> Debt outstanding
> Stock option or purchase plans
> Employment contracts
> Supplier contracts and arrangements
> Rights of first refusal

2. Audit. Historical audited financial statements and highlights of the company's operations are proof of its size and earnings. Audits of each of the past two or three years, plus an audited statement of the last fiscal year and quarter, should be completed before the private placement memorandum, or circular, is packaged.

3. Sales Marketing. Develop a list of potentially qualified and interested investors that conforms to the requirements of the specific offering exemption. Limitations on both the type and the number of investors allowed vary among different exempt private offerings (see the chart on pages 297–298).

Three Months before the Private Placement Offering

1. A planning session is held with management, attorneys, accountants and investment bankers who act as agent to the offering, if any. The purpose is to prepare the financing memorandum, also called a "private placement memorandum" or "offering circular." This document, which is governed by S-1 or S-18 requirements, facilitates analysis of the company and the offering by potential investors before they make a decision to participate in the offering. The memorandum should include the following sections:

Cover Page: Summarize proposed financing amount, timing, purpose and type.

Company Summary: Cover background data, size, lines of business, date and state of incorporation, major divisions and subsidiaries, recent financial results, and management plans and expections.

Capitalization: Review existing and pro forma capitalization based on the most recent balance sheet: long-term debt and lease obligations, short-term bank loans and usage, contingent liabilities or guarantees, equity, and percentage ownership of officers, directors and major stockholders.

Products/Markets: Detail product or service and market, historical and projected growth, sales and pretax profits by product for the past five years, new product plans, and research and development efforts.

Marketing: Discuss strategy, distribution, pricing, customers, sales volume and sales contracts including foreign distribution.

Competition: Specify the nature of the competition, major competitors, market share and company niche in the industry.

Manufacturing: Report location, nature, size, capacity and utilization of manufacturing facilities; their ownership or lease status; capital expenditures; methods and costs; raw materials and/or components; and company status under federal/OSHA, state and local regulations.

Management: Include an organization chart, biographies of key managers, compensation, company directors, outside affiliations, size and nature of staff/labor force, wage and benefit plans, and financial aspects of the pension fund, if any.

Business Risks: Assess major risks faced by the company and their historical impact, management prevention and major pending litigation.

Historical/Financial Data: Provide audited income statements, balance sheets, sources and uses of funds, and related data for the past three years; abrupt changes in financial condition; acquisitions; financial policies including dividends, capital structure, return on investment objectives, operating/capital budget and long-range planning.

Exhibits: Show annual reports and consolidated financial statements for the past five years, interim reports for the current year, recent prospectuses if any, most recent 10-K and proxy statement, if applicable, existing loan and lease agreements, and the current year's operating budget.

Forecast: Predict major changes in management, labor and operating policy: acquisitions or deletions; use of proceeds; income statement, balance sheet and sources and uses of funds statement for the next five years (incorporating proposed financing); future capital requirements and sources.

2. An investment letter must be prepared and produced by the date sales begin. This document must be read and signed by every qualified purchaser of private stock, certifying that the pur-

Public and Private Offerings

| | IPO | Private and Limited Regulation D | | |
		Rule 504	Rule 505	Rule 506
Disclosure requirements	Yes	Not specified	If one or more nonaccredited investors	
Financial statements requirements	Yes	Not specified	Variable	Variable
Issuer qualifications	Private company	Not specified	No investment or reporting companies	No investment or "bad boy" companies
Buyer qualifications	No	No	No	Nonaccredited must be sophisticated
Dollar limit	No	$500,000	$5 million	No
Number of buyers limit	No	No	35 nonaccredited, any number accredited	
General solicitation requirements	No	Yes	Yes	Yes
Resale restrictions	No	Yes	Yes	Yes
Public company	No	Yes	Yes	Yes
Private company	Yes	Yes	Yes	Yes
Self-underwriting	Yes	Yes	Yes	Yes

chase is for investment, not resale, purposes. It states the conditions and limitations of the particular exempt offering.

3. Filing: Management or its agent may have to file some registration/ disclosure documentation with the SEC and/or state regulatory bodies, depending on the type of offering.

Public and Private Offerings (Continued)

	Private Placement Sec. 4(6)	Simplified Registration Form S–18	Intrastate Offerings Rule 147	Unregistered Public Offerings Reg. A
Disclosure requirements	Not specified	Yes	Not specified	Yes
Financial statements requirements	No	Two years' audited statements	Not specified	Two years' audited statements
Issuer qualifications	Accredited investors	No investment or reporting companies		No investment, reporting or mineral rights companies
Buyer qualifications	$5 million	No	Residents of one state	No
Dollar limit	All accredited	$7.5 million	No	$1.5 million
Number of buyers limit	Yes	No	No	No
General solicitation requirements	Yes	No	No	No
Resale restrictions	Yes	No	Yes	No
Public company	Yes	No	Yes	No
Private company	Yes	Yes	Yes	Yes
Self-underwriting	Yes	Yes	Yes	Yes

Offering Date

Sale of private stock can begin on the date selected by management, when the offering memorandum and investment letter are available for distribution to potential investors. All companies that sell a private offering must file notice of sale of their stock on Form D within 15 days of the first sale and every six months, and a final notice within 30 days after the last sale.

FILING REQUIREMENTS

Filing requirements, descriptions, costs, the limitation on the number of purchasers, dollar amounts, qualification for purchasers and issuers, disclosure requirements, resale restrictions and solicitation prohibitions are included in the following chart for all types of private placement offerings.

Accredited investors are certain institutions, or individual purchasers whose net worth exceeds $1 million or whose income in each of the past two years exceeded $200,000 and who have an understanding of the risks involved in the offering.

Resale restrictions are covered under Rule 144 of the 1933 Securities Act. They stipulate that purchasers of private stock must buy for investment, not resale, purposes. Unless specifically indicated, 144 stock cannot be sold until two years after stock purchase.

The "bad boy" provision prohibits a company or investment banking firm acting as agent to the offering from participating in an exempt offering, to prevent specific acts of misconduct regarding securities laws. The provision includes management, officers, general partners, directors and/or major shareholders, and underwriters and their partners, officers and directors.

COSTS

Most private placements are only slightly less costly than a public offering. The total cost can range from $20,000 to $500,000 includ-

ing legal, accounting, filing and printing costs. A full discussion of
the costs related to a public offering are found in Chapter 1.

ADVANTAGES AND DISADVANTAGES

Advantages

1. Management can avoid some or all of the time-consuming
SEC registration/ disclosure requirements of public ownership.
2. Management can raise capital in less time and at slightly
less cost by not going public.
3. Friends, employees and associates can acquire private
company stock at a more beneficial price with a private offering.
4. More control is retained by company founders/owners/
management by remaining private with an exempt offering.

Disadvantages:

1. Regulation D limits the number and qualification of
private investors, as well as the amount raised, in some offerings.
2. Resale of private shares is restricted and lack of a public
market creates other obvious resale constraints.
3. Private companies do not receive as much media and
analyst attention as public entities do.
4. Share price may be lower because of limitations on the
number of purchasers and on resale of shares.
5. Private companies cannot apply for NASDAQ or stock exchange listing.

TESTING THE WATERS

There is no guideline for timing a private offering. A company
that has inherent value and growth potential usually can benefit
from active private investors who tend to invest regardless of
stock-market volatility.

ALTERNATIVES TO A PRIVATE PLACEMENT

1. Going Public. If management wants to raise substantial amounts of capital from a broader equity base and is willing to give up confidentiality and some control of the company, an initial public offering can be beneficial. The Institute of Clinical Pharmacology went public to raise over $7 million for a new testing facility at New York Medical College (see Chapter 20).

2. Self-Underwriting. If the company wants all the advantages of public ownership at a fraction of the standard cost, self-underwriting also can provide new capital. Hughes Steel and Tube Ltd. raised more than $4 million to expand production in California (see Chapter 21).

3. International Joint Venture. In order to maintain control of the company while expanding market share to raise capital, Television Technology Corporation did a joint venture with a Chinese firm to net over $10 million in a five-year period (see Chapter 11).

4. Limited Partnership. Low-cost syndications are turning increasingly to a growing public market. Windsor Electronics, Inc. raised $3.5 million in six offerings (see Section I).

SOURCES

Most national, regional and local brokerage firms place and sell private offerings. Firms that match entrepreneurs with appropriate investors include:

Allen E. Fishman & Co., St. Louis, MO.
The Investment Matchmaker, Inc., Los Angeles, CA.
The Venture Capital Network, Inc.

PITFALLS TO AVOID

A private placement should never be done to raise money for the upfront costs of going public.

If a private placement is not targeted to extremely compatible investors, it will be difficult to sell in either a strong or a soft private market.

A private placement does not offer the tax advantages of a limited partnership, for example. So a private offering has to provide other advantages management may not want to give up, primarily a larger amount of equity for a smaller per-share price.

Private placement investors are passive, and do not offer management, advisory or other assistance.

CHAPTER 24

Unit Offerings

DESCRIPTION

"Unit offering" is an umbrella term that encompasses any combination of stock, convertible securities, warrants for stock and/or bonds in one offering.

A unit can be either public or private, contingent on the market to which the issue will be sold. Most units that include debt are issued by public companies. Units can combine any of the following:

Preferred stock plus warrants for common stock
Common stock plus warrants for common stock
Bond plus warrants for preferred stock
Bond plus warrants for common stock
Bond plus preferred or common stock

Offerings that combine stock, warrants for stock and/or bonds are considered "junk" offerings, named for junk bonds that are unrated (or have a bond rating below, BB or Ba) and high-yielding (2.5–3.5 percent higher than investment-grade bonds). These unit securities often are issued by stable companies that (1) have a unique tax advantage like a tax loss carryforward, (2) have strong off-balance-sheet assets, or (3) need to manipulate the debt/equity structure to meet specific needs. Unit issues proposed by established, quality companies often are called "hybrid" securities (although not all units are hybrids), because they combine aspects of both debt and equity in one security. Smaller, emerging companies often sell unit offerings to sweeten the deal with combinations designed to entice investors who want an equity play in a debt offering or the opportunity to purchase additional stock at a future date.

PROFILE OF A SUCCESSFUL UNIT ISSUER

There are two kinds of unit issuers. One is a large, mature and/or stable company that has (1) off-balance-sheet assets that are recognized by a unit offering, (2) a need to combine securities in order to restructure debt/equity ratios, or (3) an unusual tax advantage that can be enhanced by a unit offering.

Also, unit issues are sold by small or startup companies that cannot attract investors unless an equity kicker is included. Although these issues can be sold, the future cost may be very high to the company. Startup issuers sell units most successfully when the company has (1) beneficial off-balance-sheet assets, (2) strong growth potential but no bond rating, (3) problems that are only temporary, offset by certain revenues, earnings and cash flow gains and/or (4) an equity kicker that is priced fairly and accurately.

Mature and successful unit issuers include:
Intergrated Resources
River Oaks Industries, Inc.
Comdisco, Inc.
Sunshine Mining Co.

RESULTS OF A UNIT OFFERING

A unit offering (1) attracts capital that can be structured to fit specific financial balances between debt and equity within the company, (2) can be a less expensive way to raise additional capital than going public, venture capital or debt financing, (3) creates a long-term financing pool to which the company can return again in the future if the offering provides fair returns to investors, and (4) can raise large amounts of capital for specialized purposes (many recent mergers and takeovers of large public companies were accomplished with junk bonds created for raiders like Mesa Petroleum's T. Boone Pickens).

WHEN TO DO A UNIT OFFERING

The most favorable time to do a unit offering is when the company needs inexpensive capital and (1) has strong off-balance-sheet assets, (2) has a unique tax advantage like a tax loss carryforward, (3) has unrealized growth potential in earnings, revenues and/or cash flow, (4) does not yet have a bond rating or (5) can absorb some future dilution of the common stock that results from a warrants unit.

THE HOW-TO TIMETABLE

Like a warrant, a unit offering must be planned when the primary security is structured. It takes about six months to prepare a unit offering with the assistance of a third-party professional like an investment banker, attorney or accountant. Most companies prefer to use a third-party professional who is qualified to analyze the complex valuation and pricing formulae that determine both parts of the unit offering. Refer to the timetable that explains the preparation stage for a stock (Chapter 20) or a bond (Chapter 18) offering.

FILING REQUIREMENTS

Public unit offerings are subject to the same federal and state reporting/disclosure requirements as any other public issue. Reporting documents include proxy statements, annual report to the shareholders, quarterly financial report (Form 10-Q), annual financial report (Form 10-K), reports about current material events in the company (Form 8-K), and other reports for audited financial statements, the sale of control shares and tender offers.

Companies that sell a public unit offering also must meet filing requirements of the states in which the security is offered, if applicable. Merit states have approval power over the offering. The NASD must approve underwriter compensation, if any, before the effective date.

Private unit offerings must meet Section 4(2) or 4(6) requirements for Regulation D exemption. In addition, states in which the private offering is sold may require certain reporting/disclosure documentation.

COSTS

The upfront cost of structuring a unit offering is included in the underwriter's or agent's commission for packaging and selling the offering.

1. Public Stock or Private Debenture Issue. If the unit issue is based on a public offering of stock or a private bond offering, the costs are roughly the same as initial public offering costs:

Commission between 7 and 10 percent of the offering proceeds

Underwriter reimbursements up to $50,000 for legal and other expenses that are paid by the company. Up to 2.5 percent of the offering value may be required for nonaccountable expenses.

Out-of-pocket expenses for third-party consultation costs between $150,000 and $300,000 for an offering of between $5 million and $10 million.

Printing ranges from $50,000 for a small offering up to $200,000 for four-color production.

Filing fees are similar to IPO costs. SEC filing costs .02 percent of the maximum aggregate offering price. NASD filing costs $100 plus .01 percent of the offering price with a $5,100 maximum. State blue-sky filing fees cost up to $15,000. Registrar and transfer agent fees range between $5,000 and $10,000.

2. *Private Unit Offering*. If the unit issue is a private place-ment, the cost ranges between $20,000 and $500,000 depending on the size and complexity of the offering and the preparedness of the company.

3. *Debenture Offering*. Public bond offerings, which start at about $15 million, generally are sold by large companies. If the unit is based on a private bond offering, the cost is similar to a private bond placement:

Agent fee, usually a minimum of $25,000 to $50,000 or from 1/4 to 2 percent of the amount borrowed, depends on the condi-tion of the company. Smaller offerings are charged a higher per-centage of the amount borrowed. Junk bonds cost between 2 and 4 percent.

Printing the memorandum usually costs between $5,000 and $50,000. Third-party legal and accounting assistance costs between a fraction of 1 percent and a maximum 5 percent of the amount borrowed.

The future cost of the unit offering, with respect to dilution and market price of the shares, can vary widely and is subject to offering terms that can be highly negotiable.

ADVANTAGES AND DISADVANTAGES

Advantages

1. Management can fine-tune the company's debt/equity structure with a unit offering that balances the need for both sources of capital.

2. Emerging companies that may not be able to attract inves-tors can obtain new capital by issuing units of common stock and warrants for stock.

3. Units offer speculation possibilities for investors. Junk yields are typically higher than market rates.

4. Capital formation with units may be less expensive if the offering is structured accurately and professionally.

5. By offering an equity kicker, a small company can save a percentage of interest costs.

Disadvantages

1. A penny stock company may have difficulty selling an offering if investors do not find offsetting advantages within the company, such as tax benefits, upside growth potential or off-balance-sheet assets.

2. The equity portion of the unit may be costly to the company in future dilution or a depressed stock price.

3. A unit that includes warrants may cause negative future consequences in financial planning.

4. A unit may not offer any advantage to the company unless accurate projections reflect growth in revenues, earnings and cash flow.

TESTING THE WATERS

If management can sell a bond offering, a unit offering that includes a bond will probably be well-received by potential bondholders. If a small or startup company wants to sell a unit offering, it should be able to demonstrate strong growth potential of at least 10 percent annually for three years, tax advantages or off-balance-sheet assets.

ALTERNATIVES TO A UNIT OFFERING

1. *Limited Partnership.* If the company doesn't need debt capital in the next round of financing, a limited partnership with buy-back terms may be a good alternative to a unit offering because partnership terms can be flexible. Energy Sciences Corporation raised $3 million through limited partnerships that financed the development of the company's data and communications products (see Chapter 3).

2. *Private Placement.* If upside potential is evident in the company's projections, a private placement may be the least expensive way to raise capital. Wilson Hotel Group, Inc. raised nearly $30 million by selling private placement interests in its con-

dominium/hotel project in Osceola County, Florida (see Chapter 23).

3. Venture Capital. If the company has enough negotiating leverage, venture capital funds that finance emerging companies also can be a good alternative to a unit offering. Triad Design, Inc. raised $250,000 in venture capital financing from Economic Development, Inc. to upgrade and expand facilities in a new location (see Chapter 1).

SOURCES

Venture magazine, "Private Placement" and "Public Offerings" columns, New York, NY.

Most national, regional and local brokerage firms underwrite unit issues.

PITFALLS TO AVOID

A unit offering should be structured for the benefit of the company, not to help the underwriter sell the issue. If it combines debt and equity, the offering must be balanced to provide the most beneficial ratio of both for future capitalization: too much equity can dilute the common or depress the per-share price; too much debt can overload the debt ratios and curtail future borrowing capacity.

There are distinct tax consequences for hybrid units that combine debt and equity characteristics in one offering and for units that piggyback separate debt and equity issues. A professional tax opinion should be sought for either offering to avoid undesirable tax consequences.

The underwriter should be paid from the proceeds of the offering, not with stock or warrants.

CHAPTER 25
Warrants

DESCRIPTION

A warrant entitles a holder to buy a certain amount of the company's common or preferred stock at a preset price before a specified expiration date. The common share price of large, mature companies often rises above the warrant price before the warrants are exercised. This means that a shareholder who has a warrant for more common can buy a $10 share for $5, for example.

But the common share price of smaller, emerging companies often does not rise above the warrant price before the warrants are exercised. This means that a shareholder who has a warrant for more common would have to buy a share that currently sells for $10 in the public market for the higher warrant price of $20, for example. When the warrant price is higher than the stock's market price, most warrants are not exercised. In fact, about half of the warrants issued for small growth companies are never exercised.

Unless the market price of the common goes down, a warrant will always be worth its intrinsic value because it represents the discount at which a holder can buy stock below the market price. A warrant will have a higher market price than its intrinsic value because of its nature. Warrants can be issued separately or as part of a stock or bond package.

(1) There are two kinds of warrants. The subscription warrant, also called a rights offering, is a less costly and less time-consuming issue targeted to existing shareholders who want to buy more stock at a future date, hopefully at a discount. Other types of warrants (2) are offered to the general public and have a longer life, up to perpetuity, than subscription warrants. Some warrants are transferable and are traded on the AMEX. Warrants also can be called "stock-purchase warrants."

In contrast to warrants, "rights" to buy common stock usually have a subscription price lower than current market price, and a life of only two to four weeks.

Warrants attached to a common or preferred stock offering create a unit (see Chapter 24). Warrants that accompany a senior debenture offering create a hybrid issue. Warrants also can be issued separately from stock or bonds, used as dividend payments or added as a kicker to sweeten other financing strategies like bank borrowing. Warrants can provide speculation opportunities, be used alone to raise capital (rarely issued to the general public, but often issued as a rights offering), or enhance a merger or acquisition with the prospect of speculative gain. Warrant terms for any purpose vary widely.

PROFILE OF A SMALL COMPANY AS A WARRANT ISSUER

Virtually any company can issue warrants. It is a beneficial tool for companies that (1) need an extra push when going public to induce buyers to purchase stock from an unknown company, (2) are almost creditworthy or do not want to pay a high current interest rate, (3) want to attract backers by issuing warrants as a sweetener, particularly when the company's future looks profitable, (3) want to balance the capital structure by offering a debt issue that is accompanied by a planned equity issue.

The most successful warrant issuers offer a maturity of three to five years and terms that are simple to understand. The warrants are not overpriced relative to company projections, which have been accurately assessed by financial professionals.

Examples of successful warrant issuers:

Mesa Medical, Inc.
Legume, Inc.
Vistar Corporation

RESULTS OF A WARRANT ISSUE

Warrants usually induce purchasers or lenders to make a final commitment to the company, either by lending capital through a bond issue or loan, or by buying stock. Warrants can attract some amount of future capital (when warrant holders exercise their right before the expiration date) for a staged financing effect. Warrants can broaden a company's capital base if projected earnings promise price appreciation in the company's stock.

The only thing the company has lost by issuing warrants is a small percentage of ownership. By contrast, if the company doesn't live up to projections, the warrant offering hasn't further eroded the company's capital structure and ownership percentages remain unchanged.

A complicated long-term warrant package can be an expensive way to raise capital in the long run if investors do not understand the package or if the market for the common declines.

WHEN TO ISSUE WARRANTS

The time for a small, emerging business to offer warrants is when (1) the company needs capital, but bank or investor lenders are hesitant, (2) interest rates are high and lenders are competing for customers, (3) projected earnings are assured, although the current economic condition of the company is not strong, (4) the company wants to sell an initial or secondary offering and stock alone won't move a reluctant market or (5) the company has a low bond rating or competition is strong in the bond market.

Larger, stable companies with a proven track record should issue warrants when the capital structure of the company needs to be fine-tuned to create an appropriate balance between equity and debt capital. If a debt issue is sold, for example, an accompanying warrant to buy common at a later date is not a sweetener, but rather a staged-capital technique that offsets excessive debt repayment in the future.

THE HOW-TO TIMETABLE

The most critical factor in the decision about whether or not to add warrants to an offering is the pricing factor. Most warrants are overpriced because of their limited supply. They must be priced accurately to do their job: add incentive to an offer sold by a small company, or provide a balance between debt and equity capital for small and large companies. In either case, warrant issues are carefully planned to provide infusions of capital at a time and at a price that is beneficial to the company.

There are many ways to price a warrant. One is to price it the same as the common. Another easy way to price a warrant is to (1) estimate the market price of the company's common stock at a future date and (2) from that date, figure the current price of the warrant based on an annual percentage return that investors may accept. This formula may result in a warrant price too low for the future cost to the company in terms of lost capital if the price jumps more than anticipated. Therefore, price should also be influenced by:

Maturity date
Nature of the issuing company
Special warrant terms

Warrants can be used in several ways: (1) packaged with a senior security (bond), creating a hybrid security, (2) packaged with preferred stock at a premium rather than at par, (3) packaged with common stock and/or (4) as separate, privately held issues. Following are the primary factors to be considered when deciding whether or not to issue warrants.

1. The time to consider warrants is when the primary vehicle of the offering (the stock or bond) is being planned. If the offering

is a stock offering, check the how-to timetables for stock offerings in Section 1. If the offering is a debt package, read the how-to timetables for debt offerings in Section 2.

2. The next consideration is how to structure the warrants: as a package, combined with the proposed stock/bond or as a separate financing instrument. Most companies consult a financial expert or investment banker who can explain the results of packaging the warrants or of selling them separately. Although advisers often suggest packaging, it is important to note that the rate on the senior security is usually not lowered and a premium is usually not obtained for common stock. The best reason to package the deal is to provide enough kicker to induce investor interest.

3. Pricing the warrant is the most difficult aspect of structuring a warrant package. The two pricing keys are: (1) what the price of the company's stock will be on the warrant expiration date based on price/earnings ratio (this price determines the price at which warrant buyers can purchase the company's stock before the expiration date), and (2) a fair warrant price, that is low enough to attract buyers despite a lack of market in the warrants and high enough to offset the future cost to the company.

A financial specialist who packages warrant offerings (investment banker, attorney or accountant) can help management accurately assess future stock value and inject reality into the warrant-pricing process.

4. Other warrant terms must be chosen carefully, as well, including:

Exercise (option) period—three to five years is optimum

Nature of the security obtained on exercise of the warrant, and the number of shares or amount received

Attachment or detachment from the security with which the warrant is offered

The eventual cost of issuing warrants is assessed by determining how much dilution the company can afford. Although an unknown amount of additional capital is obtained by issuing warrants, the stock often is greatly diluted. In addition, the company can actually lose future capital if the stock price rises beyond expectation and warrant-holders own the right to buy stock at a discounted price.

FILING REQUIREMENTS

Specific filing requirements for warrants are contingent on the nature of the securities they're packaged with. If the stock/bond issue is registered with the SEC or must meet specific federal or state statutes, so must the warrant that accompanies it. If warrants are sold separately to the public market, they must be registered with the SEC, and the company must meet federal and state disclosure/reporting requirements as applicable. Privately issued warrants must meet state and federal filing requirements determined by the Regulation D exemption under which the offering is structured.

During the course of the exercise period, which can range up to about five years, management must keep the offering in continuous registration if it is sold to the public market.

Leveraged Nature of Warrant on Basis of Intrinsic Value

| | 1 | | | | 4 | |
Column	(Common)	2		3	(Warrant)	5
Year	Market Price	Appreciation/ Depreciation		Exercise Price	Intrinsic Value	Appreciation/ Depreciation
0	$100			$90	$10	
1	110	+10%		90	20	+100%
2	100	−9%		90	10	−50%

COSTS

1. Upfront. If an underwriter or agent is used to structure and sell the issue, the cost of analyzing the use of warrants is included in the commission or fee. The commission for a stock issue is between 7 and 10 percent of the amount raised. The fee for a bond issue is about 2 percent of the amount borrowed. There is no separate cost for adding warrants to the offering.

2. *Future*. It is difficult to assess the dilution of stock that often occurs after warrant rights are exercised. If the company or its analysts misjudge the share price that must be honored at expiration date, the company can lose capital in the future, although an emerging company may acquire new investors who would not have bought the offering without a warrant attached. The key to cost containment, therefore, is accurate pricing of warrants and future shares.

3. *Ongoing*. A public warrant issue must remain in registration until the expiration date. This can cost, on an annual basis, one-third to one-half the total cost of the offering.

ADVANTAGES AND DISADVANTAGES

Advantages

1. A warrant can function as an equity kicker for small companies that need a boost to sell the security.

2. It can attract capital without depressing the stock if the exercise price of the warrant is below the market price of common when the warrants are exercised.

3. This technique offers speculation opportunities for investors who perceive the company to be in a growth mode.

4. A warrant issue can expedite an acquisition or merger, which often provides additional benefits to both the purchaser and the issuing company.

Disadvantages

1. Issued separately, warrants often do not raise enough capital to offset the cost of the offering.

2. Warrants packaged with a stock or bond may provide extra capital, but at the cost of future dilution or depressed stock price.

3. Once issued, warrants cannot be called by the company. It has no control over the issue.

4. The prospect of future dilution can depress the market price of the shares, which creates financial planning difficulties.

5. If the common stock price increases significantly, the company will, in effect, be issuing future (dilutive) common at a discount that results in a loss of capital.

6. A warrant is a leveraged security. Therefore, it can be more expensive than other forms of capital because investors will want a higher return on the warrant in exchange for the risk involved.

7. Continuous registration until the expiration date can be expensive and time-consuming. This additional cost may not be offset by the amount of capital raised through the warrants.

TESTING THE WATERS

Warrants are most effective when company projections indicate a solid increase in earnings and general market conditions indicate an upward movement in the stock price before the warrant expiration date. Aside from meeting these conditions, all warrant offerings provide an equity stake in the company for investors who want additional reassurance for their risk.

ALTERNATIVES TO WARRANT ISSUES

1. *Limited Partnership.* Often the chief attraction of warrants to investors is the opportunity to participate in the company's growth. A limited partnership also offers growth opportunities through royalties or a percentage of income. Advanced Instrumentation Ltd. raised $500,000 in limited partnerships from several individuals and companies to develop the company's hemotology instruments (see Chapter 3).

2. *Venture Capital.* Some funds specialize in startup investments. The ultimate cost of venture capital can be far less than the cost of warrants if the offering results in dilution or the price of

the stock decreases. Zytrex Corporation raised $1.2 million in venture capital financing from T. H. Lehman & Co. to expand its manufacturing capability in advanced CMOS integrated circuits (see Chapter 1).

3. *Unit Offering.* Vistar Corporation offered 6 million units, consisting of one share of common and one warrant to buy one additional common share, to raise $1 million for the development of its new electronic test instruments and to build up sales support (see Chapter 24).

SOURCES

Venture magazine, "Private Placement" and "Public Offerings" columns, New York, NY.

Most national, regional and local brokerage firms underwrite warrant issues.

PITFALLS TO AVOID

Investors in small, low-priced issues exercise their right to buy warrants in fewer than 50 percent of all unit offerings. Management should not depend on a future infusion of equity capital from units that include warrants.

Warrants should not be included in the unit in order to help the underwriter sell the issue. Warrants may be included so that a small company can sell a low-priced issue.

The underwriter should be paid from the proceeds of the offering, not with stock or warrants.

Section 7
Reorganization Techniques

Section 7
Introduction

The eight reorganization techniques described in Section 7 can be effective financing strategies for a small public or private business in the under–$25 million category. Although reorganizations historically have generated large amounts of capital for big public companies, in recent years they have become an effective way for owners to retire and cash out of a small business or to assign a market value to assets for estate purposes.

Information about standard taxable mergers and acquisitions can be extrapolated from Chapter 26, which describes tax-free mergers and acquisitions, because the process for both strategies is virtually identical.

Reorganizations also have become a favored alternative way to achieve rapid growth. As a result of high interest rates in the early 1980s, many companies expanded with product lines or technology acquired from other companies rather than from startup development financed by debt. Often, a company will divest itself of an unprofitable or unrelated subsidiary or division in order to raise additional funds for a more appropriate acquisition.

Notable failures among billion-dollar corporate reorganizations have captured news headlines since 1983, but the appetite for mergers, acquisitions and divestitures is stronger than ever among smaller-sized companies, particularly when inflation is on the rise. Reorganization is a good strategy for later-stage companies that have highly valued assets, have stabilized earnings and cash flow, and are poised for expansion.

Glossary

Break-Up Value: the perceived worth or price of a company if a subsidiary or division were valued separately, and spun off or sold separately.

Collar: a provision in a stock-for-stock acquisition for the adjustment of the exchange ratio which guarantees that the target company stockholders receive shares with a minimum specified market value.

Definitive Agreement: a legally binding merger document that specifically states the representations, obligations and rights of all parties to the merger, including termination terms.

Earnout Agreement: provides the acquired management with incentives to stay after the merger or acquisition in order to maintain or improve prior performance levels.

Golden Parachute: a compensation agreement for senior executives that provides severance payments and other benefits when control of the company changes hands. This is often used as insurance in an unfriendly takeover.

Hart-Scott-Rodino Act: The Antitrust Improvements Act of 1976 requires the buyer and seller in certain mergers to give advance notice of the proposed merger to the Justice Department and the Federal Trade Commission to satisfy waiting-period requirements before completing the transaction.

Integration: a four-staged plan to assimilate the buyer and seller, including preparation before purchase, immediate ownership actions, intermediate profit improvement plans and strategic development.

Intrapreneur: an in-house staff member or manager who functions as an entrepreneur within the corporation, with the latitude to experiment and/or spend additional funds. Intrapreneurs often are given an equity stake in a division or subsidiary in order to encourage commitment to research and development requirements.

Kelso Plan: an employee stock ownership plan (ESOP), developed by Louis O. Kelso, in which employees buy a percentage of ownership in a public or private company, although not necessarily control. This can be a mechanism for taking a public company private.

Show-Stopper: a substantive violation of law by a bidder which can result in an injunction against the reorganization offer.

Spin-Off: the corporate divestiture of a subsidiary or division by sale, merger, initial public offering, management buyout or employee ESOP which creates an independent company.

Target: the object of a tender offer, acquisition proposal or takeover attempt. TRASOP: a tax-reduction variation of the ESOP created by the Tax Reduction Act of 1975.

Two-Factor Theory: the theory that the real wealth of a nation is produced by capital, not labor: if employees owned newly developed capital, the results would be economic growth coupled with full employment, some inflation and a hard currency.

White Knight: a third-party bidder who offers a higher price for a target and precludes acquisition by a hostile bidder.

CHAPTER 26
Tax-Free and Taxable Mergers/Acquisitions

DESCRIPTION

A tax-free merger or acquisition is a transaction that restructures the acquired or merged company as a continuation of the shareholders' initial investment in the buying company. Thus, the merger or acquisition is a nontaxable event for shareholders at the time of the reorganization. (Taxes are actually deferred on a carryover basis until the company is sold outright, liquidated, or other events occur.) The definitions of certain tax-free merger/acquisition transactions are outlined in Section 368(a)(1) of the Internal Revenue Code.

In order to use a tax-free reorganization as a financing technique, an acquiring company must assess the value of the assets and cash flow/earnings potential of the acquired or merged company against the cost in stock, cash or property paid to consummate the deal. In many cases, the tax-deferral aspects of the acquisition or merger offset the costs, but it must be emphasized that to qualify by IRS standards as a tax-free reorganization, the transaction can not be structured for tax benefits alone.

There are seven ways to structure a tax-free merger/-acquisition:

1. A Reorganization. This a statutory merger or consolidation simply combines two companies under the laws of the United States or any state, territory or the District of Columbia. The A reorganization is the most flexible of the tax-frees and allows dissenting shareholders to be paid in cash (they may have to pay capital gains on the cash) or nonvoting preferred stock so that the transaction can take place.

2. Triangular A. Company 1 is merged into a subsidiary of Company 2, therefore the newly structured subsidiary is the survivor. The merger would have been an A Reorganization if Company 1 had been merged with Company 2 rather than the Company 2 subsidiary. Company 1 shareholders get stock from Company 2, not the subsidiary, because no subsidiary stock can be used in the transaction.

3. Reverse Triangular A. The opposite of a Triangular A, instead of the newly formed subsidiary being the survivor, Company 1 survives as a wholly owned subsidiary of Company 2. In this case, Company 2 shareholders generally do not vote to approve the merger. Company 1 assets are legally preserved in the

Acquisitions of Privately Owned Companies
1982–1988—Dollar Value

Number (Percent of Transactions Disclosing Price)

Value of Purchase Price	1982	1983	1984	1985	1986	1987	1988
$5 million or less	197 (47)	198 (40)	180 (41)	149 (33)	125 (23)	56 (19)	50 (20)
$5.1–10.0 million	85 (20)	116 (23)	84 (19)	105 (23)	98 (18)	56 (19)	33 (13)
$10.1–15.0 million	52 (12)	55 (11)	50 (11)	51 (11)	67 (12)	37 (13)	30 (12)
$15.1–25.0 million	35 (8)	56 (11)	51 (12)	56 (13)	87 (16)	54 (18)	44 (18)
$25.1–50.0 million	29 (7)	48 (10)	46 (10)	57 (13)	81 (15)	41 (14)	40 (16)
$50.1–99.9 million	15 (4)	19 (4)	15 (3)	20 (4)	45 (8)	21 (7)	24 (10)
$100 million or more	7 (2)	8 (1)	19 (4)	15 (3)	45 (8)	31 (10)	30 (12)
Number of Transactions Disclosing Price	420	500	445	453	548	296	251

merger, and leasehold and other relationships continue without change. Management is restricted in the kinds of consideration that can be used to close the deal.

4. *B Reorganization (Stock-for-Stock).* The stock of the acquired company is paid in exchange only for the voting stock of the acquiring company or its parent, assuming the acquiring company has control of the acquired company upon acquisition. This tax-free transaction is the least flexible because only voting stock can be exchanged.

5. *C Reorganization (Stock-for-Assets).* The acquiring company obtains substantially all of the legal assets of another company in exchange for voting stock and/or some cash or property. The acquired company generally becomes a division of the acquiring company. There are strict limitations on the amount of taxable cash or property that can be used. Only stock avoids taxation.

6. *D Reorganization.* This method combines affiliated companies or splits up an existing company.

7. *E and F Reorganizations.* These methods produce changes within one company, such as a corporate restructure or change in the state of incorporation.

Sources of Capital for Entrepreneurs—1988 (Purchased Existing Business)

Source	Number of Deals	Millions of Dollars
U.S. Acquires U.S.	2,875	159,031
Non-U.S. Acquires U.S.	446	60,808
U.S. Acquires Non-U.S.	158	6,501

PROFILE OF A SUCCESSFUL TAX-FREE CANDIDATE

Virtually any size company is a potential acquiring entity, especially (1) if management wants to offer shareholders favorable tax treatment available from statutory reorganizations, (2) because growth is less costly through a tax-free merger/acquisition if the acquisition is negotiated rather than hostile, (3) if merger/acquisition prices are depreciating, (4) if the stock price or asset value of acquisition candidates is at the bottom of a cycle, (5) if high borrowing rates prevent smaller companies from expanding—or surviving—or (6) if target industries are slowing down because of foreign competition, a soft market or obsolescence.

The reverse is also true. Any company can be a viable merger/acquisition candidate if it has (1) undervalued assets, (2) underpriced real estate, (3) strong earnings potential or accumulated earnings, (4) cash flow to finance recapitalization or growth, (5) products, services or management complementary to the acquiring company, (6) a solid niche among competitors, (7) off-balance-sheet assets or (8) tax advantages desired by the acquiring company like unused tax credits or net-operating loss carryovers (NOLs).

Tax-free mergers/acquisitions that have been successfully concluded for management and shareholders include:

Allied Nursing Care, Inc.
Network Security Corporation
Deer Park Baking Co.
Astrex, Inc.

Stock was the predominant form of payment for private companies in 1988, followed by a combination of payments and cash as illustrated in the table below.

Acquisitions of Privately Owned Companies—Method of Payment

Number (Percent of Transactions Disclosing Payment Form)

	1982	1983	1984	1985	1986	1987	1988
Cash	137 (24)	129 (20)	167 (29)	170 (28)	180 (27)	78 (23)	85 (31)
Stock	256 (44)	306 (48)	226 (39)	234 (39)	295 (45)	173 (51)	107 (39)
Combination	169 (29)	202 (31)	180 (31)	195 (33)	188 (28)	89 (26)	80 (30)
Debt	16 (3)	6 (1)	4 (1)	1 (—)	—	—	—
Number of Transactions	578	643	577	600	663	340	272

Source: *Mergerstat Review.*

RESULTS OF A TAX-FREE REORGANIZATION

A tax-free reorganization as a financing strategy must be carefully analyzed for tax and other ramifications. For example, consider the following: (1) The acquired or merged company can survive in a Reverse Triangular A or a B reorganization, but it won't survive in an A, Triangular A or C reorganization. (2) Taxes are deferred from the time of any tax-free reorganization until the company is liquidated or sold outright in a taxable transaction. (3) Acquiring company shareholders generally profit because they are paid a premium over market price at the time of the reorganization. (4) Dissenting shareholders may demand a large cash settlement in exchange for approving the deal. (5) Control and/or dilution may

Number of Net Merger-Acquisition Announcements By Purchase-Price Distribution (in Millions) 1976–1988

	$0.5– 5.0 MM	$5.1– 25.0 MM	$25.1– 99.9 MM	$100.0– 499.9 MM	$500.0– 999.9 MM	Over 999.9 MM	Base*
1976	498 (50%)	344 (34%)	117 (12%)	35 (4%)	3	1	998
1977	451 (44%)	377 (36%)	163 (16%)	39 (4%)	2		1,032
1978	417 (39%)	404 (38%)	170 (16%)	76 (7%)	3	1	1,071
1979	387 (36%)	393 (38%)	184 (18%)	69 (7%)	11 (1%)	3	1,047
1980	306 (35%)	324 (36%)	166 (19%)	80 (9%)	10 (1%)	4	890
1981	388 (35%)	433 (38%)	192 (17%)	86 (8%)	15 (1%)	12 (1%)	1,126
1982	296 (32%)	338 (36%)	180 (20%)	96 (10%)	14 (2%)	6	930
1983	321 (30%)	380 (35%)	238 (22%)	104 (10%)	23 (2%)	11 (1%)	1,077
1984	270 (25%)	361 (33%)	253 (23%)	166 (15%)	16 (2%)	18 (2%)	1,084
1985	296 (23%)	454 (34%)	300 (23%)	204 (15%)	30 (2%)	36 (3%)	1,320
1986	219 (15%)	519 (35%)	384 (26%)	260 (18%)	59 (4%)	27 (2%)	1,468
1987	92 (10%)	294 (30%)	285 (29%)	218 (22%)	47 (5%)	36 (4%)	972
1988	101 (9%)	320 (28%)	359 (31%)	267 (23%)	57 (5%)	45 (4%)	1,149

*Base: Number of transactions disclosing a purchase price.
Source: *Mergerestat Review*.

occur in a stock-for-assets reorganization. (6) A retiring owner can cash out of a merged or acquired company by creating a public market for private stock, by establishing a fair market value or by assuring continuity of the company as an intact entity within the acquiring company.

WHEN TO STRUCTURE A TAX-FREE REORGANIZATION

The strategic time to do a tax-free merger/acquisition is when (1) the merger/acquisition is a good deal without tax-free aspects, (2) the target company is undervalued or underpriced, (3) capital sources are costly or scarce, (4) expansion is more cost-effective via the existing earnings or cash flow of a merged/acquired company than by startup development, (5) the equity market is soft, or (6) the acquired company has products, management or tax credits that complement the needs of the acquiring company.

THE HOW-TO TIMETABLE

Six Months before the Reorganization

1. *Third-Parties.* Because the qualifications for and structure of a tax-free reorganization are complex, legal and accounting assistance should be brought in at the beginning to evaluate the ramifications of the deal. Legal and accounting professionals should be experts in tax-free reorganizations as well as in the company's industry. Several firms in both categories should be identified and interviewed, based on:

Fee: The fee structure should be clarified on the basis of a stated hourly fee or a percentage of asset value of the transaction. The practice of paying an attorney or accountant in corporate stock, which sometimes occurs among low-priced companies, should be avoided.

Reputation: The firm should be reputable and be recognized as expert in tax-free reorganizations.

Contacts: Acquiring companies should look for firms that can provide possible merger/acquisition candidates.

2. Legal Review. A reorganization may involve both a public and a private company. The SEC requires that public companies disclose all significant transactions between company-related associates. Although the company's private arrangements between officers and shareholders serve a private company well, they may not be perceived the same way by public shareholders or the SEC. A legal review of the following should take place before the transaction is negotiated:

Corporate charter and bylaws
Shareholder or management loans
Lease agreements
Debt outstanding
Stock option or purchase plans
Employment contracts
Supply contracts and arrangements
Rights of first refusal

3. Financial Statements. In order to evaluate the merits of the reorganization, the acquired company will require a public acquiring company to provide recent annual and quarterly reports, as well as interim reports. Private companies will be required to provide recent audited income statements. The acquirer will request the same documents of its target acquisition.

4. Prospectus. Some tax-free reorganizations require that a public buyer or seller provide a prospectus (see Chapter 20 for prospectus inclusions). Form S-4 guides disclosure in a tax-free reorganization. The prospectus can be standard length or short-form, depending on the nature of the reorganization and the relative sizes of the buyer and seller.

Three Months before the Reorganization

1. Analysis. Target companies will be analyzed by the legal or accounting experts to find a match for the acquirer in assets, diversification possibilities, earnings and/or cash flow potential, and tax credits. This process may take a variable amount of time, depending on how much homework management has done ahead of time, industry and market conditions, and the number and quality of contacts provided by third-party professionals. Other sources for leads include investment bankers and deal brokers who specialize in mergers/acquisitions.

2. *Stockholders Meeting.* When a target company has been identified and evaluated, and an offer has been made, the target company and/or the acquiring company may have to get half or two-thirds of the stockholders to approve (corporate articles of incorporation vary) before consummating the deal. If the stockholders vote yes, the deal can go through. If dissenters have to be bought out—paying shareholders in a B reorganization, for example, creates a taxable event—the third-party professionals will structure a buyout clause.

3. *Filing.* Disclosure requirements are contingent on the public or private status of the companies involved, and on the nature of the tax-free reorganization. Legal counsel will file the required federal and state documents, which may include a prospectus or proxy statement, annual and quarterly reports, and audited income statements.

FILING REQUIREMENTS

If the merger/acquisition is consummated with securities issued by the acquirer, the acquirer may have to register its stock for sale, and provide a prospectus and proxy statement (unless an exemption applies under Regulation D or other provisions for private placements).

If shareholder approval is required, a public company must comply with the proxy rules for solicitation, but it may use the prospectus and a proxy statement.

If a small company is acquired by a substantially larger company (as outlined in specified IRS criteria), a short Form S-15 may be used to simplify the registration process.

In addition, other state reporting/disclosure requirements may apply to public and private companies that reorganize. Corporate regulations vary by state.

COSTS

1. **Legal.** Most attorneys who specialize in small tax-free reorganizations charge from $50,000 to $100,000 for legal review, corporate evaluation, filing and contract development. Large, complex reorganizations may entail additional costs that add up to 50 percent to the reorganization total. Generally, the smaller the dollar amount of the reorganization, the larger the fee as a percentage of the market value of the company.

2. **Accounting.** Management will pay from $30,000 to $100,000 for an evaluation of the tax and other consequences of the reorganization.

3. **Filing.** SEC filing costs .02 percent of the maximum aggregate offering price. NASD filing costs $100 plus .01 percent of the maximum aggregate offering price with a $5,100 maximum. State blue-sky filing fees range up to $15,000, and registrar and transfer agent fees cost between $5,000 and $10,000.

4. **Printing.** If required, printing of the prospectus and proxy statement costs between $10,000 and $50,000 plus.

5. **Finder's Fee.** If an investment banker, deal broker or other third-party finds a compatible match for the acquiring company, a finder's fee of from 1 to 5 percent of the dollar value of reorganization is standard.

ADVANTAGES AND DISADVANTAGES

Advantages

1. The company can be expanded or diversified with very little cash outlay if the transaction is small and the company has updated legal and financial documents.

2. Tax consequences to shareholders are deferred from the time of reorganization until outright sale, liquidation or other specific circumstances occur.

3. An A reorganization is extremely flexible under individual state laws.

4. A tax-free reorganization sometimes results in a fresh capital infusion that is virtually cost-free, in the form of earnings acquired from the seller.

5. If Internal Revenue Service qualifications are met, a private tax-free reorganization can be consummated more quickly than other strategies to raise capital.

Disadvantages

1. A slip-up in meeting IRS criteria for tax-free reorganizations can result in the needless payment of millions of dollars in taxes.

2. In an A reorganization, the acquiring company cannot avoid the assumption of contingent or unknown liabilities because by law it will automatically assume all of the liabilities of the disappearing corporation.

3. Dissenting stockholders may require a substantial amount of cash for their shares and/or an outside appraisal of fair market value of their shares.

4. In a B (stock-for-stock) merger, only voting stock may be given in the exchange. Any other form of compensation will create a taxable event.

5. Legally unclear ownership of assets can impede a stock-for-assets acquisition in which "substantially all" of the acquired company's properties must be bought.

TESTING THE WATERS

The rule of thumb to determine whether or not a tax-free reorganization makes sense has three parts: (1) if the proposed merger/acquisition can stand on its own merits without the tax benefits, (2) if the deal is consummated for other than strictly tax reasons and (3) if the continuity of proprietary interest can be retained (to qualify as a tax-free) by paying at least 50 percent of the compensation in equity-type securities, then a tax-free reorganization probably makes sense.

ALTERNATIVES TO A TAX-FREE REORGANIZATION

1. *Corporate Securities.* Equity or debt financing can achieve the same purpose, to acquire another company for growth or to improve the bottom line, but it may be a more costly strategy. Edac Technologies Corporation and Cade Industries, Inc. sold an initial public offering in order to raise funds for the acquisition of Gros-Ite (see Sections 5 and 6).

2. *Leveraged Buyout.* Management or employees may provide a good buyout market for founder shares. The leveraged management buyout (unit management buyout) of Southwestern Pipe, Inc. by Halliburton Co. raised more than $30 million (see Chapter 17).

3. *Divestiture.* If market conditions are conducive, spinning off or selling a division or subsidiary of the company may be the most efficient way to raise capital. Dresser Industries, Inc. sold its Orillia, Ontario, plant to JKS Boyles Industries, Inc. in Canada for $5 million (see Chapter 27).

SOURCES

Information about mergers and acquisitions:

"The National Review of Corporate Acquisitions"' Tweed
  Publishing Company, Tiburon, CA.
Mergerstat Review (Merrill Lynch), Chicago, IL.

VALUATION METHODS FOR MERGERS/ACQUISITIONS

  I.   Balance Sheet Methods
         Adjusted book value
         Liquidation value
 II.   Earnings Methods
         Average of the past three to five years' income as an esti-
           mate of future income
         Estimate of future earnings under the current owners' man-
           agement, adjusted for inflation and industry trends
         Estimate of future earnings under the new owners' man-
           agement, adjusted for inflation and industry trends
III.   Pricing Future Earnings Power
         Capitalized earnings
         Discounted future earnings
         Discounted cash flow

PITFALLS TO AVOID

Many tax-free reorganizations turn into taxable events when
IRS restrictions on cash or class of stock as compensation are
unknowingly overlooked.

The tax consequences of any taxable or tax-free reorganization should be carefully studied to avoid penalizing buyers,
sellers and shareholders with excess future taxes.

Management should have a pervasive legal review conducted when the company must acquire the liabilities of the
seller to meet IRS requirements for the reorganization.

Acquisitions of Publicly Traded Companies—Medium of Payment, 1980–1988

	Number (Percent of Transactions)								
	1980	1981	1982	1983	1984	1985	1986	1987	1988
Cash	94 (55)	89 (56)	98 (55)	94 (51)	134 (65)	182 (57)	182 (57)	127 (57)	250 (76)
Stock	44 (25)	38 (24)	34 (19)	52 (28)	34 (16)	78 (25)	78 (25)	60 (27)	52 (16)
Combination	31 (18)	31 (19)	44 (25)	37 (20)	35 (17)	56 (18)	56 (18)	35 (16)	29 (8)
Debt*	3 (2)	2 (1)	1 (1)	1 (1)	4 (2)	1 (—)	0 (—)	0 (—)	0 (—)
Base	172	160	177	184	207	317	316	222	331

*Base: The number of transactions disclosing method of payment.

Source: *Mergerstat Review.*

Acquisitions of Publicly Traded Companies—Dollar Value, 1980–1988

	Number (Percent of Transactions Disclosing Price)							
Price-Paid Value	1981	1982	1983	1984	1985	1986	1987	1988
$10 million or less	20 (13)	22 (12)	16 (9)	14 (7)	58 (18)	42 (12)	17 (6)	41 (10)
$10.1–25.0 million	28 (18)	25 (14)	22 (12)	26 (13)	46 (14)	51 (15)	29 (11)	74 (17)
$25.1–50.0 million	22 (14)	31 (18(	40 (22)	36 (17)	43 (13)	54 (15)	45 (17)	74 (17)
$50.1–99.9 million	24 (15)	33 (19)	30 (17)	32 (16)	41 (13)	56 (16)	48 (18)	75 (17)
$100 million or more	62 (40)	65 (37)	73 (40)	96 (47)	133 (42)	150 (42)	128 (48)	172 (39)
Base	156	176	181	204	321	353	267	436

*Base: The number of transactions disclosing a purchase price.

Source: *Mergerstat Review.*

CHAPTER 27
Divestiture

DESCRIPTION

A divestiture is the disposition of a company asset, division or subsidiary by sale, employee or management buyout, or liquidation. Most divestitures occur when the company is unable to maximize returns from a hidden asset or when an unrelated business division saps profits from the core business. In some cases, a profitable subsidiary is sold to boost core business profits or is spun off to be taken public. Most companies spin off in order either to concentrate on what they do best, in the case of a conglomerate with too many unrelated businesses, or to raise capital or increase the price/earnings ratio by selling a portion of the business that is a financial drain on company resources.

PROFILE OF A SUCCESSFUL DIVESTITURE CANDIDATE

Although most divestitures historically have been transacted by corporations with billions of dollars in revenue, smaller companies also can raise capital by spinning off an asset. Most likely to benefit is the company that (1) has a division or subsidiary that is unrelated to the core business, (2) wants to reemphasize a management specialty, (3) can sell into a strong market, i.e., when high inflation or interest rates raise borrowing costs or the merger market is strong, (3) has on-staff entrepreneurs or management who can better maximize returns from the spin-off and want the opportunity to run their own business, (4) has a profit margin below industry standards, (5) will get additional capital from other sources only by improving cash flow or the price/earnings ratio or (6) has a higher break-up value than book value as perceived by the market.

In addition, if the subsidiary or division is profitable, or has a positive cash flow or reasonable growth prospects, there is nearly always a potential buyer for the operation.

Companies that have divested to raise capital include:

Aca Joe, Inc.
Winn Enterprises
American Research & Development, Inc.
Medrad/Intec, Inc.
National Intergroup, Inc.

RESULTS OF DIVESTITURE

By divesting, a company can (1) raise capital in order to reduce debt, recapitalize or fulfill other corporate goals, (2) sometimes qualify for new tax benefits, (3) eliminate a profit drain from the bottom line, (4) streamline the core business, concentrating on what management does best, (5) improve the price/earnings ratio for additional financing opportunities, (6) manipulate the capital structure in beneficial ways or (7) finance the acquisition of another company to increase market share or compete more effectively.

WHEN TO DIVEST

Market conditions are among the most influential factors in timing a divestiture. Management should sell when (1) inflation is high, and asset values and appreciation rise, (2) merger and (leveraged) buyout activity is strong, (3) the break-up value of the company is perceived by Wall Street to be higher than book value, (4) the company has an unrelated operation that a growth company or industry wants, (5) expansion capital is scarce or expensive or (6) the company's (public) stock is not overvalued.

THE HOW-TO TIMETABLE

Six Months before Divestiture

1. Third-Party Professionals. Whether the company is private or public, an evaluation will have to be completed on the operation for sale to establish its market value. Because of the complexity of the analysis, it should be undertaken by an attorney, accounting firm or investment banking firm that specializes in the company's business and in market evaluations. Companies with over $10 million in sales will need more extensive analysis that is best undertaken by an investment banking firm in conjunction with the company's attorney, chief financial officer and controller. Several firms should be interviewed personally before a selection is made on the basis of:

Fee, as a percentage of the sale price, a flat fee or a negotiated retainer
Experience level and reputation of the firm
Personnel credentials and style
Ability to find a buyer

2. Analysis. The evaluation of the operation to be sold is the pivotal factor on which the sale price is based. For this reason, the evaluation team, consisting of the investment banking firm and in-house or retained professionals, should document the following:

Audited financial statements for the past five years, plus interim reports
Industry guidelines, which vary; television station acquisitions, for example, usually are priced at 10 times cash flow.

3. If the company does not have current audited financial statements, the following will be evaluated:

Capitalization: Existing and pro forma capitalization must be analyzed, including all long-term debt and lease obligations, short-term borrowing with monthly usage for two years, liabilities, guarantees, equity ownership (for private companies), where stock is traded, the number of outstanding stockholders and shares outstanding, and percentage ownership of officers, directors and major stockholders.

Projections: Project planned changes, potential new product lines, product line expansion, future capital requirements, income statement and balance sheet, projected revenue, earnings, market share and total potential market.

Products: Detail by market, historical data, markets served, sales and pretax profits by major product for the past five years, and the research and development program.

Marketing: State how the products are sold, distributed and priced, customer base, sales volume concentration and sales contracts.

Competition: Specify by name for the industry, market share of each and company niche in the industry. Make performance comparisons with the closest competitor and industry leader for sales volume, margins, returns, capitalization and related ratios, and domestic and foreign trends.

Manufacturing: Describe location, nature, size, capacity and utilization of facilities, ownership or leasehold terms, capital expenditures for five years, costs and methods, source, availability and cost of raw materials, and company status under federal, OSHA, state and local environmental regulations.

Management: Present an organization chart with biographies on key management, size and nature of the labor force or staff, and wage and benefit plans with their financial aspects.

Risk: Assess historical impact, protective measures, market and industry conditions, and all pending litigation.

Historical Data: Review audited income statements, balance sheets, sources and uses of funds for the past five years, abrupt changes in financial condition, acquisitions over the past five years, management information systems, operating/capital budgeting and long-range planning procedures, and comparisons with major competitors by sales volume, margins, returns, capitalization and related ratios.

Three Months before Divestiture

1. Negotiation. If a legal or accounting firm is retained, the firm will compile a list of potential buyers to interview. Strong buyer candidates will be selected for final negotiations.

2. Contracts. When final negotiations are completed, in-house and investment banking attorneys will draw up the sales documentation and file the necessary documents with state and federal regulatory bodies if either party is a public company.

FILING REQUIREMENTS

If the seller or buyer is a publicly held company, it is subject to state and federal reporting/disclosure requirements. Reporting documents include a quarterly financial report (Form 10-Q), annual financial report (Form 10-K), reports about current material events in the company (Form 8-K), proxy statements, annual reports to the shareholders and other reports for audited financial statements, the sale of control shares and tender offers.

COSTS

1. Evaluation. To establish a market value for the asset to be divested, management will pay a legal or accounting professional or an investment banker from $50,000 to $200,000. Complex transactions may cost up to 50 percent of the value of the asset.

2. Finder's Fee. If an investment banker, deal broker or other third party finds a buyer for the asset, a finder's fee of from 1 to 5 percent of the dollar value or sale price of the asset may be charged.

3. Third-Party Assistance. Attorneys charge from $50,000 to $100,000 for legal review, filing and contract development, depending on the complexity of the divestiture. Accounting assistance costs between $30,000 and $100,000.

Divestitures 1965–1988

Year	Number	Percent of All Transactions	Year	Number	Percent of All Transactions
1965	191	9	1977	1,002	45
1966	264	11	1978	820	39
1967	328	11	1979	752	35
1968	557	12	1980	666	35
1969	801	13	1981	830	35
1970	1,401	27	1982	875	37
1971	1,920	42	1983	932	37
1972	1,770	37	1984	900	36
1973	1,557	39	1985	1,218	41
1974	1,331	47	1986	1,259	38
1975	1,236	54	1987	807	40
1976	1,204	53	1988	894	40

Source: *Mergerstat Review.*

ADVANTAGES AND DISADVANTAGES

Advantages

1. By divesting, management can improve operating profit and reallocate resources.

2. There are tax benefits associated with some divestitures.

3. The company has new capital with which to expand, recapitalize or acquire another company.

4. The price/earnings ratio can improve by selling an unprofitable operation, which, in turn, enhances future financing opportunities.

5. Divestiture can be one of the speediest ways to raise capital if the spin-off is already profitable and/or has strong growth potential. A fast sale provides the capital to make rapid changes and compete more effectively.

Disadvantages

1. The company loses an asset that may become more profitable in the future.
2. The market value of the operation to be sold may be lower in a soft or illiquid market, or in other difficult economic conditions.
3. The company may lose tax benefits that resulted from the nature of the divested operation.

TESTING THE WATERS

The best test for a divestiture is the spread between the operation's fair market value and the pricing formula used in the company's industry. If the market value of the operation indicates that the sales price should exceed industry standards, and/or mergers and buyouts are fueling price increases, it is a good time to sell.

ALTERNATIVES TO DIVESTITURE

1. *Management Buyout (LBO) or Employee Buyout (ESOP).* If the company can't get a fair market price for the operation, or managers or employees want to own it, another alternative is an internal buyout. General Electric spun-off its $2 million Genium Publishing Corporation to managers as a leveraged buyout in 1984 as well as television station WRGB in Schenectady, New York, for $25 million to Forstmann Little (who hired the station's general manager to run it in exchange for a 20 percent equity stake). See Chapter 28.

2. *Intrapreneurship.* Some companies are increasing revenues and profit by offering an equity stake to managers-cum-entrepreneurs who are compensated with a profit percentage for operating the division or subsidiary. Health Improvement Systems, Inc. was developed by a vice president of Merrell Dow Pharmaceutical with a $5 million budget.

SOURCES

Companies that specialize in the divestiture of assets in the under–$25 million category:

> Modern Technologies International, Redwood City, Calif.
> Dallas Flagship Group, Inc., Dallas
> Corporation for Enterprise Development, Washington, D.C.

PITFALLS TO AVOID

Many divisions, subsidiaries or entire companies are under-valued because the appraisal process to establish a market value for the operation was not accurate or updated, or the professionals who conducted the appraisal were not knowledgeable about the company or its industry. Divestiture can be unprofitable unless it is planned years in advance, when there is still time to clean up the books and make the operation attractive to potential buyers. Avoid divestiture as a spur-of-the-moment strategy for an unprofitable operation.

A strong acquisition market often tempts management to sell off a profitable part of the company for short-term gain, at the expense of long-term increases in profitability.

CHAPTER 28

Employee Stock Ownership Plans (ESOPs)

DESCRIPTION

An ESOP is a tax-driven benefit plan for employees who want to acquire a substantial, or 100 percent interest in the company. It is also characterized as a credit mechanism. Technically, an ESOP is structured as a stock bonus plan that can borrow money for the purpose of raising capital and acquiring shares.

A publicly held company can go private by establishing an ESOP, although it may take years because the number of shares the company can issue to employees is limited. It issues stock to an employee trust, which is subject to vesting like a pension plan. When employees leave the company, they collect the vested shares or sell them back to the trust, both of which result in tax deductions for the company and other benefits for employees: the ESOP ensures a ready market for the shares and allows stockholders to save on taxes while accumulating retirement benefits.

As a result of recent changes in the law, a company owner can defer or eliminate taxation on profits from the sale of at least 30 percent of the stock sold by the company to an ESOP. Another provision allows lenders to halve their taxes on interest income earned on loans used to acquire company stock for an ESOP. Therefore, lenders pass on some of that tax break to bor- rower/owners, enabling companies to arrange ESOP leveraged loans at up to 30 percent below cumulative interest costs.

Combined with the standard tax deduction for debt financing, ESOP rules can make employee-owned companies virtually tax-ex- empt.

PROFILE OF A SUCCESSFUL ESOP

An ESOP can be established by a company of almost any size that needs certain tax benefits. The most successful companies usually have at least a $250,000 payroll or 15 employees, and are in the 40 percent tax bracket. An ESOP is often used by companies with a large, often unionized, worker population and by family-owned companies that want to perpetuate a closely held environment or create a market for company stock.

The most stable ESOPs have been structured by companies that (1) have at least a 10-year operating history with stable revenues and a profit margin of at least 10 percent, (2) are in heavily capitalized industries, (3) have potential manage- ment/worker problems or have to compete for labor, (4) want to prevent a takeover or acquisition, (5) offer employees increasing amounts of stock each year under regulatory limitations or (6) regard employees as owners rather than hourly workers.

Successful ESOPs include:

Western Airlines, Inc.
Fred Schmid Appliance & TV Co.
Katz Communications, Inc.
Yellow Cab Inc. of Denver
Blue Bell

RESULTS OF AN ESOP

With an ESOP plan (1) some percentage up to 100 percent of the company is owned by its employees, (2) the employer corporation obtains a tax deduction equal to the shares' fair market value, (3) certain shareholders may sell their shares to the ESOP and not pay current tax on the gain, and may transfer shares to the ESOP in exchange for the ESOP's assumption of the shareholders' estate tax liabilities, (4) the company may be able to deduct dividends paid on ESOP-owned shares, (5) the company can obtain loans at a lower interest rate. Dilution may occur, however, if the plan is structured improperly.

Most important, an ESOP can be used as an employee benefit plan, as a way to raise additional capital and as a less complex way to divest a subsidiary. Many ESOP-owned companies tout improved manager-employee relationships, closer employee involvement, increased productivity based on ownership incentive, improved and faster growth patterns in sales, net profit margins and return on equity, protection from outside acquisition and long-term career opportunity.

New Issue Registrations Filed by Total Dollar Amount

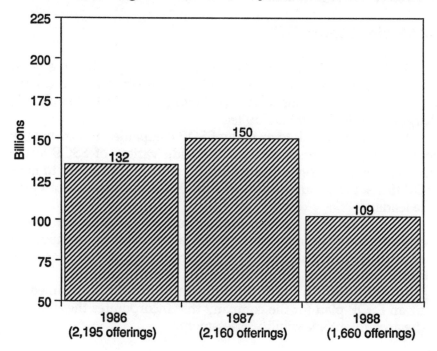

It should be noted that although an ESOP indicates some percentage of employee ownership of the company, it does not guarantee employee control of the company.

WHEN TO ESTABLISH AN ESOP

The best time to establish an ESOP is (1) before workers become dissatisfied with their relationship to the company, (2) before an unwelcome acquisition or takeover occurs, (3) when high interest rates or borrowing restrictions become inhibitive, (4) when planned management succession becomes a corporate goal, as in a family owned business or (5) when the company's financial structure could benefit from specific tax-advantaged features and deductions.

THE HOW-TO TIMETABLE

Six Months before ESOP

1. National Center for Employee Ownership. This is a good place to get information about ESOPs, modal structures, and legal and accounting referrals. The association, based in Oakland, CA, charges a modest membership fee.

2. Feedback. Talk to as many ESOP companies and owners as possible to get a perspective on the wide variety of ESOP structures available and on how well ESOP companies compare to non-ESOP firms. Lists and newsletters from ESOP associations can provide leads.

3. Accountant. An outside accountant who is an ESOP specialist should be retained to begin a feasibility assessment on the company, including cash flow projections, profit and tax consequences.

4. Attorney. An ESOP legal specialist should be retained to draft an ESOP plan for the company that incorporates the findings of the accountant's feasibility assessment.

Three Months before ESOP

1. *Valuation.* An attorney or accountant who specializes in ESOPs (but not the professional who performs the feasibility assessment) should be retained to conduct a valuation study that determines the market value of the company stock.

2. *Letter of Determination.* The attorney who drafts the plan must seek approval from the Internal Revenue Service of the plan structure by requesting an IRS "Letter of Determination."

ESOP Implementation

The IRS Letter of Determination usually takes at least six months to be processed. For that reason, a company can implement the ESOP before receipt of the letter. If the IRS objects to some aspect of the plan structure, later adjustments are made in interest and/or penalty payments.

FILING REQUIREMENTS

All companies that implement an ESOP plan are subject to various federal and state reporting/disclosure requirements. In addition, the company, which must file state incorporation documents to qualify its ESOP, is subject to annual or triannual federal disclosure reporting requirements. The attorney who drafts the ESOP plan must be an ESOP specialist who is familiar with these myriad federal and state reporting requirements.

COSTS

1. A small company that has fewer than 100 employees and a standard ESOP model usually pays from $5,000 to $10,000 for initial accounting fees and a company valuation. The initial legal fees range from $5,000 to $15,000.

Cumulative Growth of Employee Ownership Plans, 1975–1987

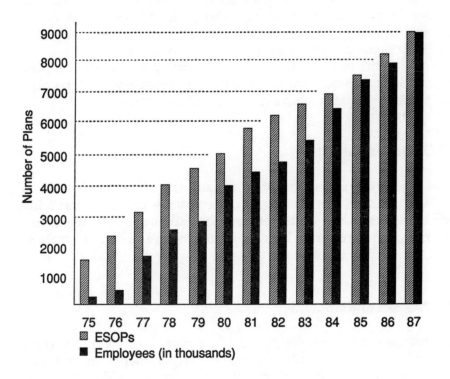

Source: National Center for Employee Ownership, Inc.

2. Larger companies with more than 100 employees pay initial accounting fees that range from $25,000 to over $100,000, and initial legal fees in the same range. Generally, the larger and more complex the company is, or the more analyses that must be performed, the closer fees are to the $100,000 level.

3. Filing fees for small or large companies total about $5,000 to meet varying federal and state requirements.

ADVANTAGES AND DISADVANTAGES

Advantages

1. An ESOP is an automatic employee benefit plan. The company most often makes fixed contributions based on a percentage of payroll.

2. Raising capital is easier because there is a built-in investor base among employees.

3. ESOPs provide an easy way to sell the company when the owner wants to cash out, because a market valuation for the stock has been established.

4. Employee relations usually improve when workers have an equity stake in the company.

5. ESOP-owned companies often perform better than non-ESOP companies by several standard indexes including sales, net profit margin and return on investment.

6. Current taxes on gains are avoided if certain requirements are met: the shares are held for one year and, after the sale, the ESOP owns 30 percent of the total value of the securities outstanding at the time of the sale.

7. ESOP ownership by employees does not always imply employee control of the company.

Disadvantages

1. An ESOP is not recommended when the company has financial difficulties or faces bankruptcy.

2. Employee pension funds sometimes are used in part to fund the ESOP.

3. Managers often benefit more than employees on the purchase of stock when a buyout occurs, creating bad employee relations.

4. The existence of an ESOP may impede later merger or acquisition opportunities.

TESTING THE WATERS

The best time to use an ESOP is when the company is profitable and has at least a $250,000 payroll, and when management must either compete for labor or wants to create a market for company stock in preparation for retirement. To some extent, general market conditions will influence the valuation of the company stock. Employees who will use the ESOP as a retirement plan want stock when it can be sold in a strong market.

ALTERNATIVES TO AN ESOP

1. Buyout. If the owner is retiring and wants to sell, sometimes a buyout can be structured with beneficial terms for management and/or workers. Choosing retirement, the owner of Dry Wall Supply, Inc. sold to Affiliated Capital Corporation for $3 million in cash (see Chapter 17).

2. Merger. A merger with a larger company can result in benefits for both a retiring owner and workers. A merger with a cash-rich company can allow the merged company, as a subsidiary for example, to compete more effectively in its industry. Flower Time was purchased by General Host for $27 million in cash. The company retained its entrepreneurial identity after the merger because the Flower Time founder stayed on to run the operation for General Host (see Chapter 26).

SOURCES

Kelso & Company, San Francisco, CA.
The National Center for Employee Ownership, Oakland, CA.
The ESOP Association, Washington, D.C.

ESOPS—Outcome of Selling Mr. Smith's Shares of Smith & Company

	To Smith & Company	To Third Party	To ESOP
Fair market value of Smith & Co. (300 shares × $800/share)	$240,000	$240,000	$240,000
Cost (300 shares × $50/share)	15,000	15,000	15,000
Gain	$225,000	$225,000	$225,000
Percentage of shares held by ESOP after sale	0	0	30%
Deemed dividend taxed to Smith as ordinary income	$240,000	0	0
Gain taxed to Smith as long-term capital		$225,000	
Gain not currently taxed to Smith			$225,000
Taxes paid on sale by Smith	$120,000	$ 45,000	$ 0
Aftertax sales proceeds available for investment	$120,000	$240,000	$240,000
Cost of RIF shares	$240,000	$240,000	$ 15,000
Smith's basis in RIF shares			

Source: Ernst & Whinney

Fred Schmid Employee
Stock Ownership Plan* (in Millions)

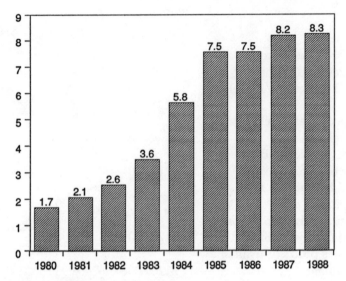

*Total value by fiscal year.

Source: Fred Schmid Appliance and TV Company.

PITFALLS TO AVOID

To get additional tax deductions on interest from funds borrowed to establish an ESOP, management may borrow too freely, encumbering future opterations with the need to repay debt and decreasing the likelihood of future debt financing.

The use of employee pension funds to establish an ESOP can result in strained employee/management relations and future lititgation.

Although employees own at least a percentage of the company, they may not be professionally capable of managing the company. The amount of stock ownership offered to employees should be planned carefully to insure the profitable continuation of operations.

Index

About the Author

As a contributing writer for such publications as *Venture, Personal Investor* and *OTC Review,* Jennifer Lindsey has been a finance specialist for over 12 years. In addition to reporting on small business management, she has been a partner in a business consulting firm since 1980. Listed in "Outstanding Young Women of America" (1971), she has won national writing awards and has acquired specialist training in bank functions, limited partnerhsips (Series 22 License) and IRA/SEP Retirement Plans.